# The Company I Kept

# The Company I Kept

Phyllis Ryan

Town House Dublin

Published in 1996 by
Town House & Country House
Trinity House
Charleston Road
Ranelagh
Dublin 6

British Library Cataloguing in Publication Data. A catalogue record
for this book is available from the British Library.

ISBN: 1-86059-028-4

Typeset by Typeform Repro Ltd
Printed by

To May Ryan, the Ryans of Millicent Hall, and Jacquie.

# Contents

# Acknowledgements

Special thanks to my dear friends John B Keane and Gerald Colgan, who supplied essential practical help and boosted my confidence. Also to that great journalist John J Finegan for constantly jogging my memory and to Tomás Mac Anna, Patrick Murray, Gregg Ryan, Mai and George McFall, Fergus Linehan, Carolyn Swift, photographer Fergus Bourke and to playright and producer Joe O'Donnell, author of *The Lads* and *Noone*, whose contribution to Gemini merits a book in itself. My sincere gratitude to Tom Murphy, Thomas Kilroy, Brian Friel, and Emma and Sarah Ryan for their serious encouragement and inspiration. Finally, my heartfelt thanks to countless members of the theatre profession who thought the book a worthwhile project and egged me on.

# 1

# *Overture*

By the age of eleven, I was a failed musician, according to the excellent teachers and examiners at school. In that same year of crisis (1934) I was introduced to Mícheál Mac Liammóir by an actress friend of Mother's and instantly fell in love! He was playing in *Liliom* by Ferenc Molnár at the Gate Theatre, and assured me backstage that I was destined for the theatre, so I instantly fell in love with that, too. I was already a veteran in the sense of awareness of the theatre, having graduated from pantomimes to weekly visits to the Abbey Theatre from the age of seven on. As my aunt was a cashier at the local cinema, regular free visits there also became part of my life. All these outings were part of Mother's plan to give me a hint of culture. But there was a time before the theatre...

I went to a kindergarten school somewhere in Crumlin, when I was four or five; a small school which taught reading, writing, the fear of God and the fear of a very cross teacher. Another lesson was that people who invited children to tell the truth didn't mean it. If you told them the truth about their ugly noses or fat bottoms, they smacked you.

I once told a lie about my homework, which I had improvised and not copied from the exercise book. Forced to kneel in front of a bleeding-heart statue of Jesus, I was invited to repeat the lie under pain of eternal damnation. Weighing up the consequences of truth and falsehood, of pleasing and not pleasing Gods and teachers, I decided that retribution would be swift from a cross teacher, but that God could maybe be placated later. So I lied, immediately felt bolts of lightning and hellfire, and knew that damnation was due to explode around me.

Nightmares oppressed me for years after this event, and Mother kissed me every night and stopped the devil from taking me. When I

1

was six, I wrote a school essay, and the cross teacher read it out to the class and said I was a genius, but also that people thus afflicted had to pray harder than the rest. The essay was about a shipwreck, and featured an impossibly brave captain who saved everyone on his ship and then drowned with the wreck, singing a hymn. Had I heard talk of the *Titanic?*

Pantomimes had been on the menu from the age of three, and when the time came for First Communion, the dress full of white flounces reminded me of the pantomime fairies. It was thrilling to wear the beautiful dress and the white handbag that went with it into which people kept dropping money. It was a mysterious, dimly understood day, and I heard some of the other mothers and teachers muttering about me looking like something out of 'bally', and how it was a disgrace to stand before the Lord in a short dress right up to my bottom. Mother laughed about this, and said that she knew for a fact that the Lord just loved me and my frock.

There was a mystery about Father, who had died or had otherwise disappeared from the scene before I was born. Mother, daughter of a Roman Catholic Republican family, had married an Enniskillen Protestant in the British army. He was, Mother agreed, handsome, charming and as irresponsible as a child. A 'Nanny' figure had told me that he was mad about the ladies, that Mother caught him 'at it' in the house one evening and gave him the benefit of no doubt at all. Mother was quite fiery, and he was reputed to be a hothead too.

I never believed the 'dead' version, and pined for my father, waiting for endless trams and buses that might bring him back, moaning and depressive enough for Mother to wish that I had vanished with him. My sister, older and bossy, often shut me up with a smart slap unseen by the adults. Despite my best efforts to emulate *la petite Dame aux Camélias*, there was a lot of laughter in the house. Mother, sister and our friends were high-spirited enough to counter my whinging, and I often forgot myself and joined in the fun.

It was the wish of my irresponsible and improvident father that his girls should go on from kindergarten to Alexandra College, an upper-crust and costly establishment. Mother had to work on the double to pay for my entrance to this enlightened school, which was considered to be ahead of its age culturally and educationally. I no longer needed to go to the private dancing, piano and elocution classes Mother had always managed to provide for us. Everything was attainable in this exciting new world, inhabited by wonderful, story-book people who spoke with the accents of ladies and dukes.

My sister, leaving me to climb trees with snotty-nosed street kids, was already at home with the mainly Anglo-Irish pupils, while she studied her elegant form and future. Doris was lissome, blue-eyed and incredibly attractive to men, even at a very early age; extrovert and good at mixing, she would today be described as cool. In contrast, I was self-conscious and awkward in the worst way, always knocking over chairs, vases, anything in my way and spoke with a strong Dublin accent.

But the world was not yet real for me, still in that strange and magical realm children inhabit until there is finally no more Santa Claus. It was difficult to talk to strangers outside the walls of my fantasy; much easier to stay quiet, and pretend that I was naive or inarticulate. This earned me lots of nicknames, and people made up reasons for their inability to understand my lack of response to overtures of friendship and ploys to draw me out. They dismissed me as shy, sullen, dramatic, affected and conceited. I hated being the butt of these undisguised opinions, but feared even more that I would be found out; that I didn't know what was real from what was fantasy.

I went into Mícheál's dressing-room after a show once, and he was sitting half-bare in front of the mirror. He looked quite like Mother after a while, and smelt like her too, and I loved him even more after that. It was so safe in the theatre, always so safe; nothing hurt me there.

I was really very grown-up before I began to accept the real world, a little at a time. There was so much pain there. Even then my two worlds tended to get confused, but less often as time went by, and the theatre gradually became my real world.

# 2

# *Childhood*

When I was four, we lived in 'The Bungalow', which had fields around it and a long, dark driveway leading to the front door. Once away from the driveway, the world was bright and warm; the sun lit up the apple trees and the pond sparkled. It looked so big, that pond. There were no fish, but lots of green plants were tangled in it, and mounds of grass surrounded its rim. I often lay there and made the stories come out of the books I brought with me, so that I could look at the pictures in the sun.

It was during those halcyon days in the bungalow that I discovered from books the relationship between hawthorn, God and the fairy people. The hawthorn bloomed all around the fields, and if I lay under the trees in summer the heavy fragrance would send me to sleep, and I wouldn't hear them calling me for tea. They would have to search for me, which made our minders irritable. The hawthorn was to have a great significance in my life, popping up at the oddest times, and no other perfume ever gave me greater pleasure. Thankfully the thorn trees were plentiful, swarming in from the hedges to invade every space, and I was never without them in the gardens of my childhood.

Our kindergarten school was small and drab, and never looked as though it could shine. There were benches and assorted wooden tables, all looking ready for the scrapheap. There was a dull yellow look about the classroom, and no pictures except the inevitable holy ones, like the rather gruesome Sacred Heart, or badly painted Virgins with vacant faces. The person who seemed to be the Principal came in only once or twice a week, and there was a tense, thin-faced lady religious fanatic in charge of the 'low babies' of five or six. This was one of the most miserable periods of my life, but I had no way of measuring this at the time.

I had been encouraged to read at an early age, so there was no worry about learning skills, and simple sums held no terrors for me.

4

But I was frightened of the Catechism interrogations, and of the terrifying teacher who assured the class, and me in particular, that no one who missed one question when the priest came would be allowed to make First Communion. There was great hostility there, and the teacher had a pretty nifty swinging smack which she used when she felt like it.

I could never at that stage convey to Mother how terrible the days were at school, and how scared I was of the thin lady teacher. Doris had gone on to Alexandra without having the woman even impinge on her consciousness, but then she had guts and such a ferocious temper that few people challenged her even then. On my last day at kindergarten, my sister held my hand as she walked me home; the touch remains in my memory. It must have been summer, but it might have been wet and stormy; all I can remember is the feeling of sheer joy. The world was warm and welcoming as I left 'high babies', and no baby was higher than I that day.

We grew up sustained by love supplied in huge quantities by Mother and our minders, and a diet of good plain food, as it was called in those days. Porridge was mandatory in the mornings, and a boiled egg – if anyone had the time to coax us to eat one. Dinner was meat and vegetables, cooked into the then customary pulp, and there were the usual kids' rows about the hated cabbage, sprouts and other suspect greens.

On Saturdays Mother gave us a bag of sweets each, and on Sundays there was always cake, treats which made life rich because we were not made blasé by excess. Things changed when we went to 'Alex' and were given pocket money. Doris always saved some of her pennies, but I disposed of mine soon after I got it, which boded ill for future business acumen.

The biggest thrill was the trip to the seaside whenever Mother had a day off, and we took buckets filled with sandwiches and apples and flasks of tea, and big fluffy towels so that Mother and our minder could hold them up to shelter us changing into our togs, and dry us when we came shivering out of the sea at Bray or Killiney. There was all the excitement of journeys by steam train, tram or bus. Some of the girls at Alex had fathers who collected them in motor cars, and I envied those girls, not because of the cars, but because of the fathers who drove them.

There were times when I would see other children playing ball with their fathers, and I would try to keep the tears from rolling down and spoiling the day for Mother. Then the sight of a ship in the distance might give me hope again, and I could imagine him sailing back to us. Doris had no time for what she called that mushy stuff. She thought that he was better anywhere else than with us, and once said that he might have had the decency to die properly. But then Doris knew the truth; Mother had told her about the separation, but for some reason had never mentioned it to me.

We inhabited, as I grew from four to twenty, four houses where Mother brought us to live until we finally arrived at 'Shangri La'. That was the house in Palmerston Road, large and imposing, roomy enough to accommodate the family, a dog, a few assorted cats, two minders, Queen Anne chairs and Sheraton-style cabinets. Palmerston Road was lined with beautiful trees. The tall houses had fair garden space front and back as well as basements, once servants' quarters, which were large enough to house four people comfortably.

We had a great childhood, and if there were traumatic moments in our teens as we changed physically, that was because of the conspiracy of silence imposed on parents by the almost Victorian times. There were things for grown-ups to know and for kids to find out. Talk about periods, pregnancy and anything to do with sex was simply not admissible. Even brave, liberal Mother had hang-ups in this direction until she found out that the silence was causing her girls hurt and confusion. Then she immediately threw off inherited reservations and became totally open on all intimate matters. While Doris responded eagerly to these new freedoms, it was too late for me. I had retreated too far into my protective shell, and it was to be a long time before I was dragged out of it.

Mother was ahead of her time. As the years brought change, she embraced the more open society with zest, building on it in her own life and widening her girls' perceptions. In the process, she added to her astonishing library more and more banned classics, as well as lighter works, that challenged the familiar conventions of artistic suppression and personal limitation. Her girls were never forbidden to read any of these authors, who included Joyce, Anatole France, Chesterton, Marie Corelli...what ever happened to her? But then Mother knew well that we couldn't tackle the literary giants until we were at least at college level. We were, however, forbidden to bring Bram Stoker's *Dracula* into the house, and, of course, went crazy to get our hands on it. Doris finally borrowed it from a girl at school, and we read it together under the blankets with the help of a flashlight – turned off whenever we heard a footstep. Mother was right, of course, and I had such nightmares afterwards that everyone was up all night for ages.

What a Christmas Mother made; always the one prayed-for present under the tree, and a big net stocking full of little toys and comic books from Santa, who had definitely been there last night because his sherry glass by the fire was empty, and only a few crumbs remained on the plate where his mince-pie had been left along with biscuits for the reindeers. Just before dinner we would gather together; the two girls, Mother and Aunt Lena, the current minder and one or two lonely people invited because they had nowhere to go on this special day.

So there we all were, an odd assortment of people, some shabby and some elegant, some old and some others of Mother's age; we girls considered most people over thirty to be on their last legs, but Mother was ageless and Christmas never changed. After dinner, we pulled the crackers and asked the silly riddles; then the pudding arrived blazing with a sprig of holly in the centre, and everyone stood up and cheered. We passed around the whiskey sauce which the girls hated, and when the pudding was eaten one of the guests always stood up and made a toast thanking Mother. He would invariably add, 'Here's to the next time, may we all live to see it next year', which sounded as if he was booking his place.

When they were gone, Mother would at last open the little gifts we had bought her. We always bought them at Woolworth's Threepenny and Sixpenny Store in Grafton Street. Poor Mother always got a cheap ornament or a brooch that went green after a few weeks, but received the gifts as though they were priceless, saying they were what she really wanted. Since she got the main gifts, we had very little money left over for the others, so aunt and minders got soap and sticky toffee bars. But nobody minded at Christmas, a time when the thought really was what counted. Woolworth's also provided mistletoe, for those who couldn't get the real kind. Ours hung from light bulbs or just about anything that could hold it, and people made jokes about how you had to marry the man who kissed you underneath it. This horrified me so much that I would not let even my uncle kiss me under the mistletoe until I was certain that the dire prediction lacked credibility. Years later, I would discover the plant's romantic properties, and make good use of them.

# 3

# *Fits and Starts*

At Alexandra College I learned that there were many Christian faiths, all jostling with each other to win the Lord's approval. I, of course, had always belonged to the one true Church, as was borne out by the huge numbers of Roman Catholics encountered at Mass and Confession. At Alex, however, I was in a tiny minority of about six, including the two McEntee children whose mother taught Irish at the school. I was in the same class as Máire (afterwards the poet Máire Mhac an tSaoi), who was regarded as insufferably goody and, even worse, brainy; attributes which did not make for popularity among a group of high-spirited ten-year-olds.

Years later, Máire, by then married to Conor Cruise O'Brien, remembered me as the ringleader of a group of dissidents up to any mischief that might enliven classroom routines. The Headmistress at Alex was a most distinguished lady known as Miss Bewley. She may have been a member of the well-known Dublin Bewleys, since being a Quaker would not have mattered in a Church of Ireland school which admitted Catholics, every kind of Protestant and a sprinkling of Jewish children. I was instantly attracted to the Jewish girls. There were identical twins, Zara and Judy, and a girl called Sybil who became a close school friend; a very dark, intense girl who went out of my life after school. Afterwards, I always had close Jewish friends, finding in them throughout the years a loyalty and sense of shared history that transcended the severance brought about by the New Testament.

Mother must have scrimped and saved to send her daughters to Alex, but could not have received a better return for her efforts than was given by that school. Apart from a superb education in the essential subjects, there were classes in deportment, eliminating stoops and bad stance, and in eurhythmics, which brought the clumsiest customer close to achieving dancer status. There were

8

music and singing lessons, art and cooking classes, as well as sessions in dress-making. Extra tuition was provided for those weak in any subject who were willing to stay on for one hour after school.

Games included netball, hockey and tennis, and there was drama; to be selected for a part in the school play was quite an accolade. There were prizes at the end of each year in two different categories – for excellence in the school course over the year, and for excellence in final exams. This arrangement catered for a 'panicker' like me, who went blank when faced with a test paper, but never failed to gain a school course prize. We were also taught a love of books, literary discernment and how to read with intelligence and insight. With this sort of education under my belt, being a failed musician at the age of eleven or twelve did not destroy my spirit for long. My bruised ego soon got a chance to heal and renew itself, and the theatre began to do more than just beckon. It started to take over my thoughts and life, especially after Mícheál Mac Liammóir had said those magical words about the theatre being my real destiny.

One day, however, the bliss of being an Alexandra girl was shattered. I went to Mass one Sunday to hear thundering denunciations of parents who defiled the minds of their innocent children by sending them to dens of iniquity to learn 'unseemly falsehoods about the Holy Father', and to lose the faith through participating in heathen rituals. Then came the awful crunch; parents who defied this ruling would be excommunicated, refused the sacraments and probably damned for all eternity. Their sin would be so great that it would be classified as 'reserved', meaning that only certain bishops could absolve it, if they had a mind to.

Mother turned out to be totally unmoved by the prospect of hellfire, telling me to simmer down and refusing to be even serious about the situation. Doris was also quite unmoved by the sermon, and attacked me for my stupidity in thinking that the Lord would take it out on Mother because of a few old fuddy-duddy bishops. But soon Mother, seeing that my fright was real, embraced me saying 'Who said that God was responsible for this new sin?' 'The bishops,' I blurted out. To which Mother replied, 'Well, He didn't tell *me*!' That night, when being tucked into bed, I asked, just to be sure, where I would go to school on Monday. Mother smiled, hugged me and said 'Alexandra, of course, unless God instructs me personally to the contrary before then.'

On Monday morning Alex was all business as usual, and no one referred to the big purge. But Mrs McEntee and her girls were missing, vanished over a weekend that affected my life for years to come. Although I developed a great fear of priests, and to avoid one would run or cross the road, I retained a great need for God in my life. Even though they had painted Him as a vengeful, sadistic father-figure, I wanted Him to be kind and loving, as my own father must have been. So into the dream-world I went with God, and there I made Him love me and approve of Mother and Doris. I even put it right about my father. He was an all-right guy who lost his memory and disappeared, so they all thought that he was dead; but I *knew*.

There was no way that I could think realistically about my defunct musical career, so I worked it out that God had meant me to go into the theatre, thus making it necessary to give up the music. He had also sent me to Mícheál Mac Liammóir, where His real plan for me would be revealed. Everything that happened from the crunch time became a direct consequence of what God wanted or didn't want. The fact that His wants and mine always coincided was no matter, and any disappointment was just God's way of saying 'Do something else, that was unimportant.'

Mother was friendly with a lady who was a relation of Ria Mooney, a famous Abbey actress who went on to become Director of Plays at that theatre (later Artistic Director). I heard via the relation that a school of acting was opening at the Abbey Theatre, and that you had to be eighteen and upwards to audition. I begged Mother to let me try, just *try*, although I was a mere twelve-and-a-half and not eligible. Then Mother heard that Ria herself would be running the school, and asked her if she would grant me an audition – not to break rules, or with a view to admitting me – just so that there would be peace in the house again. Ria was very understanding and gave me an audition time, while making it clear that eighteen was the entrance age to the school. I was to do the balcony scene from *Romeo and Juliet*, with someone reading in Romeo.

I told no one, and the tension mounted inside until I couldn't eat or sleep. Then the day came when, after school, I trudged down to the old Peacock Theatre beside the old Abbey. I was heavy-eyed and heavy-hearted, stiff with fright, wishing to be whisked away into the atmosphere and never seen again.

What a beautiful face Ria had, with her sleek black hair, almost oriental peachy skin and large, long eyes. And how gentle she was with me as I managed to blurt out a painful rendition of

Shakespeare's great love-scene. Lovely, patient Ria congratulated me for bravery, and made me do it again and again, directing, guiding, pointing out the humanity of the two characters and how young they were. Ria, who insisted that she should be called by her first name, told me a lot about the meaning of love that day, and I in turn confided my own love for Mícheál Mac Liammóir. She then asked me to come back next week and put that love into the Juliet scene.

I went home on a high, even though Ria's last words were that, whatever happened, I could not be given a place in the School of Acting until I was eighteen. What could that mean; that now only twelve, I should wait for six more years? I might be dead, *would* be dead if I didn't get in, and anyhow, I was now in love with Ria too – not as much as with Mícheál, but quite enough to want her for a stage teacher. Reading the scene again, imagining I was Juliet and using all the love, such a different feeling came over me that I got weak with emotion and tears ran down my face – and nothing was ever the same again.

The great day came, and I was back in the little theatre with the 'Peacock' painted on the inner wall, telling myself that I was now Juliet, in love with Romeo-Mac Liammóir, and willing to die rather than be parted from him. But supposing Mícheál died, or my mother; who would take me to the theatre ever again? Such an intensity of fear and confusion came upon me that I burst into tears, and couldn't speak a word.

Ria's approach was sympathetic but practical. She told me, sodden and dumpy in the gym slip, to wait and watch the other auditions, and then try again – or maybe it would be better for me to go home, and come back again when I was older, and presumably wiser? This advice galvanised me into instant action. Mumbling that I would do it now, I leaped onto the small stage and – with Ria reading Romeo whenever she could get a word in – launched into Juliet's lines with no coherent motivation other than fear of losing my chance and being banished.

Ria sat down with me afterwards, and gently told me that my interpretation was unusual, that it was essential to pause for breath between speeches, and that verse had its own special technique. As she accompanied me to the door, she said the words that were to influence my life forever, 'You broke every rule, but you have real talent.' As I grew wings and floated out the door, I heard Ria's voice saying 'There's a place here for you when you're older.'

It was probably June, but it would have been summer anyway. The air felt so good as I ran home straight into the garden to climb my favourite tree, tearing my socks and scraping my shins all the way to the top, almost delirious with excitement. I saw the birds flying in the small blue gaps between the leaves overhead, their little beaks glinting as they sang and I sang.

I had seemed so close to heaven up there, but all the time God was watching, blaming me for having forgotten Him and not having prayed that morning – and what about going to a Protestant school; did I think He had forgotten that? His wrath came upon me as I sat astride a branch, blood running down my legs, not from the scratches but from somewhere higher up, and I couldn't find how I had been hurt. Perhaps, please God, I wouldn't die till I saw Mother, I thought, scrambling and sliding down the tree screaming for her, scattering two lady visitors and a minder, as I ran into my bedroom.

My sister said 'Shut up, you're not dying. All girls get this, and it's called the 'curse'. I got it two years ago, but I didn't tell you because you were such a baby. It has to do with babies, and it comes every month.' But I cried that I didn't want it, didn't want babies, while she helped me to clean myself. I lay on the bed sobbing, because the world was no longer beautiful but ugly. How could I ever have felt so happy; everything was spoiled, and I could never go back to Ria until this thing was cured.

Summer was over, and back to school I went, only now I was changed. Girls were not allowed to swim when the curse came upon them, or to do certain gymnastics. At the back of my mind, two great questions were still unanswered. When would Ria Mooney realise that she really needed me at that acting school, which was due to open in the late autumn; and now that I knew where babies came from, how did they get there? One girlfriend thought it was all done by kissing, while others said you had to take off your clothes to make the kissing work.

We vowed not to ask our mothers, in case they might get upset, and fathers were taboo as there was a general feeling that they were the guilty ones – although not mine, of course, since he was missing. It was known that men did the kissing and made mothers pregnant, and that babies lived inside their mothers. It was agreed, too, that boys must not be allowed to kiss any of us, dressed or otherwise, and one girl got hysterical one day and had to go to confession because a boy had kissed her and put his hand somewhere. After these revealing chats we would forget and play games like 'tig', chasing, 'see the robbers passing by', skipping and, later, cycling within the limits of the safer streets. At night I would dream that I was on-stage with Mícheál Mac Liammóir, and that he kissed me; but I always knew, somehow, that he was not included in my confused ideas of boys and babies.

We were all becoming adolescents, and starting to focus on boys, what they might do and what would happen if one asked you out; who could tell us how to cope with this new mystery, since mothers were out as sources of information? All parents said, 'Don't let me catch you talking to those boys at the end of the street, or anywhere else,' and if you asked why, they said 'Don't you be impertinent to me.' Except Mother, who saw no harm at all in talking to boys, as she saw no harm in anyone until they hit her with a mallet.

One fateful day Mother got a letter. She read it at breakfast, and kept looking at me as I swallowed my toast with my homework propped up at the table. Mother told me to come home early that evening, and not to stay out playing games with friends; she had something to tell me. I didn't mind coming in early. It was a bonus to see Mother outside of weekends, and maybe she was going to arrange for new shoes or something of the sort. But when I arrived home, Mother told me that Ria Mooney had written to say that she had spoken with the directors of the Abbey Theatre, and that because of her high recommendation an exception was being made, and I was being offered a place in the Abbey School.

Heart thumping, I heard Mother say that I could attend only if I gave her my word not to neglect school or homework. Then she kissed me and said she was proud of me, and I hugged her back and wondered why I wasn't happy or moved at all by the news that I had got the thing I had most longed for. I was to learn that this emptiness and sense of loss almost inevitably follow the granting of a wish, the fulfilment of a dream or the achievement of a truly creative act.

It was a teacher in Alex, one who struggled patiently to help me with my really terrible maths problem, who gave me the response I needed to my news of Ria's letter, blurted out spontaneously during a quiet moment in the playground. The teacher was as thrilled as if the good news were her own, and told me vehemently that I must go, that nothing must stop me, and that I could talk to her any time I was worried. Dear Miss Dove was a pale, dark-haired lady, given to reading letters at her desk and looking dreamy during maths class.

That evening I told Mother that I was scared, but that I would attend Ria's class and do my homework with even greater care. Mother told me that Ria would not expect me to be a genius at thirteen, and that I needn't stay if I didn't like it; and the die was cast. Classes were not commencing immediately. There was a month to wait before the next great day, and I prepared by running little plays at Alex between classes, in lunch-breaks and after school. These never really got off the ground, because the faithful few among my friends who accepted roles dwindled as sports, girl-guides and the welcoming out-of-doors took over. I was voted by my class to direct that year's Culwick choir for the annual competition, but I had to decline because I guessed that I would not have time for that plus homework when I went to the Abbey.

I suffered agonies in maths class, as I couldn't at all come to terms with algebra; despite the efforts of kindly Miss Dove, I was always near the bottom of the class, and hated that. But I flew through English; poetry and essays were no bother, and I once made an arrangement with three other girls who were duds at English that I would write their essays and they would do my maths at weekends. This worked well enough until we were discovered one Saturday because I was tired, and wrote three essays that were strikingly similar.

Outside of school, some girls were meeting boys and going to the pictures with them, and one girl asked me to go out with her brother and his friend for a walk one evening. I didn't like the brother; he was pompous and spotty, and although he only put one arm around me and pecked, it gave me the horrors. I found, too, that I was considered boring by boys, and by some girls too, because I was really unable to talk about anything except the Abbey, the Gate and Mícheál Mac Liammóir, while they talked about clothes, films and parties. But the days rolled by anyway, taking me to the first Saturday class.

# 4

# *Auditions*

The Peacock was ablaze with lights as I entered the small auditorium to begin my first class. Up near the stage a group were greeting each other noisily and asking questions, until Ria had to call for quiet. I loitered at the back near the door, and could see about a dozen people, all grown-up men and women except for one large, untidy figure with a boyish face, whose name was Dermot Tuohy. Ria was introducing the newcomers when she saw me in the back row and called me up to join the others. She told them who I was and that an exception had been made in my case and that of Dermot with regard to age, because she felt that we both had talent and would benefit from early tuition.

The girls all looked very glamorous, and the men, who seemed quite old, were in smart suits. Ria looked gorgeous, and Dermot and myself looked like the ugly ducklings, he in a suit that seemed too small for him and me in the brown gym slip with straight hair falling over my face, and pencil and jotter in a brown paper bag. Ria appointed a girl and a man as assistants, and they gave out pieces of script to each of us, and a poem; then Ria talked about the art of acting, and asked what it meant to us. Most of her listeners were working in day jobs or attending university. Some said that they would like to make acting a career: some wanted to act but also keep a safe job; some didn't know yet. Dermot didn't know, but said he liked the thought of acting better than being in a bank or something.

I had only one way to go, and said that I wanted to be a part of the theatre always, and yet not to be famous; just the best I could be. This was said in such an inaudible, muddled way that twice Ria had to ask me to speak up, and averred that one thing we would have to learn was voice projection. She was a fabulous giver, who knew more than any stage authority I have since met; more about her subject, more about imparting her knowledge, more about the need one has to be performing and not just listening to lectures or reading books on theory. She gave us a little time to study a short poem, and then, one by one, we had to get onto that stage and say it, trying to interpret the poetry and to be heard. However it came, Ria wanted us to be up there working.

Afterwards she gave a general run-down on what we had to learn. She noted early signs of weak areas to be dealt with, sent some of the class to movement lessons and others for extra voice production classes, as well as her own exercises and comments. No one was ever downed or made to feel a culprit, unless for laziness, and the slightest progress was praised. The only threat was that we might some day find ourselves in other hands, and be lost without her. During that time, the Stanislavski and other methods evolved in Europe and America. Ria always pointed out what was useful in these novel ideas, but didn't spend too much time on experiments. We were rarely asked to imagine ourselves as trees, growing flowers, lamp-posts, octopuses, rabbits or prowling tigers. She knew that these games had their value, and that trainees needed a few of them. But they needed more of what she gave in plenty, being director, voice teacher, guide and confessor.

All that Ria had told me about voice projection was swallowed up in a wave of self-consciousness, and I began to retreat in voice and intelligence, to blush and stammer and wish that I could fall through a hole in the stage. Dermot Tuohy must have been having the same feelings, because he walked up and down, turned his back so that he could not be heard, then turned around and shouted his last lines, making everyone jump.

Ria made no comments then, but gave us all parts to read and learn, and suggested that we read aloud at home for voice training. We all trooped out into the evening full of elation and despair in equal measure.

As a twelve-year-old, and right through my teens, I resented any set-backs, and fought passionately against the injustices and heartaches inherent in being young, thereby adding to the personality problems which caused my troubles in the first place. At that time I was a veritable pain in the neck, always preoccupied with the 'Universe' and 'Me', moody and boring, impossibly full of myself. I read loudly whenever I had time, telling anyone who would listen that I was producing my 'Voice'. I played classical music on the gramophone, and the bit I knew of the 'Moonlight' Sonata over and over on the piano. Homework was done with a bad grace, as an unfit occupation for artists. We were in the third house in Edenvale Road by then, and the minder, whose name was Lizzie and who stayed with us until her death, almost quit with the constant reciting, the noise of my sister slamming doors and the rows until Mother came home from work and we subsided.

People often gave parties, for birthdays or any other reasonable excuse. But we didn't give dances or have parties at our house, because Mother was so busy, and it wasn't expected of people who had no father. I wondered where he was and why he did not even send a letter. Perhaps Mother was right, and he was dead. Doris told me that, as he had been gone for seven years, he was dead as far as we were concerned, and Mother was not just a grass widow, but a real one. None of this explained or healed anything. I persisted in my dream, and no one told me the truth, not at that time. There were difficult times ahead. Something had happened in Mother's life, and we didn't catch on to the real meaning of it for a very long time. It had a tremendous effect on us as a family, and became absolutely clear around the time of my joining the Abbey School.

When I was about seven, we were about a year out of the bungalow and living in Charleston Avenue, Rathmines, a small cul-de-sac with terraced houses and only a small garden space. Mother told us one day that a very special friend was coming to tea, and that we were to wash our hands and behave as nicely as we could. We were duly scrubbed by Lizzie, a frail little lady stunted in growth, probably from malnutrition; a story in herself. She came from a family of twenty children, most of whom died early from tuberculosis and pneumonia, only a handful struggling through to survive into adulthood.

So, with faces washed and shiny, wearing clean frocks and with hair brushed into neatness, we waited for the visitor. We whispered about the chances of a small gift or cash donation from him, being as mercenary as most children about such matters. Eventually Mother came into the drawing-room looking like a girl, flushed and particularly elegant, with a tallish and somewhat portly gentleman whom she called Joe, informing us that we could call him Uncle Joe or Mr Anderson. He had a kindly face and a soft, unfamiliar accent. Joseph Anderson came from the Glens of Antrim and was, Mother told us proudly, a very important person, the editor of a newspaper. We had tea in comparative silence, mostly from shyness; even Doris was less talkative than usual.

It transpired that Joe loved animals, especially cats and dogs, and was fond of strays. We took him into the garden after tea to show him our cats, of which there was always a selection. There had also been Flossie, a white hairy dog who died of old age before we left the bungalow, and a beautiful collie called Shep who stayed only a week and had to be given to some dog-lover with more garden space than we had. We told Mr Anderson all about the cat and dog problems. He listened and smiled, and gave us sweets from his pocket and a whole sixpence each – more than we got from grown-ups even at Christmas. We thought he was the nicest friend Mother ever had, and that night, whispering in bed, talked about whether we might see him again, and if he should be called Uncle or Mr A. We had no relations other than our aunt, and the occasional lady who said 'You may call me auntie if you want to.' We didn't have cousins, and I never remember any grandparents; we were cut off when Mother and Father married, as their families bitterly resented the marriage and didn't want to know about us.

Uncle Joe came in and out of our lives at odd intervals. Sometimes we didn't see him for months; sometimes he would come to tea, and stay for a while in the spare room. He was always generous and kind, and we liked him and by this time really believed that he was our uncle. Once Mother told us that he was ill, and was coming to stay with us until he got better, as he lived alone and needed care. He arrived rather red in the face, singing the 'Old Orange Flute', and was led to the spare room; we were told to keep away and not disturb him, The doctor came, and talked to Mother downstairs for ages. She was very quiet and serious when she came in to talk to us that evening. She said that Joe had taken certain medicines and they didn't agree with him, but he would be all right in a week or so, and the doctor would come again. The medicines made him sing and stagger about his room a lot. We crept about the house until Uncle Joe appeared one morning at breakfast, looking a little wan and not really fit for work; but he did go out, and that was the last we saw of him for a long time.

Doris said that Mother met him often, and she always knew when they were meeting because my aunt and Mother talked about him at night, and she crept downstairs and listened. Mother began to look happy again after a while, and one day told us that Joe was completely recovered and that we were moving to a new house, a bigger one, and that he would be staying with us for a while. Doris instantly flew into a rage. She told Mother that she wanted to have her own friends to stay, and that Joe was in the way and spoiling everything. Mother looked dreadfully hurt and told her she was being selfish; then Doris turned to me and asked did I not know that Mother was going out with Joe like engaged people did, and neither of us would get a look-in if Mother was getting soppy about Joe.

I ran from the room, not thinking of Mother's feelings, but only selfishly that I might now lose her love and have to run away, and hating poor Joe for having ever come into our lives. Oh, the imaginary crimes committed by poor, unsuspecting Joseph Anderson in my heart as I hid in the stumpy tree that was all the garden could offer a climber. Joe had plotted to steal Mother's affections, that was it; and my real father would kill him if he tried to supplant him. But I knew that I could not sustain that particular fancy; Father had not come for me, had not written, had made no attempt even to see me.

My thoughts became chaotic as I sat shivering in the dusk, wondering if Mother was going to leave home and if we would have minders instead. I knew I couldn't possibly live without Mother, so I rehearsed how to die, how to make myself die. Then I heard Mother's voice asking me to come in and talk to her, and scrambled down into her arms, and we went indoors together.

Doris was having tea, laughing and chatting to Lizzie as though the world had not ended a short time before. I couldn't follow this change of heart. While Mother went off to make lots of buttered toast, Doris made a face at me and said that she would never tell me anything again. 'But', I protested, 'you said that Joe was spoiling everything and going away with Mother.' 'Oh, shut up', she retorted, 'you get everything wrong; Mother's not leaving, and Joe is coming to be one of the family, like a real relation.' 'But what about our real father?', I started to say, when Doris suddenly ran over and slapped my face so hard that I couldn't even cry. 'Don't', she said, 'mention that bloody man to me ever again or I'll damn well break your neck.'

After that, life returned to near-normality. I went to school, and to acting school at weekends, and plotted to get as many visits to the Gate as I could, in the hope of talking to Mícheál afterwards. It wasn't easy, because of all the lessons and work, and the usual outings to school friends and their return visits to our home. We had moved to Edenvale Road, to a house aptly named 'St Jude', after the patron of hopeless cases. It was in Ranelagh and had more rooms and a bigger garden, and Joe came to live with us, to be Mother's friend and the best and most understanding uncle any girls could have adopted. I gradually became glad that Mother had the company of such an intelligent and sensitive man. He never intruded on us, or entered family discussions or rows; he was always there when we got into trouble at school, or were short of cash for a visit to the cinema.

Nobody in Alexandra, not even my closest friends, was told about the advent of Joe. He did not exist in the Abbey School, either, where I was beginning to find one or two people I could talk to. How many children invent a home life that simply bears no resemblance to reality? At thirteen, I succeeded in painting a picture of a home where my sister became a stranger to me, where there was no father and no relatives (my aunt disappeared from this version), and my wraith-like mother wafted in and out, too delicate for me to intrude upon with problems or confidences. Mother was in fact a well-built woman, extremely handsome, and nothing remotely like the picture I had painted of a frail 'lady of the camellias'. I just needed to have a mysterious background, and if I made my family seem strange, at least I didn't make them seem bad or unkind.

In fact, if the sympathetic adults at the school had known, the only strange being in our house then was myself. Sometimes when my voice was too small, and Ria called for more projection, a student full of concern would explain to the others that I was forced to whisper at home, and rarely spoke to my weird family. Dermot Tuohy had a strange home life, too, they said; but there was real tragedy in his home, and, although I felt sorry for him, he made me feel insecure. He was still big, and shambled about rather than walked, but he was beginning to emerge as a very good actor, with a strong, clear voice even then.

Being the two youngest members, Dermot and I were left to our own devices a lot, but I disliked his crazy bursts of laughter and his horse-play, which was loud and noisy. He in turn disliked my attempts to float around like a 'blooming ghost', and often said nastily that I would do better to try improving my *stage* acting. But we became the best of friends in the end, working together on numerous occasions, and I learned to respect and be genuinely fond of him. He had enormous faith in God, and that carried him through the hardest times of his life, when he was trying to come to terms and cope with the more bizarre expressions of his homosexuality.

The two-year gap between my sister and me was of no great

significance until Doris reached her teens; then it began to seem enormous. All sorts of privileges go with being the first-born *and* a teenager. Doris could stay up longer at night, and stay out later. She had more pocket money and new clothes, and became closer to Mother, who confided in her and told her secrets that I was considered too young to know about. They knew that anything I couldn't handle became larger than life to me, and might be escalated into a drama for more than home consumption. Once I accused them of whispering things about me, threatened to run away and find my father, and locked myself in my room, refusing to come out until hunger drove me to sneak down for food.

Mother tried reason, then greeted the tantrums with weary resignation. She actually ignored my most strenuous efforts to get attention, and worst of all, Doris laughed at me. I really wanted something terrible to happen to Doris; not bad enough to kill her, like poison, but something that would keep her away from Mother. At school, at dancing class and at the Abbey I thought of little else but how to restore my status at home. Someone up there must have been listening, because the downfall of Doris was drawing near as I prayed my nasty little novena.

Doris and her friend Patty Broughal were allowed to go out dancing occasionally to places which were properly supervised, and which closed early. Then one day word spread throughout Dublin that a pleasure steamer called the *Royal Iris* was about to operate at weekends from O'Connell Bridge, and that there would be a band playing on board. Doris and Patty asked Mother if they could go for a short cruise and listen to the music. She thought it a good idea, and even suggested that they might take me, a suggestion promptly rejected by Doris who didn't want to look after a 'kid', especially one who disliked modern music and was into boring old classics. So they went, apparently for more than just one trip, because they were back late. Even though the summer evenings were bright and she was with Patty, Mother was not at all pleased, and scolded both of them.

I was secretly thrilled at their discomfiture, but the tiff did not last long; the duo were soon laughing and chatting about the band and the fun it all was, and Mother even said that she might go with Joe one weekend. But Doris got her pocket money in advance on some pretext, and went back on the *Royal Iris* for one more trip the next day. This developed into several secret outings with or without the redoubtable Patty, who could be counted on to imitate a clam when awkward questions were asked. Doris, wearing all her limited store of finery, with flowers pinned to her bosom and her thick auburn hair in masses of tonged curls, listened to the band on the *Royal Iris* often enough to be able to sing their entire repertoire. She explained her absences at weekends by pretending that she was learning the latest ballroom dances at Patty's house, or studying dress-making there, or going on long nature walks in the countryside. She was in fact studying a quite different life-form on the pleasure steamer.

One day Mother came home late to find no sign of her. It was certainly after eleven, because I was in bed and heard Mother knocking on Joe's door and whispering to him. Then she put her head round the door of my room and said in a grim voice that I was not to worry, she would soon be back, and Aunt Lena and Lizzie were in the house. It emerged that Mother and Joe went first to Patty's house, there to learn that Patty had not seen Doris since tea-time, when they left the delights of the *Royal Iris*, and thought that she had gone home. Under cross-examination, however, Patty blabbed that Doris had fallen for the trumpeter in the boat's band, and he for her, and they had made a date at an O'Connell Street venue.

The posse caught up with the love-sick pair gazing into each other's eyes in a coffee-house, he with a head of black Brylcreemed hair and a jazzy suit, she in Mother's new silk jacket and her best fake pearls. All hell was let loose. Doris roared crying, and Mother threatened the young man with arrest if he ever laid eyes again on a child of mere sixteen – he had thought she was twenty. Mother was impressive when she got going, and Doris was yanked home.

Soon afterwards she was on her way to a convent in Deal, in Kent, supposedly to 'finish' her education. Looking back, it was clear that the *Royal Iris* affair had triggered off a worry Mother had about the way men looked at Doris, and how she flirted with them; the convent seemed the best answer. Doris went reluctantly, vowing that she would never come back, and accusing Mother of ruining her life. But she knew Mother very well, and got her revenge for her sentence in a most unexpected way.

Almost a year passed before Doris played her trump card. A letter arrived from the Superior of the convent, demanding to see Mother. It seemed that Doris had undergone a total change of character, had taken to prayer and fasting, and wanted to join the Order as soon as possible. Mother took the first boat and descended on Deal like a bolt of lightning. Despite her pleas and those of the Reverend Mother, Doris was whisked back, home and dry. She had won, and thereafter Mother denied her nothing. Doris made no secret to me about her plan to get away from that convent; she had as much interest in becoming a nun as I had of going into a bank. She was highly intelligent, but her interest was in earning a living, not in college. There were ideas of being a beautician, a secretary or a designer, and she did part of all three in her 'working' life. But eventually she had one of the happiest marriages I have ever known, to a lovable man who adored her until his death in 1987.

While Doris was in Kent, Ria decided that it was time to show the Abbey Board and other interested parties what her students had achieved. We started to work on two plays, *Cradle Song* by Gregorio Martinez Sierra and Yeats's *The Land of Heart's Desire*. They were to go on at the Peacock, and then there would be a 'weeding-out' process, so that only the most talented would be invited to stay on. This was a terrifying scenario in my mind, already certain that I would be first to be thrown out of the school. Home was full of uncertainties caused by my craving to expel everyone else out of Mother's life, and I was also finding it difficult to study at Alex. My dismal record in maths reached new lows, but my dramatic essays improved greatly and kept me out of real trouble.

I was confused, and began to retreat into my dream-world, taking whatever talent I possessed with me. Every emotion I felt for the characters I was portraying at acting school went inwards; my improved vocal powers dwindled into mouse-voice. Worst of all, I couldn't speak verse, so being cast as the 'Faery Child' in Yeats's play was just another hopeless challenge, a means of exposing to Ria and the Abbey class how little I had to offer. I was also cast as Sister Joanna of the Cross in *Cradle Song*, a middle-aged nun who was dotty about an orphan girl brought up in the convent. Maureen Jordan, older and taller than I was, played the orphan; a hilarious situation if you weren't dying of loneliness and inadequacy. The words 'low self-esteem' did no justice to my despair of getting through even a day.

# 5

# *Growing Pains*

How quiet the streets were in the evenings, dark with no brightly lit shops, and so little traffic – and the lamplighter going around, putting out the gas lamps on the top of the street lights. I remember the lamplighters only dimly, but I remember Lizzie's father, a kindly old man who often gave us a penny which I now realise he couldn't possibly have afforded. He had a long stick with which he doused lamp after lamp, and Lizzie told us he had terrible rheumatics.

As we grew older, living on the Southside, Doris and I often walked into town. It was an easy stroll to O'Connell Street from Ranelagh, and the only dangers after lights out were crossing the roads without care when buses were running, or encountering a drunk who would shout out funny remarks as we passed. It was such joy to walk through Dublin over O'Connell Bridge in the mellow evenings (as long as we were home by nine o'clock) and look at the Liffey, dark and gleaming under the final lamplight or early moonlight. We would listen, too, to the last cries of the flower sellers under Nelson's Pillar, and gaze into shop windows caught in whatever light there was left.

Once, in our teens, we went to a fun-fair with two lads we knew from parties. It was so beguiling on the rides and swings that we lost the run of ourselves and went for an ill-considered walk in the direction of the Dublin mountains. Time was forgotten until we began to feel cold, and the evening's joys were quenched in a drizzling rain; then we all wanted to go home. The lads piloted us back in sullen silence, because we had started to blame them unfairly for keeping us out late.

Mother was waiting at the door; the lads turned and ran as if a mad dog was chasing them, and we were let in. With the door closed, Mother said, ice dripping from every word, 'I've sent for the police.' Doris wanted to know why, and it emerged that, at midnight,

Mother, Aunt Lena, Uncle Joe and Lizzie had concluded simultaneously that there had been an accident, or worse. As we tried to explain, there was a knock on the door, and it *was* the police.

Next morning Mother had words with us, and she didn't mince them. We were forbidden to go out for a week, or until we could be trusted, except of course to school and other classes. Doris refused to accept this at all; she had a birthday party and a trip to the cinema planned, and she and Mother had a ferocious row about it. Both of them were hot-tempered and impulsive, terribly alike. Doris used her worst words, 'damn' and 'bloody' and 'blast', but Mother won by walking out of the house and leaving us both to simmer in our different ways. Out of this came new rules; Doris could stay out occasionally until 11 pm, but I had a 9.30 pm limit until I too was sixteen.

In a sense I grew away from my family as the activities of acting school took over more and more of my thoughts, and leisure time turned into long walks with Maureen Jordan from the Abbey school. She was a lovely young actress, just a few years older than I, and we had common ground in music and poetry. She seemed isolated insofar as her home background was not remotely theatrical. We shunned people who scoffed or sneered at our lofty ideals, and spent our time communing with nature or rehearsing our parts for Ria.

Part of our schooling was to go to rehearsals at the Abbey as often as possible. We loved this, sitting there quietly watching the greats – M J Dolan, Eileen Crowe, F J McCormick (that great, great artist, whose match I have never since found), May Craig, Maureen Delany, Barry Fitzgerald, Arthur 'Boss' Shields. Watching them, we learned more than we realised, because their professionalism and versatility were rubbing off on us.

The Abbey then ran what was virtually a weekly repertory, with many popular shows repeated each season for audiences who could not get enough of them. Favourites included *The Fort Field*, *The Passing Day*, *The New Gossoon*, *Professor Tim* and others by George Shiels, comedies peopled with bitter, cunning characters; Shiels was an invalid, and was never seen. Popular also were the works of O'Casey and Yeats, Lady Gregory's *Spreading the News* and *The Rising of the Moon*, Synge's *The Playboy of the Western World* and *The Well of the Saints*.

Amidst all these glorious events, I would worry lest Mícheál would feel annoyed that I was not part of the Gate, where I was surely destined to star with him one day. Their plays were so different, by classic authors such as Molnár, Shakespeare and Ibsen (regarded as dubious, if not decadent, by the Abbey company). There was glamour, style and gorgeous settings, plays like *Death takes a Holiday*, *Berkeley Square* and *Children in Uniform*, madly romantic and in complete contrast to the 'peasant' plays at the Abbey. I longed to be in the Gate plays, *and* in the Abbey plays; and I longed to be grown-up. We were all young enough to think that everything would fall into place, nicely pat, no problems.

There was a lot of fun in the Abbey School because of our disparate ages. We had to play the parts of much older people, as in a working piece called *The Long Christmas Dinner*. Ria gave me the role of a lonely spinster who was withdrawn and docile until someone made such a hurtful remark that the floodgates opened; then the poor lady broke down in torrents of emotion. Everyone thought it was a scream to see me playing the part in my gym slip, but we all laughed when some of the girls had to emulate aged grannies and the lads had to climb into grandpas' shoes, going all quavery and doddery. Ria laughed, too, but added that she had never seen sixty-year-olds tottering into their living-rooms, speaking in gummy tones or high-C tremolos. Once she said that playing one's own age was hardest of all and she was right.

One day, in my spinster role, I came to the emotional breakdown and the skies opened; I stood there choking with the heartbreak of that lonely woman, and the speeches came out all wrong. Everyone was quiet when I stopped speaking, and Ria told us to go on and finish the piece. Afterwards, she gave us notes. Once more, everyone got praised for their best qualities, until she came to me. She said that, as usual, I had neither coherence, technique, breathing nor vocal projection – but that I had given an example of what really mattered. The rest could be learned, but the depth of emotion I had shown could not. I had wings again, but something told me I couldn't fly with them, no matter how much technique I practised. They didn't have enough power. I had never found it hard to cry.

# 6

# *Graduations*

One day at the Peacock, Ria called me aside and told me that the Abbey had decided to revive a very popular play, and that a child actress was needed for a key role. The play was *The Moon in the Yellow River*, by a young avant-garde writer called Denis Johnston. The part was that of an eleven-year-old girl who had been rejected by her father, a lonely child seeking his love and approval.

The custom in those days was to have children's parts played by younger members of the Abbey Company, normally in their twenties or early thirties. (For instance, the two schoolgirls Pat and Ducky in Lennox Robinson's popular comedy *The Far-Off Hills* were always played by 'mature' performers.) Ria told me that Denis Johnston wanted a real child, and that she had informed him that she had a fourteen-year-old in the school, who was only in her first year of training. However, a reading of the part was arranged with the author present, and Denis said that he was very pleased, and that I had the right quality and appearance for his character.

Mother was duly telephoned and formally asked if I could accept the role. She agreed, and promised to give me all the back-up necessary as long as school rules were observed. I could rehearse with the Abbey after school each day, and study the part and do my homework in the evenings; and I would have to get up early to do my school work when the play was actually on. So it was settled, and I was to play my first part ever with the Abbey Company. The other school members were very nice to me, and there were many congratulations, together with pieces of advice about not getting a swelled head.

The part seemed made for me. I had a rapport with all the other characters, and with the heroic idiocy so well portrayed by Denis O'Dea in the play, which was ahead of its time in more ways than one. I related to the Chinese poet Li Po whose poem, quoted in the text, provided the title. ('Li Po also died young – he tried to embrace the moon in the Yellow River!') The father in the play could not come to terms with the loss of his young wife, who had died giving birth to their child. He did not want to set eyes on the girl who had deprived him of the only person he had ever loved, so he grew bitter and withdrew into his work, leaving the child to grow up as she pleased. Barry Fitzgerald, a marvellous comic personality much loved by Dublin audiences, was to take this part, his first really serious role.

Denis Johnston was an extremely handsome, tall man who was enormously kind and encouraging; sensing my nervousness, he went out of his way to befriend me, making me feel very special. Understanding the part presented no problems; I *knew* that girl. But the techniques – including the handling of props, moving on certain lines, and making it all seem perfectly natural – did not come easily, and I frequently held up the seasoned performers while I struggled to get movements right. Ria had taught the mechanics of the stage, but it was quite different when one came to apply the lessons while working with a team of super-professionals. My voice had to project further in the larger theatre, and timing had to be adjusted to the rhythm of the production. I gabbled from nerves, slowed down monotonously and fell between every possible stool.

The players were helpful, if a little distant, gritting their teeth at having to put up with a student, and a child at that, and who could blame them? Their life was not easy, although they were the star players of their time. They worked all day in the theatre, with only a break for a cup of tea, until the scene or act was as good as they could make it. Both rehearsal and playing time were short, usually one week for each. The repertoire was huge, and they were always either repeating a play or attempting to fit in a new one which might require two weeks' rehearsal, but seldom got it.

I talked very little at home, just telling Mother that it was going fine, and my sister that the players were nice and the author a dream. She was quite interested in my description of his looks and charm, but of course I had to add that he was oldish (in my eyes), which put him out of her league. But mostly I worked, fretted, lay awake and longed for each new trial at the part. Gradually I began to get benevolent smiles, Eileen Crowe would say I was improving, F J McCormick would pat me on the head and tell me to ask him if I was worried about anything. I was too much in awe of the players to know whether I liked them or not; indeed, it was to be some years before I was permitted to share the Green Room with them, and call them by their first names.

The dress rehearsal, before which costumes were approved and fitted, proved to be a revelation. Scenery appeared and was set up while lights were focused and adjusted, and the actors went over their lines. Everyone was admonished to cease the rehearsal mumbling and play as though the first night had arrived. This amazing injunction struck me like an electric shock; I thought everyone was wonderful at rehearsal, and where did that leave my efforts?

There was little time for soul-searching. Denis Johnston passed out a few notes, none for me, and the famous Abbey gong sounded three times. The curtain rose, the performance started. I stood in the wings at the side of the stage, with too much happening around me to take stock of my feelings or anyone else's. My cue came and I was on-stage with the Abbey Players, and I didn't faint or forget anything. Sometimes it seemed as if it were all a dream, and I had little recollection at the end of just how I had performed, but at last the curtain came down. The dress rehearsal was over, and the players sat around the stage waiting for notes and comments, and so did I.

While I was shaking at the back of the stage, Denis Johnston's towering figure loomed in front of me, and he beamed, gave me a big hug and said I was splendid, just what he wanted in the part. I felt such a rush of relief and affection for this dear man, a gentle giant by any definition. I was happy as never before, going to play, at fourteen, in my beloved Abbey with the best company in the world. Mother would be proud, Ria would not be let down by her pet student, Mícheál Mac Liammóir might hear about me and some day we might play together, and a brilliant writer had become my friend.

At school next day, everything was just like any other ordinary day. Of course I did not mention the 'Big Night' waiting at the end of the maths, geography, essays, and the break when I did not rush for the swing in the playground. I stood alone trying to eat a sandwich and to remember lines, a fatal mistake in the middle of all the other activities, for none would come. I had forgotten the words, and I wouldn't be able to swot them during French or Latin, not until I left for home – and then there was homework. I got the bus home stiff with fright and picked up the script; memory flooded back, and I relaxed again, and did my homework somehow.

Mother said that she would not be going to the play that night, explaining that sometimes it is an added burden if you feel you have to do better than your best for your family. I wanted Mother and Doris to be there, if it was a success, but in a perverse way also knew that she was right; I didn't want to think about them on that special night. Mother had a lovely picture card for me with all her love and good luck written on it, and Doris had added her name at the bottom. Doris said loftily 'Give them hell' as she was going out to the bus. Lizzie thought it was a school concert, and shouted 'Enjoy yourself' as I left.

Then I was somehow in the safety of the theatre, in the little room off the main dressing-rooms, which were spartan enough but well lit with bulbs all round the mirrors. Ria came in to wish me well and give a few last minute tips. She also made me up, but very little because she said that I must not look too made-up from the front, and the footlights were quite bright. I felt composed.

The Abbey Players, one by one, knocked on the door, wished me luck, and said that I had nothing to worry about. Nobody gave me a hug; they were not like that, more like Victorian aunts, anxious for your good, but not exactly warm. The men were more friendly, but in a gruff sort of way, except for F J McCormick, who was kind to everyone and possessed a humility out of keeping with his unique abilities and reputation.

The call-boy shouted at each door, 'Fifteen minutes', 'Ten minutes', Five minutes', and then 'Beginners, please', so that those who appeared early in the play were on-stage before the gong sounded. (When there was a small group of musicians under Dr Larchet, the distinguished composer/conductor, the call became 'Overture and Beginners, please'.) After the five-minute call, Denis Johnston came into my room with a bunch of flowers, said 'You'll be great' and kissed my cheek. I wanted him to stay, but could not say a word. After the last call I went down and stood in the wings beside Udolphus, known as 'Dossie', Wright, the stage manager, who muttered 'Good luck' and gave me a pat on the back. The three gongs sounded, and still I felt nothing.

Finally the curtain rose, the play started, my cue came and I walked out into the light. The cue came again, and I opened my mouth – and nothing happened; I could not make a sound. As though I might not have heard before, the cue was repeated more loudly, and I could hear a noise in the wings – Dossie swearing? At last a voice said my first line, timidly but gaining in strength as I knew it was mine and felt my way into my role.

At the end of the play, there was loud and lasting applause. I had been told where to stand in line with the company, and to take my bow from the centre player. Then the curtain was down for the last time, and I stood rooted to the stage, tears running down my cheeks. The whole cast tried to comfort me, saying nice cheering things, and Denis Johnston said he was happy with everyone, especially me, and was horrified that I was so upset. Ria came and brought me to the dressing-room, telling me that I had done very well for my first time, and would be even better by the end of the week.

I couldn't tell them that I wasn't crying for something that I might have missed or mistakes I might have made. It was because the play was over, and the magic world I had inhabited had been dissolved at the last curtain. I was so strung-up that I felt I couldn't go back to school and home and pretend that everything was the same as before.

Next day there were reviews in the papers. They said nice things about the play and everyone in the cast, and were especially nice about the 'little girl' who showed such sensitivity in her role. I was shown the reviews that night in the theatre; no one at home mentioned them, although I knew well that Mother had read them. She came to see me perform during the week, and thought I did quite well, on the whole. I learned afterwards that she was saying more complimentary things about me to her friends, but didn't want me to get 'notions', as I had enough problems. Uncle Joe came to see me too, and was absolutely bowled over by the whole thing; he did not stint his praise of the production or of me.

During that enchanted week I had to correct faults nightly; pull back when I was gabbling, and strive to be heard without losing the character. Dossie and the players were quick to tell me when I mistimed and spoiled someone else's lines, and I nearly died on those occasions; but I learned more in that week than I could ever have learned in six months in any acting school. Denis Johnston was there nearly every night. I talked to him more easily than I could to anyone else I knew, and felt confident somehow that I would be with him again in a play, or in some other field of work, in the future. He felt this too, and talked to me about his plays, and his plans to direct.

Later I realised how privileged I had been as a child to have known the beauty of the words 'a big man, in every sense'. Denis remained a hero to me for the rest of his life, and we did work together many times in radio and television until he left the theatre, along with writing and everything that had previously been foremost in his life, to become a brave and distinguished foreign correspondent during World War II. After that we lost contact, and I saw him only on social occasions, and again towards the end of his life when *The Moon in the Yellow River* was revived at the Abbey by Tomás Mac Anna. We met then, and reminisced and talked as though the years between had not made any changes.

Getting back to ordinary life was difficult. At home, no one behaved as if there was any difference. But I *was* different, going inwards again, not responding with any grace to good-natured gibes from Doris and my friends, making heavy weather of increasing school demands as I moved into a higher class and got more home study. My friends were unchanged, involved with horses or dogs as much as I was with plays, but no longer willing to join me in theatre games. At the School of Acting all the students congratulated me, but older ones such as Cecil Barror and a couple of others were critical as well as kindly in their comments.

There was an edge to some of the compliments that made me insecure. Ria could take me and everyone else apart when necessary, and we would only try harder, but the other students, probably because of my youth, went the wrong way about keeping me from the sin of vanity. After a big event – and playing in the Abbey was a 'big event' in anyone's book – there had to be 'down' symptoms, and criticism is not helpful to one in this trough of depression. Things started to go wrong in the Peacock.

Ria had worked hard on the school plays, and I had two leading roles in the major dramas. Suddenly I found myself unable to express the feelings I had for the characters, and could not bring the age-old malice and wisdom of Yeats's Faery Child to life. It was locked away inside me, as was the sadness and love of the sister Joanna in Sierra's *Cradle Song*, who could not face losing the orphan girl the nuns had taken in and reared. Maureen Jordan was my one hope; loyal and unselfish, she kept trying to find the words to unlock the floodgates that were building up inside me. I knew that the students meant no real harm, but the fact was that they were now making sharp comments in my hearing about young ones seeking attention.

Ria had us all to contend with, and had to ask the students to rehearse at home, or to come into the Peacock on days she would arrange and go over their scenes. She could not reach me, as I could not tell her what was wrong; indeed, I did not understand myself. The gift had deserted me, and I simply could not act any more. One day I was rehearsing with Maureen when a young man with a very English voice walked into the Peacock and, having watched us for a while, asked if Ria was coming in. He was of medium height with a thin, intelligent face, bright brown eyes and hair burnished like chestnuts, so handsome that we stared at him before telling him that Ria was at the Abbey rehearsing her next play, and that we were students. Maureen said all this as I just looked, and we wondered who he could be.

At the next Peacock meeting, Ria told us that he was the new Director of Plays at the Abbey (this position was later to be known as Artistic Director). She said he had done great things from Cambridge to the West End, and that the Abbey directors thought a change was needed. His name was Hugh Hunt. He came to the school one day when I was struggling through the Faery Child in *The Land of Heart's Desire* and asked Ria if he might have a word with the 'little girl'. He spoke to me about the part and the verse, and I told him about the feelings I had locked inside which would not come out. He laughed and said, 'Well, I've just turned the key, and all you have to do is believe.'

He asked Ria to run a scene from the play so that he could see the other students at work – and a miracle happened. I became carried away with the words, floating and 'dancing on the mountains like a flame', calling the young bride to leave her husband, the dull house, the old woman and the wise old folk, to come where 'the lonely of heart is withered away'. Ria, the other students and indeed I myself were speechless at the end of this demonstration, quite the most extrovert outpouring ever seen or heard in class before. The mouse had roared like a lion! Hugh Hunt whispered to Ria, then came up and told us that he was delighted with the scene he had witnessed. We were to work hard, as he was looking for new young talent to add to the Abbey Company, and would keep an eye on our progress. To me, now fifteen, a new enchantment had come into the magic world I longed to be part of forever; I had fallen in love.

With my busy life at real school and acting classes, I did not get much chance to see the exciting dramas at the Gate Theatre. I thought I would tell Mícheál Mac Liammóir about the forthcoming Peacock plays, and one day confided in Ria about my feelings for Mícheál, and how he had inspired me. Ria was an old friend of his, and promised to tell him about the school plays and invite him to come. Ria said that love took many forms, and that she herself had, when young, had desperate crushes on actors; these were real and sometimes painful emotions, but they didn't last. There was another love that some people were lucky enough to find that was unselfish and lasting. She said that Mícheál was a genius of the theatre, and that it was all right to worship at his shrine; but he was not romantically inclined towards women, and preferred them to be friends. But somehow I had always sensed this, and knew I would love Mícheál forever regardless.

Hugh Hunt came into the classes quite often at the beginning of his reign at the Abbey, and one day asked Ria if he might send me to a special dance instructor, as a stylised movement would give the role of the Faery Child an added dimension. I took lessons from a teacher called Sara Payne, who was given the task of matching balletic movement with the lines Yeats had written. There was a volcanic relationship between us, with me unused to the classical positions and Sara not used to having to devise steps for a virtual beginner, let alone follow the verse with its varying rhythms. I would dig in, resolutely doing as little as possible, and Sara would fling the book at me, until we both decided that whatever we were trying to do just would not work. Ria finally accepted the situation and decided on the minimum amount of stylized movement. Still, experiment was essential, and we had at least tried.

Miraculously the key had also turned in the lock insofar far as *Cradle Song* was concerned, and I was able again to get inside the character. After all, it was to do with love, an emotion I was beginning to feel in a real way. My heart soared when Hugh Hunt entered the room, and I was conscious of loss when I did not see him. I told no one; this was too precious and private. It did not matter if he never noticed me, so long as he was there to be noticed; I had it bad, all right. First love, never to be experienced again, and just as well.

Passion was not yet a word associated with love in my mind, although perhaps I had felt it about poetry and plays and performers; certainly about music, always in the background of everything I did or experienced. Sex did not occur to me, either. I still had only a sketchy knowledge of the subject, and it was assumed that I understood the facts of life; certainly I was not going to learn much about sex from the school plays or the Abbey repertoire. At that time the Abbey Theatre was known as the 'Monastery' by those sophisticates who favoured the Gate. But the Gate people were also inhibited as far as the spoken word was concerned when the subject was delicate, and although sex might be lurking underneath, limits were imposed.

It was a time when little could be overtly expressed that was real or raw, and movement or gesture could not be too revealing. Romantic love was the big attraction. Tragedy, classical and modern, thrived, and comedy was born out of gentle satire and observation of characters. O'Casey's *The Plough and the Stars*, the Abbey's most popular repertory revival, showed clearly that only the poor could speak and behave on-stage with the searing reality of their daily existence. Their humour, hunger and solidarity were given a savagely poetic voice by O'Casey, one of their own. Rosie Redmond, the prostitute, demonstrated clearly to the smugness of the age that only low, drunken women had casual sex with men. The word for the virtuous was respectable; it had to be shown in dress, in married or single status, in conformity to the norm.

We were not strictly respectable at our house, what with the theatre looming in my life, Mother's 'single' state ('Was she a widow or what?' you could hear the whispers) and Alexandra College, where conforming Catholics did not go. But no one was sure enough to label Mother and her brood; people may have been a little afraid of her reaction. I had discovered where Mother worked about a year earlier. She brought us to meet a Mr Morrison who owned Dublin's Olympia Theatre and Belfast's Empire. Mother was his agent for both theatres, finally helping to book shows for the Olympia only, while she completed her studies in chiropody, the work she really wanted to do.

The Peacock plays were to open in a week, and I lived on the desire to do my very best for Ria, and on my growing fear that Hugh Hunt might go away and not bother with the students once the term was over. I would have to see him again, and I longed for the plays to be on so that he might see and speak to me. My ballet teacher had refused to attend any further rehearsals since the movements she had devised had been largely abandoned, and this was a relief. Even Dermot Tuohy, who teased me unmercifully most of the time, told me that I was better off without the 'dying swan' bit, adding that I was not half bad.

The senior students were always chatting about what they would wear, how they were dying of nerves and whether their fellows would enjoy the plays. They tended to close ranks when I tried to join their conversations, wanting to keep their talk adult; a gym slip is a symbol of immaturity, but I still felt that they were very stand-offish at the time. I had Maureen, however, my friend through all the school years. I shall always remember with gratitude her friendship and counsel at a time when I was going through a most difficult phase.

The dress rehearsal was on a Saturday, and needed a whole day, with two plays on the bill. Costumes came from the Abbey, reasonable fits based on measurements sent earlier to the wardrobe mistress. *The Land of Heart's Desire* was first, and Ria stopped and started as the lighting plan was adjusted, so that it was impossible to get a complete run at the play. My dress was traditional faery garb, filmy green material with berries and leaves woven into skirt and bodice, and a head-dress of leaves and silver cobwebby stuff. Arms and legs were tanned from a bottle, and my face made up eerily with winged eyebrows and green eye-shadow. The others wore flowing robes and, as they were young people playing at being aged, they had beards and lines put on their faces. As Ria said, the rest had to be acted. Moya Devlin, a sister of the poet, Denis Devlin, played the young bride, and looked fabulous. But then everyone was marvellous or seemed so, although I did not think of them or myself as being on a par with the Abbey Players.

As the day wore on, and we broke for sandwiches I realised that Hugh Hunt had not appeared. I asked Ria if he would be along later, but she said that he was busy, but might come to our opening night on Monday. I felt utterly miserable, thinking that he could not have cared about the students after all, or he would not have left them at the dress rehearsal when they needed his guidance. But the break was soon over, and I had to don the nun's costume and veil, having creamed off the Faery Child's strange face and applied a more normal one.

I used my disappointment and disproportionate misery at Hugh's absence to good effect in *Cradle Song*, weeping buckets when there was time for it. This brought a note from Ria; tears were fine, but too much moisture could saturate make-up, or even costume, and sorrow could be conveyed with less waterworks. We all sat down for notes; Ria was pleased enough, but wary of complacency. Once again I had gabbled in two speeches and fallen over my feet. Dermot had boomed through the small theatre; others had been too young in their movements and so on. I went home half-elated, resolved to spend a blameless weekend so that God would look after us all on Monday, and make Hugh Hunt appear.

The day of the opening of the Peacock shows I must have asked the time interminably from every girl who had a watch. At last I was free to gather my books, and fled straight to the theatre to be in the atmosphere of the place. Of course I was nervous; backstage, as other players arrived, I did not want to talk. Ria came to help with the difficult make-up for the Faery Child. There was a lot of chatter and laughter in the small dressing-rooms that had to hold so many, but it was all a bit strained. Everyone was on edge, no one untouched by the excitement. Ria came in again to wish us all good luck, and to tell us that she had forbidden any other visitors before the play, as actors had quite enough to contend with. But she also told us that all the directors of the Abbey wished us luck, and would be in to see us before the shows were over.

So he might be there; I didn't dare to ask. The five-minute call had been given, and the stand-by was imminent. I would do my very best tonight and play for him, because I felt he was there. With his help I could dance in the woods and seduce the young bride with a promise of eternal youth, defy the priest and reduce his prayers to mumbo-jumbo. I could steal the soul of the young bride and go off singing, while the cries of the bridegroom were lost on the wind. Then the play was over, and we bowed to the enthusiastic house, and rushed to become nuns for the second half of the programme.

Ria came in to give a hand with the nuns' habits, and said that she was very pleased. She spoke about the mood of *Cradle Song*, telling me to relax before the curtain rose again, and to wipe the memory of the first play out of my mind as though it had never been. She said that she was sitting with someone very important who had loved the first play, and my heart soared. It must be Hugh Hunt; who else could it be? I went on-stage with a light heart, although feeling a little sick with butterflies, but this was forgotten as the play unfolded. Although trying to concentrate on my own part of Sister Joanna, I noticed how Maureen Jordan lifted the play when she entered, and how everyone responded to her superb rendering of the orphan girl.

Maureen and I played together as though no one else existed, and afterwards hugged each other as if the feelings expressed in the play had become real for us. Such a buzz of excited noise and talk, and people crashing through the door to the tiny backstage space to congratulate their sons and daughters – except for Dermot, Maureen and myself, who knew that our families would not be coming. Dermot's parents were both ill, and he was being brought up by some elderly relative. Then Ria appeared to tell us that we had all done her proud, and to come in early next evening for notes. No one came with her. She said that the Abbey director thought we were all very talented, and that if we worked hard we might be chosen some day to join the Abbey Company.

# 7

# *Starry-Eyed*

I said goodnight, and Maureen walked me to the bus stop. My heart was broken, and there was no feeling of anything to be happy about; only a sick ache in my stomach, and a head ready to burst from all the nervous tension I had created to supply both roles. Maureen could not understand why I was not over the moon as she was.

When I got home I felt even worse, and Mother was concerned when she learned that I had not eaten anything since school break. She scolded, and would allow no talk about the play until every bite of supper was eaten, and then packed me off to bed so that I could get up early to do my homework. Eventually she saw the plays herself before she heard about them from me. She put my bad form down to hunger and nerves, but I broke my heart crying in bed that night over the missing Hugh Hunt. How stupid I had been to think he would continue to have an interest in students. He had Ria and all the Abbey players to work with; why would he be interested in watching a bunch of beginners? I fell asleep whispering 'the play's the thing', as it seemed like the only remedy I could think of, and Mícheál had told me to read *Hamlet* before seeing it in the Gate. In the morning I didn't want to get up, not for any reason. Mother told me to stay in bed if I was ill, but that would mean not turning up for the play that night, so I tumbled out of bed and washed as if in a dream. I was low in energy, in the aftermath of the performance, and felt an ache somewhere like a nagging tooth. Somehow I got through the day.

Then I took the bus to the Peacock, anxious not to be late for Ria's notes. Maureen was already there, and showed me the newspapers, which contained some reviews of the student dramas. We were both praised highly for *Cradle Song*, as were the others, and I got very special mentions for the Faery Child – with a reference in one paper praising my 'pose' over my enunciation.

(I *had* gabbled, after all.) There was a slightly critical mention for everyone in the Yeats play about the quality of the verse speaking, but otherwise the plays and Ria's direction were well received. I could only think miserably that Hugh Hunt would read the bit about my enunciation, and think I had no talent.

Ria thought the papers were excellent on the whole, and told us that she did not blame us for not mastering the verse; this took a lot of time, and we had been rushed into a most difficult play. She opened another paper which contained a wonderful review of both plays, read them to us and then sat us down and went over our faults. She smiled kindly at me and said 'You know what you did, don't you? You got carried away and forgot the clarity.' I nodded miserably.

She spoke of the courage needed by actors to carry on even if things went wrong; and she spoke of her own colleagues in the Abbey, some of whom had continued playing their parts when their fathers or mothers had died, and of one actress who went on the night her child died.

This little homily galvanised the students, and I realised that I must put my misery behind me and strive to do better, because, after all, nobody belonging to me had died, and that must be a much greater sorrow than loving someone. That night the shows were better, and I was more controlled. Each night afterwards there was an improvement, and Maureen would listen to me from the wings and tell me if I fuzzed my words as the Faery Child.

Finally one night I gave a performance in which everything jelled – movement, pace, feeling, clarity – and I felt on top of the world again. I blotted out the memory of the young artistic director who had touched my life so briefly and painfully, and went home that night with Mother and Doris each holding my hand and praising me. It made me blush in a happy way, although Doris liked the other students just as much, especially Maureen, and Mother said we were all good, so I didn't get special mention in case I got a swelled head.

On the last night all the students made up and dressed before the show with the usual sadness when a show is ending. All my life I have sensed that deep regret, when a company have become a family, a team dedicated to a play, a director and each other. The last night of the run brings a sense of breaking up no matter how successful the show has been and no matter what other exciting work lies ahead.

At the Peacock that night, we all determined that we should make the last show the very best, not only that we would always remember it, but also to reward Ria for all she had given us, for the work she had put in while having to act in the Abbey herself nearly every week. With that sort of esprit, the shows were good, and at the end we folded and packed away our stage clothes with at least a sense of having done our best. We were just about to turn out the lights and leave for home when Hugh Hunt came backstage, smiling at us all, saying 'Well done', and once again it was as if all the lights had been turned on, and I was lost in a flood of joy.

I had intended to get the bus with Maureen, who was in a hurry that night, but heard her shout 'Goodbye, see you next week' while I was still there, standing without a word while he spoke to the remaining students. Then he asked me if I could wait awhile so that we could talk; I nodded and went down into the auditorium, sitting in case my trembling knees might give way. He came down from the stage and said goodnight to the last students left in the building; then said that they were about to lock up the theatre, and asked if I would like a lift home, and that we could talk in his car. I managed a mumbled thanks, and, as we were getting into the car, asked where Ria was. He answered that she had to go out to supper and had sent him to see us off on our last night, adding that he had been coming anyway.

It was a lovely warm night, and we sat for a while just talking about the show; then he started the car and drove quickly away from the city. We would drive a little way out of town and look at the lights, he said; looking back on a city was much nicer than living in one. He had rented a house on the Howth Road with a view of the sea and a sizeable garden. I loved him even more with each word he spoke. Once he turned to me and said that he liked being at the Abbey, but that he was lonely. I asked him if he was married. He laughed, and said that wouldn't come for many years until he had achieved something worthwhile in the theatre. He didn't know anyone here who could be his friend, someone he could talk to about the things that mattered. He could have friends in the Abbey Company, but they were working together, and he was not on their wavelength outside of the work. He thought Ria was the nearest to his ideal of friendship.

He stopped the car, and we stared at the lighted houses, like twinkling palaces of coloured crystal, and I said, 'Could I be your friend?' And he smiled and said, 'I was hoping for that.' He asked if I was ever lonely, and I answered 'Yes, all the time, really.' I told him that Mother was out working, that I saw little of my sister, that we had a minder who cooked for us and that nobody really wanted to hear me sounding off non-stop about the theatre. He took my hand and said we would meet soon again, but that it would have to be our secret because people in the Abbey and the school might misunderstand and think I was a favourite of his, and that he would not assess my work honestly.

I wanted it to be a secret too; it was even better that way. I could love him secretly and sometimes be with him, and nobody would know. He drove me home then in case Mother would be worried, and left me a little way from the house. He said that he would see me next week, and put his arm around me as he opened the door. We whispered goodnight, and he said that he was very happy that we were meeting again, and he would look forward to it. I went up the street tingling from his touch, blessing the dark that he did not see my face ablaze, my heart light as never before. He was beautiful, clever and talented, and I was his friend.

Memories of that year, when summer seemed more rich and fragrant than I could ever have imagined, remained long after the seasons changed and the magic ran out. There was no acting class until autumn, yet we managed to steal away, meeting out of sight of houses and theatres where we might be noticed, driving away to explore woodlands, to walk through meadows and lie in the sun, laughing like children and sometimes embracing, rolling over in the warm grass. He quoted Rupert Brooke and Shakespeare's sonnets, and said that 'Shall I compare thee to a summer day?' was written for *me*. We talked of our hopes and dreams, and I tumbled hawthorn blossoms over his head, shaking the branches until he was covered in the petals, and we had to pick them out of his hair and clothes before he appeared in the Abbey that night.

He told me to read as many plays as I could and, realising my painful shyness, tried to build my self-esteem. I still blushed easily, and often buried my face in his chest when it happened, but he told me it was nothing to be ashamed of; in fact, he said, it suited me because I was normally pale. We both loved nature and went for long walks holding hands and finding wild blooms hiding in the undergrowth; we lay by lakes, and listened to the sound of water.

I would tell Mother that I was meeting a friend, and she would assume it was a school friend or Maureen. But Doris grew suspicious because she knew I had normally no interest in my appearance, and here I was borrowing blouses and skirts, and brushing my straight hair until it shone. I had to be careful when Doris was around when I was going to meet him. Our meetings were always a few weeks apart because of his rehearsal schedule and board meetings, and I spent the time in between reading poetry, listening to music, meeting Maureen and going to Abbey and Gate plays. We left Mac Liammóir alone that year, content with silent worship from the stalls.

I went to Abbey rehearsals, often chatting to Anne Yeats, the great poet's daughter, who was an artist studying theatre design, and we had a brief, rewarding meeting of minds over the work and actors we admired. Once Anne brought me to her house, where I was greeted by Mrs Yeats, a charming lady; Anne warned me that we would have to be very quiet, as 'Daddy might be working'. I hoped to get a glimpse of W B, but he did not appear; and I thought it curious that this great man had a house and family just like ordinary mortals.

I enjoyed Anne's company while she was at the Abbey. We went to films together, including one called *Mayerling*, which starred a very young and attractive Charles Boyer. We both swooned over him while we were in the cinema, and laughed about it when we came out. We sometimes went to a restaurant before or after the cinema, pooling our pennies and ordering what we could afford. Tea or coffee with a chocolate biscuit was really living it up, and Anne was used to restaurants and ordering meals, so that my own gaucherie didn't trouble me. Of course I couldn't go to a restaurant with Hugh; we would certainly be seen and talked about, and I felt that even Mother would not understand.

Hugh always brought a small picnic for us if we had enough time to bother with food. Once I made him laugh by trying to cook watercress for a salad the first time I went to his house. I had never prepared food before, and he was astonished at how little I knew about cooking – not that he was an expert, a salad and cold meat being the height of his culinary achievement. After we had eaten a little, we sat listening to music while the sun streamed in through the windows; and after the record had stopped and we had fallen silent, he drew me close and kissed me. It was a long, hard kiss, and I opened my body and spirit to the surge of feelings it aroused.

When it was over, he sat with his arms around me, staring at the pool of sunlight pouring in from the window. I couldn't speak, nor could he. I turned in his arms and kissed him, and suddenly there was a wildness in the way we clung to each other, caressing each other. Then he pulled me to my feet and said that he was sorry, and he drove me back to the city without a word. He said 'I'll see you' as I got out of the car, but we made no plans. We had been overcome by age-old emotions that had changed everything for both of us. It was impossible to think straight, when my love for him had become confused by the physical impulses released in me by that first kiss.

Whatever happened, I knew that I must protect Hugh, sensing that if anyone discovered our relationship, he would be blamed, and this was not fair. I may have been younger, but I was the one who had loved first, wanted to spend every moment in his company and deceived everyone about my whereabouts when we were together. I never thought of parting from him; things would, I supposed, be different between us, but I would run away if anyone tried to stop us from meeting. I practised a kind of composure on the way home, although my heart was beating hard and I felt like blurting out my wonderful secret to them all.

At tea-time I chatted to Mother and Doris, and was very co-operative when Mother said that she had plans for that weekend; she wanted to bring us to Mr Morrison's house. She explained that she would be leaving the Olympia soon, and warned me not to mention this. Mr Morrison's daughter, 'Baby', was to be married later that year, and had asked if Doris could be one of the bridesmaids, and if I could be a flower-girl. We would have beautiful dresses and be allowed to stay for the reception, and Mother wanted us to meet the Morrison family so that they could discuss the wedding plans.

I knew that there was no chance of seeing Hugh for at least a week, so fell in with these plans, and even agreed to stay in so that Doris could go out that evening. Lizzie was off for the day, Aunt Lena was courting, and Mother and Joe were going to the pictures. Doris was meeting her friend Patty, or so she said, but she was older now and entitled to go out with a boy if Mother knew about it.

Doris came home that night before Mother, and shouted at me to find the eau de Cologne, for God's sake. She was a bit rosier than usual, and I thought her a little frightened, which was very unusual for such a carefree and confident person. I found the eau de Cologne in Mother's drawer in her bedroom, and to my amazement

Doris filled a glass with water, poured a little of the cologne into it and drank the mixture. Then she opened her mouth, asked me if I could smell the scent on her breath, and I could; so Doris splashed a little around her neck and down her jacket saying 'There, I think I'll get away with it, but you shut up!' I put the cologne back, and Doris told me that she had gone with her friend to a party where they had met two boys who danced with them, and dared them to have gin and lime-juice from the drinks cabinet which was strictly for grown-ups.

Doris and her friend had a small gin-and-lime each, but as she was still only seventeen, she knew that Mother would be furious, and left early to cover up the smell of the alcohol. Mother once told us we could drink what we liked when we were twenty-one, but in order to save us from turning into alcoholics because drink was barred in the house, she adopted the continental method of bringing up children to drink wine with a little water at Sunday meals.

Doris and I were in bed when Mother came in on the eau de Cologne night, and Doris whispered that she really fancied the fellow at the party who had given her the dare, as he was just like Clark Gable without the moustache, with gorgeous black wavy hair. I whispered back that I had met a fellow who was also gorgeous, but more like Rupert Brooke. Doris said 'You're too young to be thinking of boys, no one will go steady with you at your age.' I hugged my knowledge close to my heart and said 'Ssh, here's Mother.' Mother came over to kiss us goodnight, and did not suspect a thing, remarking only that Doris should not use so much cologne.

I thought of my own dearest Hugh, so different from the fellows my sister and her friends admired. He had told me that one day we would have a candle-lit dinner with wine on the table, and there would be blue sea and sunshine late into the evening, warmer than it was at midday in Ireland. But we would have to go abroad, he said, and I was still too young.

Some weeks went by, and I didn't hear a word. He used to send little notes, because I had told him that Mother would never touch anyone's letters even if you were very young. She thought that was a dreadful betrayal of trust, opening another person's post, and advised us never to do it. I got letters from pen-friends and school-friends on holidays, so there was no special interest in the odd small envelope that nestled in my meagre post now and then, always signed 'love, H'. No letter came, no word at all. I began to have nightmare visions of his having departed from the Abbey, or worse still, having been injured in a car crash.

I could not endure these terrible thoughts, and told Mother I had to attend rehearsals, which was a routine when I was at acting school. One hot, dusty day I walked into town, saving the bus-fare for contingencies, and arrived breathless at the Abbey to find that the players had broken for lunch. There I bumped into the Secretary, Eric Gorman, a small, lively man who was usually very cross whenever the students addressed him, but was said to have the warmest heart in the business. He also acted from time to time, and was the best Uncle Peter in *The Plough and the Stars* that I have ever seen. I gathered the courage to ask whether the company would be rehearsing with Mr Hunt that afternoon, and he said, 'Oh, they'll be there all right, but Hunt is gone to London.' The world came to an end as he spoke.

I walked across O'Connell Bridge and looked down at the water shimmering in the sun, low enough through lack of rainfall to smell a little. There was no need to hurry anywhere now. Ria was busy rehearsing; Mícheál was at the Gate, but even if he was free I could not tell him. God was the only one I could tell, and He knew anyway. I turned and made for Nelson's Pillar. I had a whole sixpence, and maybe they would let me climb up; I could think better looking over the city.

They let me in for threepence, and I climbed the narrow winding stairs, up and up, until I reached the top. I looked over the railings at the pygmies below, with their tiny splashes of colour and their muted cries of 'Tuppence a bunch of violets'. Somewhere out there, across the city and river and sea, he had gone, so suddenly ... why? I knew he would not be staying in the Abbey more than a few years, but surely he should have finished his term – he was on contract. Had I anything to do with his flight? How could I, he hadn't even written to or seen me, and surely kissing would not have such a drastic effect on a grown man? If he really wanted to stop seeing me, he had only to say so; he did not have to leave the country. Eventually, I came down from the Pillar and took the long, lonely road home.

Then Mother received a letter from the Abbey asking if I would be permitted to take the part of a page-boy in Hugh Hunt's forthcoming production of *Hassan* by James Elroy Flecker. She read this to me as I lay forlornly in bed; immediately I jumped up, demanded the dates and hugged her. Mother feared that I might be delirious, and I was. Rehearsals were to start next week. He was coming back, I was not deserted, and life was very sweet.

I arrived at the Abbey for the reading, and there he was, in command of play and cast, introducing us to the designer, Tanya Moiseiwitsch. She was a beautiful Russian girl he had worked with at Cambridge and in London, and was now a top designer in the West End. Tanya was tall, slim and olive-skinned and had impeccable English. The world-famous pianist, Benno Moiseiwitsch was her father. (I had heard his records, and was already a fan.) I said a polite good-morning to Miss Crowe and Mr McCormick and Ria, who seemed pleased to see me, and to any of the other Abbey players with whom I had already worked. Then we all sat down. There were four page-boys (girls, really), and again I was the youngest. Others were singers, as Hugh was doing the West-End version of *Hassan*, with incidental music and a few songs.

The play was read, and I thought the verse beautiful, being just at the age for lush poetry. Ria was playing Jasmine, a beautiful lady with many lovers, and Denis O'Dea, who was macho and good-looking, was playing the hero. I did not have many lines, but had more than the other page-boys, and we all had to sing the songs to back up the principals. 'We take the golden road to Samarkand' was one of the songs we sang to cover a scene-change. We pages had to run in and out of the action all through the play, and I found this much harder than sustaining a longer role; it was easy to miss a cue or entrance, and one had to wait and watch and never lose concentration.

During rehearsals, Hugh was oblivious to anything but the work in hand, and I thought this quite proper. After all, that was what dedication meant, and you could not be thinking of other things when you had an immense production to put on, with a cast who doubted the wisdom of choosing such a strange play. Most of them hated it and their roles in it, and I fretted about Hugh, and often had to bite my lip. I wanted to tell them how beautiful the play was, and how all they had to do was trust Hugh, and they would be splendid and different. Certainly this play was not in the usual Abbey mould, but I loved every minute of it, and when the dress rehearsal came and I saw the sets, I wanted to hug Tanya and Hugh. There wasn't anyone to hug among the players I had met so far, although Maureen Delany looked like a good bet. I felt a motherly warmth from this rather stout actress who could play such wonderful comedy roles, and then could knock you out with the death scene in *The Plough and the Stars.*

The first night came, and I thought it was all magical. I listened in the wings, and voted Ria the best verse speaker ever. Even though my voice was small and piping, I sang in tune and ran about paging and happily projecting my few lines. We pages had to colour our arms, legs and faces brown, which meant a long hot wash at home, and three baths instead of the usual weekly one. On the first night, I shyly told Tanya that she was wonderful, and when Hugh came to see the cast, I just smiled at him like the others, then left for the bus with a few of the cast. I felt happy for him, and believed that the play would be a huge success.

But the next evening in the Green Room, when the cast assembled for notes, the players were talking about the poor reviews, and some of them had not come well out of it. Hugh came in and gave us a pep talk about the ways of critics, and how they took time to accept change in an institution like the Abbey. He told the company to be confident, to accept new experience and stretch themselves, because they were really one of the greatest national theatres in the world. When he left, the grumbling started again, and I found myself getting angry with the players and sorry for Hugh, who had given them the chance to break out of their ordinary routine. But it was all right to feel that way if you were young, in love and not carrying the good name of the Abbey, which is how the players must have felt.

One night when I went into the wings to watch the actors, as I did every spare moment, Hugh came and stood beside me and whispered, 'Can I pick you up tomorrow, usual place?' I turned and smiled 'Yes', and he was gone. I met Hugh the following day, and we drove along the sea-front towards Killiney. The autumn day had a frosty feel to it; summer was ending, and I was due back in Alexandra in a week. I told him that I wanted to leave school, to concentrate on acting, but he grew quite stern, saying that I must finish school and go to University. 'You'll need all the learning you can get hold of,' he warned.

I did not have to be a brilliant scholar, he said, or to be laden with degrees, but I must gather information like a squirrel from my studies; and, after all, I was going to the most enlightened school in the country. I would have one more year in the School of Acting, and then there would be changes in the Abbey. His own contract would run out next year, and he would have to leave to take up a new position in England. He saw the stricken look on my face, and said that there was plenty of time to talk about that, that here and now was more important.

He parked the car at the edge of the Vico Road looking down into the breathtaking blue of the bay. He wiped away my tears, which I could not hold back when he spoke of leaving; and as we were alone, he took me in his arms and kissed me again, holding me tightly until the tears had gone and a surge of fierce joy overcame all other feeling. I clung to him, kissing him, wanting him in some way I could not define, knowing this was not enough for either of us. We tore apart from each other; now *he* was crying, and I tried to comfort him without knowing why he was so sad, and could find no words to help either of us. We drove back, holding hands whenever possible, and he decided to risk a little house that said 'Teas', and we sat in a corner of a small room with coloured linen table cloths and chintz curtains, drinking tea but unable to eat the scones he had ordered.

Hugh talked about *Hassan*, and his new plans for the Abbey, which included an adaptation of a short story by Frank O'Connor. He wanted to adapt the story himself, and also wanted to do a different version of *The Playboy of the Western World*, with a rather unusual Pegeen Mike. He knew there was unease among the company because of his new approach, but thought this natural as they had lived in a sheltered world for many years, where little change had been possible. He thought that he would be more appreciated after he had gone, and hoped to come back for future productions, as he had grown to love the Abbey and Ireland. His family had a very strong influence on him, and he explained that he would live in England, and travel as much as possible. He said that I, too, would travel one day with a theatre company, and was to contact him whenever I was in London. He would always help me.

We talked about books, about Mother's unique library; the love of the very smell of books and of browsing in old shops hoping to find rare editions. We held hands without speaking again of our inner tumult, but it was there, in every look and pressure of clasped hands. When he had driven me home in silence, stopping the usual distance from the house, he asked me to write to him, giving me a safe address to which to post the letters.

He gave me a book of Emily Bronte's poems inscribed 'for Phyllis, because she is my friend', and signed it 'Hugh Hunt'; it was best to be formal, as books could be mislaid. We hugged each other and parted. I went straight to the bookshelves and took down books of poetry, Browning, Tennyson, anything that would help me to write to Hugh with style and eloquence. In the end, I wrote a very confused love letter including bits of all of them. I hid it under the pillow that night, posted it next day and then wished it back lest it might make him laugh. He did not answer this.

School term began, followed by the renewal of acting school. I found to my delight that there were some new students, two of them around my own age. One was Maureen Kiely, later to marry the great Cyril Cusack, who had joined the Abbey Company some years before; and the other was Madge Heron, wonderfully gifted but quite undisciplined when it came to taking instructions. She abandoned acting to become a poet, and we lost touch with her. But Maureen, a small girl from Derry with large eyes, became a good friend. She had incomparable charm, an elfin quality that was quite irresistible. Moya Devlin had been called into the Abbey to take part in a Yeats play, and some of the other girls also got small Abbey roles, so things were getting exciting.

Ria used that year to polish our various abilities. She demonstrated how to improve movement, voice and grease-paint techniques: how to develop the mentality of age so that movement and voice would follow; how to time a line; how to achieve clarity while speaking rapidly; how to look at the back of the Abbey Theatre when we got a chance to work there, and pitch our voices at a spot in the furthest wall; how to cope with a bad 'dry' (forgetting lines during a performance) by keeping cool and waiting for the prompt. It was a year in a technical forcing-house.

At Alexandra, I worked harder than I had in the previous year, remembering what Hugh had said, hoping to go on to University and keep on acting as well. Occasionally I would catch a glimpse of him as we came into the street from the Peacock, and my heart would jump and the yearning rise again. But I was able to convince myself that I was working for him, in school and acting class, and this helped to fight the loneliness of being without him.

At home, things were going well. Joe was such a good companion for Mother that I no longer felt envious; Doris had finished school, and was taking a secretarial course. Lizzie had settled in through the years and was, though somewhat frail, happier and healthier with us than she could have been in her own home. We were an untidy lot, and Lizzie would grumble but go on picking up the debris we left about the house. She did some cooking, too, and loved to hear about our comings and goings, warning us not to go out with 'fast' fellows or girls.

One day I got a formal letter from Hugh, on Abbey notepaper, asking me to come for an interview to the Abbey at 3 o'clock one Friday afternoon. It was signed 'Hugh Hunt, Artistic Director, Abbey Theatre', and though I knew those letters had to be business-like, I wondered why he hadn't included a little note to say what the interview was to be about. Still, I would see him, and it could not be anything bad, or Ria would have warned me at acting class.

I went to the Abbey after school, passed the stage where the company was rehearsing and went up to the small office, knocking timidly on the door. A voice said, 'Come in', and I stepped nervously into the room. Hugh was sitting at a table with Lennox Robinson and a tall man I didn't know, and F R Higgins, the poet, was standing at a window. Hugh got me a chair, and introduced me to the third man, who was Frank O'Connor. I had met Lennox Robinson before during Denis Johnston's play, and F R Higgins had been introduced to the students by Ria after they had performed extracts from *The Plough and the Stars*, when F R had told me I was the best 'Mollser' he had seen. It was scary sitting there with all those famous men.

Higgins, who seemed to be the head man on the Board of Directors, told me they were anxious to know what my plans were when I was finished at the School of Acting, as there would be a vacancy in the company next year, and they needed a good juvenile player. Would I be interested, or did my parents have plans for my education that might clash with a position as a full-time member of the Abbey? I managed to say, 'Thank you, I want to be in the Abbey.' Lennox, who spoke with a cultured drawl, elongating his vowels and sounding utterly fatigued and bored (which he never was) said he thought I should finish my education before entering such a dreadfully difficult profession, but I said that I would continue with my studies if Mother would let me join the company.

I overcame my nerves sufficiently to tell them that I wanted this chance more than anything. Frank O'Connor twinkled and said 'That's the right attitude.' Hugh pointed out that I would not be in every play, and should be able to combine College with my career. They all seemed happy with this, even Lennox, although he huffed and puffed a little before saying that I would be a perfect 'Ducky' in his own play, *The Far-Off Hills*, and that all the other 'Duckys' were far too long in the tooth. Then I was outside the room, with stars in my eyes and feeling that all my Christmases had come together.

I crossed the stage on tiptoe, although there was no one left to disturb, and stood looking out at the darkened auditorium imagining myself playing all the great parts. I hardly noticed Hugh standing beside me. He took my hand, and we walked across the stage and out into the lane. We drove in the direction of Grafton Street, and he parked the car at Stephen's Green, and we went into the park. It was a chilly autumn day and there were few people about, so we sat by the big pond under golden trees that were shedding their leaves. Hugh told me that he was glad the directors had decided to take me into the company, and then said that I must be very brave and try to understand what he had to tell me.

He would not be able to see me again in the way we had been seeing each other. I would have to dedicate myself to my career for the present, and he would do the same. Our friendship would not change, but until I was some years older we could not meet secretly. or be alone together. I saw the leaves falling into the pond, and the willow tree drooping over the still pool at the back of the little island, reflecting my desolation. I turned to him, asking why he did not love me any more, and he answered that he did love me, that I must trust him. He would still be there to help me in every way, and would think of his 'little friend' often.

He had told me that my lack of guile, unaffected youth and ability to love with no thought of gain, had fascinated him from the beginning, and made me easy to talk to, to confide in. He had loved my sense of wonder, my excitement when he gave me a small gift. I knew he would be lonely, too, so I smiled at him and said that I would grow up some day, and maybe then we would not have to hide and pretend, because, of course, I believed that love was forever. He left me in Stephen's Green, because I asked him to. I wanted to think, and did not want him to see me break down, because that was inevitable. As I walked home through the park, autumn was not advanced enough to have done more than touch the trees with colour, the yellows and crimsons that looked as though some artist had been at work on the leaves.

When Mother heard about the offer I had received from the Abbey directors, she wasn't exactly over the moon. After all, she pointed out, I was still at school, and even in a year my education would not be complete; she thought I should wait and get some qualifications for earning a secure living, which was not to be found in the theatre. I told her that I would seize my chance regardless of education, and accused her of trying to ruin my life. This built to a degree of hysteria that unnerved us both, with Mother trying to reason with my childish threats to run away, or worse.

Next morning I thought of a plan that might ease my problems with Hugh. I would attend more Abbey rehearsals; he would know I was there, and there would be some consolation in being near him even if we didn't speak. Ria had made it clear that she wanted students to attend Abbey rehearsals as much as possible. I put this plan into action, and was always to be seen at the back of the stalls as soon as I got out of Alex, watching them work, watching him.

Then one day he came and sat beside me when the company had gone to lunch, and said that he was going away for a holiday in Switzerland, and would write to me from there. That was all, but it was enough. I could live on that. But at the Peacock during class that week, I heard some of the girls talking about Hugh Hunt and his latest lady friend. Apparently he had been seen with Shelah Richards, Coralie Carmichael from the Gate and God knows who else. There was usually a lot of gossip about the Abbey Company, and affairs were very much on the agenda, largely because they were typically so staid and proper that the gossips had nothing to get their teeth into until handsome Hugh came along.

Maureen Kiely wasn't interested in Hugh, being mad about Cyril Cusack from the moment she saw him; he was a splendid actor and had many female admirers. My heart turned over when I heard the prattle about Hugh, but I still had my secret, and although I suffered pangs of jealousy because I couldn't go out with him, I believed that the older actresses were just friends, and not special as I was. Then Ria told us she would be away for a fortnight; she was going to Switzerland with Hugh Hunt. Ria had been talking a lot about Hugh at that time, and it occurred to me that she might be in love with him too.

I had to know something definite, but where could I learn the truth? I was frightened, so confused that I was in danger of throwing away all that I had worked for by leaving the acting school, the Abbey and all the heartbreak behind forever. I crept quietly into the Abbey stalls, and there was Hugh, discussing a point with one of the actors. He saw me and, when the actor left the stage, came down, knowing there was something wrong. He said I looked haunted, and I whispered to him all that I had heard, and that I wondered if he loved Ria now.

He laughed and said, 'Not at all, but I like her immensely!' explaining that Ria was going to her friends in Switzerland, he was going to his, and they would hardly see each other until the journey home. And he told me that gossip was a very dangerous weapon, that people could be destroyed by it, and warned me always to seek the truth in any story before jumping to conclusions. Then he grinned and asked me if I really wanted him to live like a hermit, without adult company? I smiled back at him, and it was all right again. He took my hand and said, 'It was different with you, didn't you know?' then told me to go out ahead of him, teasing me about the need to avoid gossip as I left.

He wrote from Switzerland, a brief note saying that he was enjoying the break, and wished that I could share the beauty of the Alps, the majesty of their white peaks, the blue gentians growing wild in the grass; he was sure I would love it. He made an appointment to see me when he got back, as though he had never closed the door on our meetings. I met him for a short while in the Peacock, one afternoon when no one was working there, and he gave me a brooch, a circle of blue and pink flowers on a gold base. It was simple, and the loveliest thing I had ever owned.

We did not embrace. He asked how I was and I said that I missed him very much; he told me to try to be happy, since there was so much ahead for both of us in our work. He told me to go to a circus whenever I could, and wished he could take me to one. I must learn about laughter and comedy, and this would help when things looked black. People thought he had no sense of humour, because he was not very good himself at seeing the funny side of things. But he had laughed with me, and my solemn face and childish excitement at small happenings he took for granted had lightened his spirit.

We left separately, preserving our secret. It was also to be a secret (except, of course, from Mother) that I had been called to see the Abbey directors, for the time being anyway. I was oppressed by all the things I could not talk about; there had been secrecy in our home for as long as I could remember – about my father, Uncle Joe, our lack of relatives, Mother's connection with the theatre and the new career she had now begun to pursue full-time.

# 8

# *Shadows and Substance*

**M**other had qualified over the years as a chiropodist and masseuse, and had a small number of clients each evening between six and seven o'clock. She continued to work at the Olympia Theatre, and explained to us that she would leave that job when she became more expert in her new career. A room had been equipped for this in the building in Anne Street where she worked for Mr Morrison. Mother had, she said, always enjoyed work which involved healing people, and would have liked to have been a doctor; this was the closest she could get to it at her age.

Uncle Joe brought a lot of his newspaper work home in the evenings, and smoked cigarettes non-stop while he pored over it into the small hours. I often used to call into his room for a chat, in the course of which he would give me pocket-money, telling me never to go short of it. He talked to me about writing, and read my attempts at poetry, urging me to keep it up and doling out small amounts of criticism and large dollops of praise.

I had been very lucky with most of the men I knew. As well as Joe there were Denis Johnston, Denis O'Dea and Cyril Cusack, the last two rising stars of the Abbey and very easy to get on with. And there were Mícheál Mac Liammóir and Hugh Hunt, so wonderful in every way. Many years were to pass before I realised how exceptional Hugh really was. Even now I remember his triumphs in the theatre, in Dublin and overseas, and wonder whether his reticent nature kept him from seeking world acclaim.

Doris sometimes invited me out when her current beau had a friend at a loose end. I went to parties with them, but quickly unloaded any youth who tried to kiss me, or indulged in smoochy talk. I found them boring, with nothing to talk about except film stars and the girls they fancied. Sometimes I spent the evening watching my sister waltzing or doing a tango with such grace that her partners seemed inept. It was a relief if my date went off with another girl, but Doris would hate having me tag along home by myself, being a 'gooseberry'. The truth was that I had already spent so much time in the company of mature men that I felt light years older than the boys we met at parties and dances, whose conversation hardly ran to poetry or books. Of course, they were probably feeling awkward and shy, trying to be men, but I much preferred going out with girl friends, or just sitting at home playing music and dreaming.

So the year wore on. Christmas Eve came, and was enlivened as usual by Uncle Joe pretending to be tiddly and coming into the kitchen with a bottle of sherry for Lizzie and Mother's friend, Mrs Broughal, and to exchange gifts. Aunt Lena stayed in for a change that Christmas; she seemed preoccupied, and frequently called Mother aside for long whispered talks. Doris thought that Lena's latest love affair was on the rocks and that it might be because of the way she dressed. I didn't see much wrong with her pink dress and the angora cardigan, all fluffy and soft, worn with the usual bead necklace.

Doris always made me laugh. She was inherently carefree, rarely down in the dumps, and managed Mother with ease. Ever since she had wangled her way out of the convent in Kent, she had Mother's ear and could do no wrong. She brought a lot of gaiety into the house, and I know now that it helped Mother to have one extrovert and uncomplicated daughter. But Doris had a really terrible temper, which did not surface much, but cleared everyone out of the way when she really got going. When we were older, she once, in a fit of fury after a row with Mother, blurted out a secret that had been kept from me. Uncle Joe was not now an uncle but a stepfather; Mother had married him years before. Another mystery explained at last, for it had become clear long ago that not even Mother would lavish such attention and care on a mere uncle.

The new year brought the last few months at Alexandra and the last few months at the School of Acting. Hugh had directed the Abbey Christmas show, and then gone home for the holidays. We did not exchange cards, although I dearly loved them and had chosen a pretty one for him with a loving message written in it. He was drawing away from me. I knew it in the way that these things are known to lovers, young or old. I had no heart to follow him, to press my case; he had, after all, been honest with me. This was his last year, and I would have to get through it, but the hurt was there, very deep, and there was no way to ease it.

I was rehearsing with the students one Saturday when he walked in, had a brief word with Ria, and formally called to me to come off the stage. I stood for a moment, then obeyed him and came down into the theatre, following him as he walked to the exit. There, at the door, he handed me a script, asked me to read it and bring it back to him tomorrow. He said that it was a new and controversial play, and that he thought I was right for the leading female role. Then he walked quickly away, leaving me with the script clutched in my hand, not having grasped the import of his words.

I felt no elation, and did not even know whether I wanted this opportunity. It meant I would have to read for him with the players present, would have to face him as a stranger and work with him as though there had been no love between us, no secret too precious to expose to outsiders. There would be no sharing his thoughts and company as I had done in *Hassan*. I was terrified that I might break down in front of the company, and make fools of us both.

Once at home, I straightaway read the script, *Shadow and Substance*, by Paul Vincent Carroll. My role was that of Brigid, a simple girl of twenty-one who saw visions of the saint for whom she was named. The play was set in the saint's legendary district of Faughart, and there was a towering role for an actor, that of the Canon who employed Brigid. There were also a radical young schoolmaster named O'Flingsley, who was trying to get better conditions for his pupils, and two curates who were foils for the Canon's sardonic wit. It was a fascinating play, and brought tears to my eyes. There was no doubt that the Canon and Brigid were the leading characters, and no doubt either that I could play Brigid under normal circumstances – but things were so horribly wrong. Hugh had not seemed friendly when he handed me the script, but cold and distant.

I went into the Green Room in the Abbey the following day. Arthur Shields was there, Cyril Cusack, a man named Austin Meldon, Fred Johnson, a pretty girl called Aideen O'Connor who played juveniles in the Abbey regularly, Ria Mooney, Maureen Delany and other cast members whom I did not know. Hugh Hunt was also there. He told us his thoughts about the play, said that the author was from Dundalk but lived in Scotland, and started the reading. Sheer panic overcame me, and I stammered out the lines in a monotone. At the end, Hugh gave the cast the rehearsal time for the next morning, and told me to be there after school. He made no comment on my abysmal reading, but left abruptly, leaving me to trail miserably home.

The next day we read the play again, and he gave us a few moves. I read even more monotonously, displaying no understanding of the words or the character; he said nothing, and my depression grew ever deeper. At the next reading I was deplorable, and he waited until the end of the first act, then asked what the hell I thought I was doing. In front of the company, he said caustically that it was about time I started to put some life into the part. They had a little longer rehearsal time for this play than was usual, he said, but they did not have to spoon-feed *anyone*. Then he stormed out of the theatre.

I got the bus home and went into the bedroom, quite unable to eat. My mind was made up, but I wanted Mother to know, to make sure that I was doing the right thing. When I heard her footsteps in the hall, I called her in to my room, and told her that I couldn't even attempt this part, because I was just not experienced enough. It would be only letting everyone down, so I would go in early in the morning and give the part back to Hugh Hunt, and ask him to replace me. I needed Mother's permission to miss morning school so that I could do this. As I shook with sobs, Mother held me and told me to do what I thought was right, that no part was worth such unhappiness, but that I should think it over again in the morning in case I should have second thoughts.

In the morning, I went to the Abbey just before the senior players arrived; Hugh would be there first. I approached him timidly, and told him I had decided that I wasn't able for a leading role yet, that I did not want to spoil such a beautiful play, and wanted him to get somebody more experienced. I was not prepared for his reaction. He turned white with fury, told me that that was a coward's way out and that he certainly would not take back the script. He had cast me in the part, and I was going to play it and play it well. He had put his head on the block for me to get this chance. The author was in Scotland having hysterics because he, Hugh Hunt, had assigned the principal role in his play to a schoolgirl, and even the Board of Directors thought he was wrong.

He stopped for breath, and although he was quieter when he spoke again, his voice was icy. 'Since you can't get hold of this character from my directions, would you like to talk to anyone in the cast about it?' He knew that Cyril had been especially kind, so I supposed he meant me to go to him for advice. I was just about able to reply 'I'd like to talk it over with Ria' not looking at him at all. 'Right', he said, 'do it this afternoon.' I took the script, and walked into the Green Room.

A little core of defiance, with pride mixed into it, began to rise in me as I thought about his furious words. There had been no need for all that anger. I had not set out to fail in the part, and surely he must know that he was part of the reason I couldn't come to grips with it. If he was afraid that the author and the board would blame him for casting me, why had he done so? Anyhow, he was leaving the Abbey in a matter of months. These feelings propelled me into a more animated version of the role, but I still wanted to talk it over with Ria. That afternoon in the Peacock we read the play together, and discussed the accent I should use, explored the changes of mood, decided how to handle the comedy and how to approach the death scene.

Then I told Ria that Hugh Hunt had been so angry with me, and that I had tried to give him back the script. She said 'I bet that scared him! He wants you to be a great success in this part; after all, he fought hard for you to get it.' I thanked her for her help, saying that I would be all right now. Ria told me to show them what I could do, and I replied that I would, if it killed me. The next day I was in character from the beginning of rehearsal, and I could sense the relief of the rest of the players.

I did not look back after that. There were, of course, lots of things to overcome, including my awe of playing with Arthur Shields, so tall and imposing, and quite magnificent as the Canon. Cyril was O'Flingsley to perfection, with all the fire and passion the part required. He was so generous to act with, giving so much, and feeling seemed to flow between us like electricity. He had to pick me up and carry me on-stage in the last scene, and kept threatening to have me fired if I put on an extra ounce. In a later revival, I actually had put on some puppy-fat, and he was hard put to lift me. We would laugh about it, and he would warn me not to eat chocolate biscuits until the play was over. I was blessed playing opposite Cyril and Arthur 'Boss' Shields in my first big role.

I found that Hugh Hunt was not in my mind any more. For that period, there was no room for him; I had too much to achieve. He was the director, I followed his instructions, and that was all. He was nice enough to everyone, but although I went over some scenes with him when the others were gone and we were quite alone, I never wanted to reach out to him or talk to him in any personal way. Sometimes I caught him looking at me with a puzzled expression, and once or twice I thought he looked sad as I said a polite goodbye, and headed off to the bus. The great day grew nearer and nearer, and then the dress rehearsal arrived.

Hugh told us that Paul Vincent Carroll was coming over for the 'dress'. He said that he should be pleased with the acting, if not the direction, and that the last run-through had moved him to tears; we would meet the author after the rehearsal. Then, backstage, I heard the players talking quite angrily about Hugh, who apparently was not going to attend the first night, going instead to some special occasion in Manchester. They were annoyed, thinking him disloyal to be absent when a new play was being produced, and leaving a mere child to face the music on her own in a part that size – and he was supposed to be so fond of her, and so on.

It was a good dress rehearsal, and there was a positive reaction from the senior players, who usually knew what was what, as the stage crew always did. We were introduced to Paul Vincent Carroll, a small man with a layer of Scottish on his native brogue, who was hopping up and down with delight and congratulating everyone. He came to me and said 'You know, if I hadn't liked you, if you were not my Brigid, I wouldn't have let the play go on.' He said I was exactly what he had imagined when he wrote the part, then rushed out and soon came back with a big box of chocolates for me. We all stood talking to him, and asking about the play. He told us that he actually was a schoolmaster, and had worked for years in run-down schools with filthy toilets, and had many quarrels with the clergy who managed them. That part of the play was based on reality, and he did know a cleric who resembled the Canon, but St Brigid and the visions had come out of the blue.

Hugh drew me aside, and told me that I was splendid in the role. He said he would be thinking of me the next day, my first night; he was proud of me, and glad that he had cast me. Some day, he said, I would understand why he had acted so strangely, but I must be brave tomorrow night without him, as there was no way out of his other obligations. He hoped I would be all right, to which I replied quietly, 'I *am* all right; thank you for giving me such a wonderful part.' I had no special feeling about his coming or going. My concentration was already on the next night, on what would happen with an audience present, and whether I would pass the test that could make me truly professional.

It was a strange feeling, the morning of the most important day of my life so far. Mother said that I could lie on for a bit if I liked, and she would explain to the teachers at Alex, but I wanted to go to school, to be occupied. I even stayed on to play netball. Mother and Doris were coming to see me later in the week, but at tea I found a small bunch of flowers and two lovely picture cards from them. The butterflies had total control of my stomach now, and I was beginning to feel sick.

In the theatre there was a card from Hugh for everyone, and the dressing-room laughter and chatter was on that high pitch that denotes strain. I stayed quiet, stiff with nerves. I put on my dress, make-up, and apron, combed my hair, and was ready far too early. I wished everyone in my room good luck, knocked at the doors of the other dressing-rooms and wished them luck too. Cyril came out to take my hands, and tell me not to worry; we would be great together.

I went on-stage and walked around the set, walked in and out the French windows and sat in chairs, and stood beneath the garish picture of the Sacred Heart that was the cause in the play of some of the Canon's spleen. I opened doors and closed them, as I had been trained to do, and checked my props. There were several trays to be carried in, and I made sure that they were placed in proper order on the prop table. My stomach churned, and my heart was beating too rapidly. I saw the cast gathering outside the flats, and knew it was time; I prayed, a last desperate plea for myself and for the play. Then I took my position beside the door with Cyril and, when the third gong sounded and I heard the curtain rise, I opened the door and walked into the Canon's dining-room, talking brightly to O'Flingsley who was following me. My nerves disappeared, and I was in control. I had passed the test.

There was an overwhelming response from the audience when the curtain came down. It was a wonderful feeling, listening to the applause and cheers that greeted the play, and the curtain rose and fell many times before the audience would let the cast go. The actors stayed on-stage for a while complimenting each other; everyone sounded very happy, and they all thought that I had done very well.

Cyril and 'Boss' Shields were especially nice. There were a lot of people backstage that night; they came into the dressing-room, told me that I had moved them to tears and made other nice comments. Frank O'Connor, F R Higgins and Lennox Robinson came in, too; O'Connor said 'Tonight is only the beginning,' and the other two said that I *was* Brigid. The author wanted to take me out with Pearl, his attractive girlfriend, but I told him that I had to be up early for school. The truth was that I felt shy about going out with them. I was still insecure with people I didn't know well, and going into restaurants without my friends was still a bit of an ordeal.

My last caller that night was a critic of one of the newspapers, who was carried away by the whole evening, and could not believe that I was only sixteen. She insisted on driving me home, and next day wrote the most amazing review of the play, mentioning me especially. The other papers raved, too, and called me 'little Miss Ryan'. I saw the papers when I went into the theatre, and although the company were in a happy mood when I arrived, they didn't mention the reviews, so I didn't either. I was not bowled over by all the written praise, but was glad that I had not let the play down.

Paul and Pearl had left for Scotland that morning, as he had some important meeting to attend, and I felt as nervous as ever. Ria had always warned her students that the second night of a play was dangerous for a performer; you could relax too much, and then the energy would drop and the play could fall flat. You had to work harder the second night, she told us, so I did just that, and Cyril said that I was even better that night. For the first time since my audition in the school, which seemed years ago now, I really enjoyed playing a part and felt the bond between myself and the audience.

The houses were full every night. There were queues, and the play had to be retained for an extra week; then it would go into repertory, and I would play it again. This was a comforting thought, especially towards the end of the run. Mother and Joe and Doris came to see me and liked both me and the play. There were some critical letters to the papers calling the play anti-clerical (which the character of O'Flingsley was) and even anti-Church. At the mass I attended on Sunday, the priest warned his parishioners not to go to this play, which was 'near to blasphemy'.

When the show ended, I felt flat and dispirited, but this was only to be expected. During the run I had met some really famous people, and they had all made a fuss of me. Once I went into the

Green Room to ask Cyril something, and saw a middle-aged man with a stout build and greying hair sitting there chatting to Maureen Delany. I was called over and introduced to Count John McCormack, who said I was a beautiful child, and wished me a happy career. W B Yeats was in the audience on another occasion. Cyril told me he was there, and I acted my heart out for him.

I did not get a chance to meet Yeats, but next night Cyril said he had been shown a note from the great man, which said that the actors who played Brigid and O'Flingsley were both quite admirable in their roles, but that he wished they would take the audience more into their confidence. This alarmed me so much that I asked Cyril if I should use even more voice, but he grinned and said 'The old man is a bit deaf now, you know,' then laughed mischievously and told me to change nothing. It seemed that every prominent poet and writer came to see the play, as well as business managers from London and America. And, best of all, I got a lovely note from Mícheál Mac Liammóir addressing me as 'La Ryan', and promising me that he would send his partner Hilton Edwards to see me as 'alas, my dear, one of us has to work to keep the Gate open.' That note was my companion for years, until it literally crumbled from old age.

After the play ended, there was a lull, and I tried to concentrate on school studies; but I missed the feel of the stage and the interaction with the audiences. There was news about the Abbey, that Paul's play was going to Broadway, and that Hugh Hunt had been asked to direct it there with a cast of American stars. Ria told me that Hugh had suggested that I, who created the role, should be brought over to play Brigid, and had told the American producers that my performance could not be equalled. But Ria, who knew the American scene, said that the producers were bound to want stars in the cast, as that was how they raised money in the States for their hugely expensive productions. In Irish theatre the play was the thing that drew audiences, and there were no stars in the American sense. The ensemble that was the Abbey team of players brought in the punters, but no actor, director or designer was ever singled out in billing or advertising.

Following *Shadow and Substance*, Hugh Hunt's most notable works at the Abbey were his collaborations with Frank O'Connor, the famous short-story writer and a director on the Abbey Board. Hugh adapted one of his stories called *In the Train*, and made it a very novel one-act play which was produced in the Abbey in May

1937. In October of the same year, a full-length play called *The Invincibles* was co-written by the two men and produced. This was very successful, and many people felt it was a pity that Hugh did not go further down that road; but his talent for assessing scripts, and his great contribution to the development of new playwrights, were widely recognised.

Tanya Moiseiwitsch remained with him during his stint at the Abbey. They worked wonderfully well together, complementing each other's creative drives, and new and exciting ideas unfolded between them in the settings for Flecker's *Hassan* and *The Man in the Cloak* by Louis D'Alton, as well as in several others. Tanya was bright and sympathetic towards me, and I often watched her in the theatre as she painted. Sometimes she talked to me about the plays, other times about Russia.

Back at Alexandra, some of the teachers congratulated me on my success in the Abbey, pleased with the achievement of one of their girls, but they also urged me to concentrate on my schooling. Well, Hugh had spoken to me about that, and I would not forget anything he had said, even though I no longer felt anything when I thought about him. I remembered all the happy times. Somehow I always thought of those days in terms of spring and summer; my recollections were of days when the sun was warm, and there were colour and fragrance around.

But our story was not quite ended yet, because now I was in the Abbey Company which had been invited to play in Cambridge, England for a week, and the directors asked Mother if I could go with them. There was a small comedy role for me in a play called *The New Gossoon*, by George Shiels, a great favourite in the Abbey repertory. The Abbey promised that I would be properly chaperoned, that digs would be arranged for the players in first-class houses, and that the stage manager would collect me and bring me to and from the theatre.

I rehearsed with the company under M J Dolan, and Mother helped me to pack, putting in a new white dress in case I needed something especially good. The company went by boat and train, and I was glad I had brought books to read, because although I was in the same reserved compartment as the rest, nobody spoke to me much. They were the 'Abbey Company', and I was still a schoolgirl, and while they were never unkind, the feeling of sufferance was very much in my mind. When we arrived, we were met and taken to see the theatre. We were to be given lunch at a hotel, and could then go back to the theatre to run through the play, or return to the digs.

I had only a small part, so wandered out into the grounds surrounding the theatre – and saw Hugh Hunt disappear into the theatre entrance as I sat on a bench under a clump of trees. This was such a shock that I sprang up looking for some place to hide, in case he came out again and saw me. I had felt nothing for so long that I was totally confused by this new rush of feeling. I had expected him to be in London or America, and had not even dreamed that I might see him again here. And now here he was coming in my direction, bounding out of the doorway and running to where I stood near the bench, under the trees. He was breathless when he arrived beside me.

He drew me down so that we were sitting side by side on the bench, and said that he had come to wish the company luck, and would be leaving again shortly. He had come to see me especially, and hoped that I would listen to him very calmly, as he did not wish to upset me in any way. Then he explained how, when he first saw me in the Peacock, he had wanted only to develop my talent, and had recognised my extreme shyness because he, too, was shy and vulnerable. He had wanted only to help, and had not realised that he was falling in love. I turned to him to stop him saying things I was afraid to hear, but he went on, saying that he had such a desire and longing for us to be together that he would, had I been of age, have asked me to go away with him. And I would have gone with him, anywhere.

Despite his feelings of loneliness and desperation, his integrity would not allow him to compromise anyone so young, but I was not the only one to have been hurt by our parting. While seeming to be cold in my presence, he had longed for me through many sleepless nights. He smiled and said 'I had to bully you abominably to make you strong enough to play that part – and I really didn't care if I got into hot water for casting you. I just wanted you to find yourself, to know what you were capable of.' I was crying, but also glad, because now I understood everything, and I told him that I had been selfish and thought only of myself when we had stopped meeting; it had never occurred to me that he also might be affected.

Now we were standing close together, looking into each other's eyes, and he looked sad and somehow unsure. He told me to look him up in London, adding, 'You'll be older when you come, and you won't remember how you used to think of me; but there were some moments worth keeping for a rainy day, weren't there?' He kissed me gently on the cheek, and I touched his hand. We walked together to the theatre where some of the company were taking a break in the air, and we did not care that we were seen together, now that no amount of gossip or conjecture could harm us. It transpired that there was a certain buzz in the company, and that there had been suspicions, but we had kept our secret well, and interest faded fast once he had gone.

During the week in Cambridge, I met an undergraduate called Maurice Craig who invited me to his rooms and wrote a beautiful poem for me. He was really taken with me but, of course, I could not be reached on that level and spoke enigmatically of there being 'someone else', a phrase I had learned from the cinema. It must have sounded a bit ludicrous coming from someone not yet out of her sixteenth year, but it was then the simple truth.

# 9

# *A Time of Learning*

As time went by, and my career progressed and took a different shape, Hugh's words came true. I frequently found myself in England, both as an actress and a producer, but I never tried to contact him. Courteous enquiries, conveyed to me through other people, went unanswered. I fought off any attempt by mutual friends to bring us together on social occasions with a ferocity that caused some astonishment, and it was assumed that I had unhappy memories of Hugh's time at the Abbey, and that I neither liked nor admired him.

When Hugh returned to the Abbey in 1967, first to direct a superb production of *The Shaughraun* starring Cyril Cusack, I was busy with Gemini Productions, then in the process of taking over the Eblana Theatre, and also presenting plays at the Gate. I heard from a friend that he was stunned to learn that I was now in charge of a highly successful company, and had crossed the line between acting and management. He must indeed have been amazed, remembering the insecure, waif-like creature he had nurtured at the Abbey so many years ago. Still later, when he returned for a short stint as Artistic Director of the Abbey, I did not go to many of his productions.

Only now, in this journey back through the years, have I tried to explain to myself why I constantly avoided contact with Hugh, when we were both working in the same relatively small city. We were both children of the Abbey Theatre tradition, and were both artistic directors of acclaimed companies, although the Abbey was the National Theatre and Gemini was a freelance operation. I now believe that I was overcome by an irrational fear of losing something irreplaceable that had been entirely my own. I did not want us to be friends or acquaintances, or acknowledge the reality that renewed personal contact might bring.

Back in the Abbey in the aftermath of Hugh, things were a bit

chaotic, but the Abbey tradition, which was to get on with the work
according to the ideals laid down by the theatre's founders, enabled
the company and directors to move forward. That splendid actor M J
Dolan and playwright-director Lennox Robinson took over the
directing tasks between them, and although Anne Yeats, (then not
much older than me) lacked the experience and sophistication of
Tanya Moiseiwitsch, her sets worked extremely well. But it was
undeniably a patchy season, when there was no clearly discernible
plan and things just seemed to happen. There was the usual quota of
popular revivals, and I got plenty of experience in these, learning at
least what not to do, but feeling that I was for the most part just
marking time.

I played 'Mollser' in *The Plough and the Stars*, managing to look
so outrageously corpse-like that some of the audience felt that the
character should have gone to her eternal rest at least an act earlier.
The truth was that I did not have much of a clue about stage make-
up. Ria had taught us basics in the Abbey School, but now that I was
a member of the company, I was on my own in such matters, and
had applied cream sticks of Leichner for a deathly pallor, and brown
shadow-stick to hollow my eyes and sink in my cheeks.

One night I was introduced to a remarkable gentleman called Dr
Bob Collis, who greeted me warmly, said my performance was very
moving and then burst out laughing. 'You should really be dead,' he
said. 'Do something about that make-up.' Coming from a doctor, this
was enough to send me running to Maureen Delany. In my usual
self-conscious, stammering fashion I told her what Dr Collis had
said, and begged her to show me how to put things right. 'Cream all
that stuff off, child,' she said, and when I had done so, she applied
the merest hint of flesh-tinted make-up, made my lips pale, and told
me to look in the mirror. I looked delicate, but not alarming. She
pointed out that I was quite thin, with 'more eyes than face', and that
I did not need make-up to help me build the character. The distance
and the slight figure, she said, and most of all the acting, would do
the trick. After that, Maureen Delany made a special pet of me, and I
adored her in return. She was altogether marvellous as Bessie
Burgess in *The Plough and the Stars*. Her natural bent was for
comedy, and her timing was legendary, but in the part of Bessie she
remains unrivalled.

On the subject of stage deaths, during that season, a play called
*Fohnam the Sculptor* came into the repertoire. It was by a famous

Cork professor, Daniel Corkery, and was directed by a young man named Frank Dermody. This was a strange, poetic play, and I recall little of it, no doubt because its full meaning always eluded me. The advice of my peers, which I gratefully followed, was to 'just put your head down and say the lines with confidence – no one will be any the wiser'. There were three young maidens in the play, one of whom was played by Eithne Dunne, one of the great friends of my young years, and surely one of the best actresses ever to come out of Ireland. My role was that of a young girl betrayed by Fohnam, who was played by Fred Johnson, a mature, handsome actor who was a huge asset to the strong but ageing company of players. I cannot remember having a single scene with Fred, but must have felt sufficiently betrayed (in the character) to kill myself persuasively enough with a knife on-stage. Someone got a lighting cue wrong one night and, instead of fading down and blacking my death scene, left me to die in a blaze of light clearly illuminating my 'corpse' being pulled off the stage by my long-haired wig, which parted from my head just before my disappearance into the wings. The applause for my exit was deafening.

I should say that the playwright was in no way neglected, nor was there a less than serious effort to perform his play to the best of everyone's ability. In fact, the cast worked even harder than usual in *Fohnam* because of a guilt stemming from a total lack of understanding of the author's purpose. Frank Dermody, who was now directing regularly at the Abbey, must share some of the blame for the lack of cohesion in the production. He had come up through the Gaelic theatre, and was a fluent Gaelic speaker with a teeming imagination. Ideas burst and crackled around him like fireworks, but he was, in my recollection, unable to tame his often unruly fantasies.

He was apt to confuse his actors by throwing several concepts at them during rehearsals, and then failing to select a key one in time for opening night. Mícheál Mac Liammóir once described him as 'a genius without talent'. Frank Dermody was undoubtedly highly endowed with theatrical vision, but he was also a hysterical little man who lost control of his own greatest moments. Had he learned discipline, he might have joined the ranks of major Irish directors.

My own work under Dermody's direction was a strange progression of two steps forward and one back. I began by snatching greedily at every suggestion, but ended up rudderless because he did not steer a steady course. When I realised that I was making no impact on the role despite endless brainwaves from Frank, I began to fall back on displays of emotion in order to get some result. Fortunately, I was more often directed by M J Dolan or Lennox Robinson, because I learned from them not to use energy in an emotional sense when it was not required. Since there was usually only a week or less to rehearse revivals with which the rest of the company were familiar, I did not get as much coaching as I felt I needed. I was constantly holding up the seasoned players, and asking everyone for approval, from the director to dear 'Dossie' Wright, the stage manager.

I was also fighting off the image of the innocent Brigid, the Canon's little friend in *Shadow and Substance*. During the rehearsals for Teresa Deevy's *The King of Spain's Daughter*, M J Dolan told me that I looked like a schoolgirl, and instructed wardrobe to make me a long dress instead of the knee-length provided originally. This did not help much, so my hair was put on top and taken down, a wig was discussed but rejected. We experimented with make-up, too much and then too little, until Dolan got irritable with this ageing process, and pronounced that my performance was fine, and we would just have to live with my appearance.

Later on in the 1940s I performed in two more plays by Teresa Deevy, on radio and television, this time directed by Denis Johnston, and always felt a special affinity with her work. I had the privilege of meeting her on several occasions, and she told me that I acted her heroines as she had seen them in her dreams. She was a brave, sensitive lady who had become deaf after contracting Meniere's Disease while she was an undergraduate at University College, Dublin. Her great tragedy was the death of her beloved sister, Nell, in 1954, who had been her ears and voice for many years.

During the run of *The King of Spain's Daughter*, Lennox told me that he was producing a new play by the great Abbey playwright T C Murray. 'And', he said wickedly, 'you will be playing a very mature young lady, and I will show you how to appear sophisticated.' Lennox was very charming, but also extremely eccentric, and as the rehearsals grew nearer, I wondered what was in store for me. On the few occasions when I got home for any length of time, I did my own experimenting with maturity, dropping languidly into chairs and assuming a 'lah-di-dah' drawl that resembled Lennox's own.

*Illumination* was not to prove one of T C Murray's greatest scripts. From the writer of *Autumn Fire*, *Birthright*, *Maurice Harte* and other classics it was disappointing, and I heard murmurs to this effect from the company. Even that most good-natured and charitable of the players, Maureen Delany, did not think it would do anything to enhance his reputation. I liked my part of Christina, the girl who loved and lost to her beloved's preference for a religious vocation, and I liked the man in the case, a charming young actor called Joe Linnane who had recently joined the company. Joe became a broadcasting star in later life, but he began as a gifted actor with a great sense of comedy, and it seemed that he was on the road to fame in the theatre. He was in his twenties, and the age difference did not help me, but I tried to become older inside, and waited impatiently for Lennox to produce his magic method.

After a few days of rehearsal, Lennox asked me to have tea with himself and his wife that evening; he wanted to work with me on the script. I went along somewhat nervous of meeting Mrs Robinson, and wondering what she might think of me. She was a lovely, motherly sort of person who gave us a huge tea with cakes and scones and then left us to work. Lennox, who smoked like a chimney, produced a packet of cigarettes and offered me one. I told him that I did not smoke. 'Ah', he said, 'but you will learn to, because Christina smokes, and it will give you a different persona.' He roared with laughter as I coughed and spluttered my way through that first cigarette. At seventeen a lot of girls did smoke; it was quite fashionable then to do so, but I hated it and couldn't get out the lines of the play, let alone hold the thing so that it would not burn my fingers.

He gave me a packet and told me to practise until it came naturally; he would find lines for me to light up the cigarette on, and it would give me a sense of being grown-up and so on. I was utterly miserable. This was the magic formula that would solve my difficulty, and give me poise and confidence! But I persevered as directed, smoking the wretched things at rehearsals much to the amazement of some of the company and the amusement of others. Eileen Crowe muttered darkly about 'that fellow making the poor child into a smoker', and wondered did my mother know. She did, and was not pleased, but no one thought of cigarettes as a health hazard at that time, and she assumed I would just smoke them for the duration of the play, and then drop them.

The outcome of Lennox's experiment was that the play got reasonable reviews, and I got splendid ones, except for one which remarked on my youth. Nobody mentioned the cigarettes, except for a few friends who thought that I was dreadfully awkward with them. Lennox pronounced himself delighted with my performance, and said that I hadn't really needed the cigarettes after all. I ended up hooked on the noxious weed, and only kicked the habit some seven years ago.

How wonderful those years were, when I was accepted by the company and could run home on Friday with my little brown envelope containing four whole pounds in my hand to give to Mother, who always gave me back enough to enjoy myself with. I think I felt that my wages were supporting the household, but I was so in love with what I was doing that the money hardly seemed connected with it. I never developed any great enthusiasm for money, although in later years I sometimes needed it desperately for family reasons, and never seemed to have any talent for raising it.

Whenever I had time off, I went to the Gate Theatre, where I sat enthralled by the magnificence of Mícheál's settings and costumes, enriched by Hilton's evocative lighting. Everything about their productions suggested style and opulence, and it was hard to believe that they operated on a shoe-string. To the end of his days, Hilton lamented the modern tendency to do away with the curtain, believing that to show off the set to the audience, as they seated themselves amid the familiar pre-show conversational buzz, robbed the theatre of a necessary mystique. Allied to Mícheál's charisma and Hilton's superb direction of an excellent company, the Gate seemed to have found the secret of the totality of theatre, that wholeness of execution where each separate art combined to give the text the maximum of meaning. But then Mícheál always regarded his settings as a background to the play and performers; sets and lighting were never allowed to take over the actors or the plays. Some of the productions I saw at the Gate have never been surpassed for me. *Hamlet*, *Peer Gynt*, *Berkeley Square*, *The Old Lady Says 'No!'*, *Liliom*; the list is awesome.

The Abbey had outstanding actors, a large repertoire of old and new plays, and many other virtues, but there was no emphasis on the technical surrounds, which led to rather drab sets and uninspired lighting. The Gate highlighted this lack in the national theatre, so when W B Yeats brought over the young Hugh Hunt, the 'Old Lady' was lifted for a while onto a level comparable with the Gate's standards of technical brilliance. Inevitably, when Hugh departed, the Abbey temporarily declined, but it has known many peaks and troughs throughout its long and distinguished history.

In 1939 I was cut off from the usual teenage romances, acting full-time and going to Alexandra College part-time. Mícheál was always there, but now I needed to see him, on-stage and off, as often as possible. I went to the Gate at lunch-times, and waited to see if he might come out for a break after rehearsal, but he never did. So I wrote him sentimental love-poems, begging for more privileged back-stage visits, leaving small boxes of sweets as bribes. Mícheál would laugh and say I cheered him up, and lie about my terrible poems, saying they were good because they were sincere. I told him I was not improving as much as I had hoped, and he gave me some excellent advice. He believed in reading aloud to strengthen the vocal chords, and to extend the range and variety of the voice. He also advised more comedy roles, as this would help me with timing. He said I would undoubtedly end up in the Gate, but would have to make arrangements with the Abbey concerning my contract.

Hilton did send for me when I had been a year in the Abbey and asked me to join the Gate company, ignoring the fact of my contract. But I could not ignore it. Although the thought of working with Mícheál made me weak at the knees and I was overjoyed to be asked, I really felt that I could not leave the Abbey. After all, I had been given my training there and had grown to love the place, and I had made great strides as an actress despite the pedestrian approach of the directors. Frank O'Connor, F R Higgins, Lennox Robinson and Walter Starkie were joined on the board by Ernest Blythe, but there was no meeting of minds, and no change in the complacent policies that made the Abbey at that time so lack-lustre.

So, I turned down the Gate and remained loyal to the Abbey. Loyalty is high on my list of the things I need to give and receive in life, despite the rage I often feel when I see artists of stature betrayed by cold-blooded materialists. I do not know even yet if I regret having missed out on the Gate, but on the whole I think not.

I met quite a lot of young men, at first nights in the Abbey and elsewhere, who invited me out. Some were aspiring writers, some university students and others budding actors in temporary jobs. We would meet for weekend walks in the country or by the sea, having taken the bus out of the city; few of my suitors had cars. It was an idyllic time and place for eye-gazing and hand-holding, when undying love could be declared after the first date. I always encouraged passionate declarations if the declarer was half-way decent looking, and had something in common with my chosen way of life. Mother was furious when love-lorn youths turned up claiming they were engaged to me, and wanting to discuss marriage. She told me that my behaviour was thoughtless, cheap and utterly selfish. I had lived through a profound experience with Hugh at a very tender age, and none of the subsequent romantic by-play seemed serious enough to hurt anyone. But people were hurt, all the same. I wept as much as any of the young men who felt let down, because I could not hold on to love, and ended up for a time without friends.

If I had not been somewhat warily accepted into the inner circle of the Abbey Company, I would have been the loneliest teenager imaginable. At home, Mother was busy with her job and with Joe, Aunt Lena had finally married her long-time admirer Cecil, and Doris had her own busy social life. I had been weaned too suddenly from the acting school and Ria and Hugh, and I needed guidance. For some of the time I shared a dressing-room with two other girls, Aideen O'Connor and Frolie Mulhern, who had acted in the Abbey before I had even joined the school. Aideen was a pretty and lively juvenile actress, and Frolie a quirky young comedienne. They felt they were being pushed out by the new arrival, and their attitude naturally lacked warmth.

Seeing me as something of an intruder, they often whispered together, so that I took to spending time in the Green Room or in the wings talking to 'Dossie', who never tired of my questions, and gave me tips on how to make the best of myself. Ria worried me, though. She left me to fend for myself, and was rather cool when I tried to approach her on the old footing. One night I heard from the girls that Ria had some idea that I had been carrying on with Hugh Hunt, and they laughed when I began to blush horribly, and asked me if it was true. I wondered what Ria had meant, and why she should be upset about Hugh and me, even if she did know about our secret meetings. Much later malicious stories went around about how unlucky Ria had been with her love-life. When I joined the company, she had been madly in love with F R Higgins, and that had ended in tears. I owed this remarkable woman so much, that nothing could alter my gratitude and affection, and nothing ever has. It seemed desperately sad to me that she never had real joy in her private life, and ended up leading a very solitary existence despite her great work for the Abbey.

To my great joy, F J McCormick, by everyone's reckoning the greatest actor of his generation, began to take a fatherly interest in me. He was a gentle, almost anonymous person off-stage, interested in all sorts of things, like building hutches for rabbits (I wanted one) or asking tram-drivers to explain the workings of their vehicles. He had enormous humility, and never talked about acting except to congratulate others, and he readily gave his time to those who sought it. I recall an occasion when a brash young actor in a tiny role ventured a minor criticism of the way McCormick was playing the lead. To my astonishment, McCormick politely asked the callow idiot to explain his point, and they had quite a serious discussion. The players fumed about this, calling the young critic impudent, ignorant and arrogant, and indeed they blamed F J for listening to him and giving him notions.

# 10

## *With the Abbey Greats*

I was now on first-name terms with the company, although I still hesitated to use this privilege in some cases. May Craig remained Miss Craig and Eileen Crowe, Miss Crowe, although May in particular was most affable, and fussed over me lest I was working too hard, or lonely without other young people. She was noted for her stylish clothes and splendid hats. On-stage, she was the most moving Mrs Tancred (in O'Casey's *Juno and the Paycock*) that I have ever seen.

I don't know why I never hit it off with Eileen Crowe. She was pleasant to me, and I certainly admired her, but somehow I always felt scared that I might say or do something wrong if I came too close. Her husband, F J McCormick, was just the opposite, easy and natural to talk to. I realised how extraordinarily lucky I was to be able to work and associate with such a fine company, and tried to show my gratitude by observing their codes of behaviour and emulating their methods.

Cyril Cusack was mischievous and theatre-wise, and we got on really well. I can never forget the thrill of watching his brilliant development of so many roles, approaching each performance like a cat moving stealthily into position to hunt its prey. When he had found the core of the character, he was suddenly transformed into a raging tiger, often reaching a crescendo of power that made audiences catch their breath. Cyril believed in under-playing and perfected this art, and could seem so natural that other members of the cast might appear to be slightly over-the-top in contrast. To be on-stage with him was for me double heaven, especially in Synge's *The Playboy of the Western World* in which I played Sarah Tansey. He had such mastery of the poetry's rhythms, and was able to sweep the poet's imagery onto the highest peaks of genuine passion. I still tremble at the memory of his love scene with Pegeen Mike, surely one of the most beautiful ever written. The recollection of Cyril as

Christy playing opposite Siobhán McKenna as Pegeen Mike will always haunt me, to the detriment of other portrayals.

Then there was Denis O'Dea, with whom I played in *Shadow and Substance* when the original Canon, Arthur 'Boss' Shields was not available. Although this was not the kind of part Denis would normally play, he was extraordinarily good in it. He was tall, handsome and very friendly to every one. He was also a renowned practical joker, and once I shook hands with him on stage to find myself grasping a mess of squashy chocolate cream. But Denis was hard to know, and did not really mix with the rest of the company. A lot of girls fell for him, and Maureen Delany used to say that he was too cute to be caught. But Siobhán McKenna proved too much for his cuteness. She was so gifted and beautiful that, when she arrived at the Abbey, Denis courted her with patient perseverance until she agreed to marry him.

Maureen Delany remained my favourite person, and I spent hours in her dressing-room. She loved hearing about the young men I met and the letters they wrote, but she warned me against flirting, saying that it was always unkind and sometimes dangerous. I was still awkward meeting new people. It was agony to go into a restaurant with a young man, bumping into things and knocking them over, then having to listen to his life story until the inevitable love-talk began.

Although home life had ceased to be the centre of my existence, Mother was still the only one who could solve all things when trouble was brewing. She heard me out on the subject of boys, the roles I was to play in the current season, my relationship with esteemed company members and my devotion to Maureen Delany, whom she invited to dinner to thank her for her kindness to me. She was puzzled about my attitude to the state of my career; I knew I was still marking time, and I wanted to fly. I wanted to release a great surge of activity that was waiting to explode inside me, but nothing came except a certain fey quality that seemed natural, and a depressing adequacy in the work I was given. Uncle Joe listened sympathetically to me on this issue, but he felt that I was perhaps too impatient. He was sure I was suffering from a natural humility; after all, I was the youngest member of the company, and there was time enough for me to grow up and play leading parts in the Abbey classics.

I didn't want leading parts; I wanted to perfect the ones I had.

Sometimes I would meet one of the Abbey directors going into the theatre, often the great Frank O'Connor, and we would have a chat in the foyer. He had such a warm personality and always encouraged me, noting that I was growing and would soon be a young woman. F R Higgins would smile absently and pass on by.

I dreaded meeting Ernest Blythe, even though, when I first played Brigid in *Shadow and Substance*, he had welcomed me into the Abbey and indicated that he would ensure there would be a place for me in the company. On one occasion he asked me about my schooling at Alexandra, and I told him that my mother was working to support us, and that my father had been a British army officer. I sensed that this piece of information registered badly, because his fat Buddha face, stretched in a perpetual smile, went purple, and he went off muttering in Irish. Although I didn't understand a word, I gathered that I had not passed the test. Instinctively I did not like or trust him. How right I was as Ernest Blythe was to darken my horizon more than I could have anticipated.

Aunt Lena married, and graduated with her husband from a flat in Rathmines to a house in Glasthule. She seemed quite willing to settle for a life of domestic bliss. Doris had left secretarial work, and was studying to be a beautician. She was as usual surrounded by throngs of admirers. I always knew that Doris had someone special in mind if she was unusually silent when we met at night. She had tales of fast girls and faster fellows at the dances she went to; one girl rejoiced in the name of 'Jungle Jennie' because of a reputation for letting her boy-friends go too far. How this was known, and what going too far meant, was anyone's guess. Our knowledge of the facts of life was too limited to recognise danger zones, and the urge to learn more about this forbidden topic was irresistible.

At the theatre, I was rehearsing *The Far-Off Hills*, Lennox Robinson's famous comedy. I was playing 'Ducky', a schoolgirl of about fourteen, and Shelah Richards was Pet, her elder sister by a year or so. I remember Shelah's blonde hair, her not quite beautiful but oddly attractive features, her slim figure and the overwhelming charm she possessed all her life. I loved her then and always, and who could help it? She teased me unmercifully about my extreme youthfulness, and bewailed the fact that she had played Pet many times, but never before with a real schoolgirl. All the previous Duckys, she said, had been as old as herself.

I could never think of Shelah as old, even when she was in her eighties. I learned during the show that she was about thirty-six when we played these roles together, but nobody would have believed it. We became very friendly, unusually so given the age difference and her status as a leading actress. She was so frank and open about her love-life that I timidly talked about mine, or rather my lack of one. Shelah told me about her love affair with Denis Johnston, and how he chased her all the way to America to propose. She adored him (so did I) but could not decide whether to keep her career going for a few more years or to marry. Denis would travel anywhere to seek new outlets for his compulsive creativity, and might uproot wife and family without warning. But she was passionately in love with him, and in the end they married and settled for a while in Dublin, long enough to give birth to Jennifer, now a famous novelist, and Michael, a film and TV producer.

I had graduated from playing Mollser in *The Plough* to Mary Boyle in *Juno and the Paycock*. I was conscious of a casting hangover from my role as Brigid in *Shadow*, and secretly I studied the part of Rosie Redmond, *The Plough and the Stars*. I learned all her speeches and begged Lennox, M J Dolan and Frank Dermody at least to hear me, but they all thought it was the funniest thing they had ever heard.

Dermody, who had tunnel vision, told me to get sense and play what was in my range, like everyone else. Dolan, who still grumbled a bit about my youthful appearance, said there might be another riot in the Abbey if they cast a schoolgirl in that part. Lennox just dismissed the idea out of hand. In despair I consulted some friends I had met in a little theatre workshop, to which I had been introduced by Liam O'Leary, who later founded the famous film archive. Liam liked my work and thought I should be in films; but then he thought that film was the only real medium for truthful interpretation. However, he and his friend Seán O'Meara, who ran the studio workshop in the evenings and were civil servants by day, were nothing if not honest. They believed that most professional theatres were producing pseudo-actors in phoney plays.

So I sought out some truth about myself in the little studio, reading Rosie Redmond to Seán, Liam and a few of their devotees. They were enthusiastic to a degree that astonished me. Liam said if I could shake off the image of child-like innocence and purity, I might one day touch greatness. He warned that being typecast might earn me a lucrative living for a while, but that I would eventually get jaded and lose my spontaneity, and perhaps even my liking for the art. Seán agreed, and I resolved to try again, maybe with another less extreme role, to persuade the Abbey directors to 'let me fly'.

Apart from these concerns, life was good and we enjoyed our simple pleasures. The Abbey players did not go out to supper parties at night, or for drinks after the show. They went home to their spouses or lodgings, as the case might be. Actors were poorly paid even for those days, yet I never heard any of them complain about pay or conditions. Even if there had been an actors' union to fight their battles, I doubt if that particular Abbey company would have changed its attitude to standards or tradition.

In Lennox Robinson's *Ireland's Abbey Theatre, 1899-1951*, published in 1951, he describes the coming of the Black-and-Tans in 1920, and how in the spring he was forced to summon the company members and tell them that the theatre could not stay open as the curfew, originally enforced at ten o'clock, had been moved back to eight o'clock. He hoped that the theatre might open again in Horse Show week, in August, but there was no guarantee. 'One actor,' he wrote, 'F J McCormick, sold all his books to keep himself alive, and an actress, Maureen Delany, with tears running down her cheeks, declared she would willingly play the part she hated most (it happened to be in a play by myself) if the theatre might remain open.' The rest were of the same mind, and happily in 1923, the advent of O'Casey's first production at the Abbey, *The Shadow of a Gunman*, kept the unthinkable from happening.

Over in the Gate, the story was similar. The management and actors lived on 'the clippings of tin', yet there were scores of good actors queuing to carry a spear for Mícheál and Hilton. There was, of course, no such thing as subsidy at the Gate; the only reward for being involved in the arts lay in achievement.

F J McCormick, whom I regarded as a king and who never spoke about theatrical things off-stage if he could help it, once asked me if I knew anyone who could teach him the fingering necessary for using a typewriter. I said my sister was a splendid typist, and since he couldn't get free time during the day, being in every play and rehearsal, I said she could come in at night and teach him in the dressing-room. He was as overjoyed as if I had offered him a gold typewriter and a magic wand to make him proficient.

I asked Doris, and she was thrilled. She did not want to act, but was eager to meet the great actors. F J borrowed a typewriter from the Abbey office, and I can still hear the two voices chatting about the keys, and F J's anxious murmur when his fingers slipped. Doris came in frequently, until he had nothing more to learn. Like the gentleman he was, F J gave her a box of chocolates for her help, and when she asked him why he had wanted to learn typing, he said 'I don't really know, I thought it might come in useful sometime.' Like the rabbit hutch he wanted to build, or the knowledge of the insides of trams that he just had to have.

He always looked startled whenever he was complimented, which was often, and shied away. But I think that inwardly he was pleased, and he always did express thanks. He was the hardest working actor I have ever encountered, and was yet so generous with his precious time. He rescued me, too, on occasions when I cut across someone else's lines. There was a dreadful night when an actor paused longer than he usually did; I thought he had dried and rushed in with the next line and it transpired that he hadn't dried at all. He was *acting*, and I had dashed in with the wrong line, cutting at least two of his best speeches. F J got me out of that trouble when the actor, Fred Johnson, put me back in my box.

The worst experience I can recall from those Abbey days was in George Shiels's *Professor Tim*, in which an emigrant uncle, having supposedly prospered in America, returns to his family in Ireland and turns out to be a down-at-heel drunk. Things went wrong with that play each night it was performed. Gerard Healy, playing a young squire down on his luck, referring to his future should have said it was as 'black as the inside of a cloud', but he actually said 'my inside is as black as the future of a cloud'. I was his sympathetic sweetheart, but on hearing this was seized with uncontrollable laughter, and had to turn away, unable to speak for a time. This delayed the action, and when I came off I was met by a raging M J Dolan, who treated me as if I had murdered Gerard. He declared that he had never seen such amateurish behaviour, that corpsing (laughing illegitimately on stage) was not permitted in the Abbey, and that I had better not do it ever again.

Another night Gerard and I were left on-stage waiting for Professor Tim to arrive; we gave his cue once, twice, three times, but there was no sign of Fred Johnson's Tim. Gerard walked offstage to investigate, leaving me to wander around examining the set, panic welling inside me as I sensed the audience growing restive. I had just decided to run off when Fred burst in through the door, panting like a spent greyhound, and flung himself across the table, knocking crockery in all directions. At least I now had a cue, and carried on until he took up the play again. It transpired that he had gone out into the lane beside the Abbey for a breath of air, and misjudged the timing of his cue. M J took him aside to berate him, but Gerard and I ran upstairs, helpless with laughter.

In another play, Lennox Robinson's *Drama at Inish*, I really came unstuck. I was having fantasies about saving a whole play, with everyone clapping me on the back, saying that the play could not have gone on without my prompt and decisive action. Dreaming of this in the wings, while holding a tray as the maid Helena and ready to bring on tea in a carefully orchestrated routine, I dashed on too soon, dropping the tray with a crash and screaming 'give me back my baby'. No one had yet mentioned a baby, and my precipitate climax brought down the whole scene.

I had one more small entrance with Michael the Boots, played by Cyril Cusack, and I was terrified to go on. I wept all over Cyril, telling him I was sure to be fired and that I had been dreaming of being heroic and saving everything. He said gently 'Phyllis, you let your concentration go, and you can't do that even for a second, ever. Only the play you are in now is important. If you have only one line, that's the most important line in your life. Never let your mind drift. It's fatal!' He got me through our entrance, then took me to the dressing-room to apologise to all the players.

Sometimes I would not be cast in a new play, and might have a whole two weeks off; then I could attend Alexandra College again. The authorities there had generously agreed that I might attend classes in the subjects I needed, such as history and languages. They knew I had already embarked on an acting career, and afforded me privileges; in return I took a role in the college play, an adaptation of *Pride and Prejudice*. I also wrote for the college magazine, poems (imitation Yeats) and essays (after Chesterton).

Sitting in the small, underlit Green Room at the Abbey, I would watch Eileen Crowe knitting, and listen to the conversation which sometimes contained spicy bits of gossip. I loved being in that room. I had no close girlfriends at that particular time, even though other names began to appear on the Abbey's cast lists. But with the arrival of Eithne Dunne I found a true friend, both on-stage and off.

Eithne was dark and willowy, quite beautiful, and the most talented newcomer in the Abbey school. Although she was, like everyone else, a few years older than me, that did not matter. We suffered through Corkery's *Fohnam the Sculptor* together, and I played Ducky to her Pet in *The Far-Off Hills* when Shelah Richards packed in the latter 'kid role'. We were not likely to be rivals for the same roles, and I longed for her to share every play with me. We had such fun, supported each other when sad things happened and faced disappointments and successes with a united front. I did not tell her about Hugh – but I did tell her everything else, and she laughed uncontrollably on hearing about my 'past' and all my brief 'engagements'.

Men, young, old or middle-aged hovered around Eithne like flies. They cultivated me, too, perhaps to intervene for them, or because they sensed that she would not go out with virtual strangers unless I went also. So I was asked out a lot in between shows. Eithne never left me out of the chat, and we would share private jokes, eat enormous teas if the men were flush with money, and then dash back to the Abbey, either to perform or to see if we were cast together in the next production. There was a list published in the Green Room, from which we learned what play was coming next, and who would be in it. We did not act together much at that stage, because I was a member of the company, and Eithne was one of a small group used intermittently by the theatre.

Other students began to come into the Abbey from the School of Acting. Ria was trying to spread the opportunities evenly among her more talented protégés. Cecil Barror took part in quite a few new plays, and a tall blonde girl named Joan Plunkett also joined. She had a sense of comedy like that of languid screen ladies, dead-pan dumb blonde types, quite different from the more earthy humour of Maureen Delany. Eithne and I watched nervously lest we find one of them upsetting our desired casting in the same plays, and that did happen now and then.

# 11

# *Theatre and Politics*

With F R Higgins at the helm, the Abbey approached the 1940s with no policies other than to keep the theatre going on very much the same lines as those established by the Yeats/Lady Gregory partnership. Lennox Robinson, Frank O'Connor, Roibeárd Ó Faracháin and F R Higgins were all creative writers and it was inevitable that artistic rather than practical considerations would be uppermost in their minds, and that disagreements on the nature of future Abbey productions would arise. M J Dolan was the person mainly in charge of the theatre activities after Hugh Hunt left, with Lennox Robinson helping him, and both of them directing many new plays and revivals. Frank Dermody was also prominent at this time. Eric O'Gorman, secretary and part-time actor, was the one you saw in the office when 'the Ghost walked', which meant when the wages were paid every Friday, but the identity of the real boss was anyone's guess. F R Higgins was dreamy and distant, Frank O'Connor warm and friendly but not managerial. When F R Higgins died in 1941, his fellow poet Roibeárd Ó Faracháin managed to get the board to appoint Ernest Blythe as Managing Director.

Blythe's record in government was that of a ruthless politician. He was an Ulsterman in some respects in the mode later made familiar by Ian Paisley, and could see no farther than his nose in matters of imagination and creativity. As Minister for Finance in the Cosgrave government in 1924, however, he was able to secure a small annual grant for the Abbey which enabled it to pay its actors at least a living wage, to purchase some scenery and improve its tattered wardrobe. Lady Gregory and Yeats had offered the theatre to the nation, so that it might survive, but the government was reluctant to create a national theatre in the aftermath of the Civil War. After negotiation, the Abbey was granted £850 per annum, and so became the 'first state-subsidised theatre in the English-speaking world', to quote Lennox Robinson.

In 1939 Frank O'Connor resigned from the Abbey board. W B Yeats died in that same year, and I mourned his passing – not least because he had all but managed to overlook my existence, so that I could never boast of having met him. Whatever disagreements occurred among the remaining board members, it seemed certain that Ernest Blythe was intent on taking over. I listened well in my corner of the Green Room, and heard that Blythe was determined to take bi-lingual actors into the company, so that Irish language plays, then badly neglected, would form a vital part of each season. That was not unreasonable, but there were fears that Blythe's politically motivated commitment to the Irish language posed a threat to the current Abbey players. They spoke of him in hushed voices as if afraid they might be overheard criticising a dictator.

Blythe began to be seen around the theatre more and more. He had no time for creative people, unless they shared his tunnel vision and Ulster Protestant righteousness. He spoke Irish incessantly to the cronies he brought in to view his new domain. He often spoke to himself if he could not find someone fluent in the tongue, and prowled about the auditorium muttering, a dark-clad decidedly sinister figure.

In 1941 Louis D'Alton, a young playwright who already had three successful plays produced at the Abbey, was made manager. These plays were *The Man in the Cloak* and *Tomorrow Never Comes* directed by the author, and *The Money Doesn't Matter* directed by Frank Dermody. Also in 1941 his new play *Lovers' Meeting* was produced, which was a tragedy in more senses than one, since I was cast as the juvenile lead and found myself caught between the intentions of the author and the wishes of the establishment.

The plot, which had more than echoes of Greek tragedy, revolved around the plight of a respectable married woman in a rural community. Years before, she has had an extra-marital affair, resulting in a daughter who was accepted in her home as the child of herself and her husband. All goes well until Mary, the young daughter, falls in love with a wild and charming young man, Joe Hession, who is in fact her half-brother. The fear of an incestuous relationship drives the mother to reveal the truth to her unforgiving husband. The tragedy is compounded when Joe is arrested for murder, convicted and sentenced to hang. Mary continues to love and grieve for him, and her parents decide to marry her off to a rich, elderly farmer so that she and the dust can settle. Mary appears to accept their plan, but on her wedding day, as Joe is being executed, she hangs herself at the same time, joining him in death.

Frank Dermody was, as usual, full of ideas about each of the characters, but he was up against a formidable array of Abbey players who would not chop and change once they were on course. There was little he could add to the strong creations presented almost from the first rehearsal by Eileen Crowe, F J McCormick, M J Dolan, Denis O'Dea, Maureen Delany and Seamus Healy (the brilliantly talented father of Shay Healy, a versatile artist of today). I was the only one left on whom he could experiment, and even I was sure of myself in this role – and, if I had not been, the author was around to oversee this very important departure in his writing career. For all that the play had some rich comedy scenes, it dealt with serious issues raised by social attitudes of the day, including suicide.

Louis took me aside one day and said that Mary, as written, was quite sane when she decided to take her life to be with her lover, rather than marry the repulsive old man forced on her by her unloving parents. He was of the opinion that the Abbey directors wanted her to go out of her mind so that her terrible end could be attributed to madness, and he was not having any of this. The whole point of the suicide was to expose the lack of compassion and Christianity in rural society, particularly from an all-powerful Church obsessed with sin and damnation. Louis argued that Mary had made a sane decision to die with Joe, rather than live in a sordid, loveless coupling.

Frank Dermody was converted to this view, and rehearsals proceeded. But the clouds were gathering, and one day Dermody came down from the office and said that the board insisted that Mary should be played like Ophelia, driven mad with the shock of all the tragedy that had befallen her. Frank really agreed with Louis, but he was mortally terrified of authority, whether that of the board or of the Church. He pointed out to Louis that Joe was Mary's half-brother as well as her ex-fiancé, and that she had to be out of her mind if she expected to have an incestuous love-affair in the next world. Louis stuck obstinately to his argument. In the next world, if there was one, he declared, the two lovers would be spirits, and that transcended everything. Mary was sane; she was not a simpering idiot, and he would not have her made into one.

Frank changed his tune again, and agreed with Louis. Ria Mooney had one of her finest roles as a spinster aunt, cigarette hanging from her mouth, who had been jilted at the altar and never recovered mentally. She told me that I should follow my instinct. Maureen Delany was, however, furious, feeling that I would be in trouble whatever way I interpreted the part, and that it was most unfair. I did not discuss my plight with the rest of the company. Eileen Crowe didn't really approve of the play, and I could not see myself mentioning anything anti-Church to her, or even to F J McCormick. The company would naturally have sided with the board. To play the last scene as a sane person would have seemed little short of sinful to most of them. So, whenever that scene was due for rehearsal, I had Louis giving me instructions on the one hand, and a strangely subdued Frank Dermody saying nothing at all on the other.

Left to myself, I should probably have plumped for the insanity theory. I barely knew what an incestuous relationship was. This was not a problem I could bring home, being so intensely personal, and the importance of the decision began to cast huge, sinister shadows on my position as a junior member of the company. At rehearsals, I practised playing the scene insanely some days, and on others with a bright, cold logic. I could not concentrate on the early scenes, being altogether preoccupied with the right way to interpret the ending. No one came from the boardroom to watch or to threaten, yet I felt threatened.

This was a part I had been looking forward to playing so much, and I knew that the final scene, when Mary appeared in her bridal dress, could be critical for all concerned. I was enchanted with the beautiful dress and flowers designed for the wedding of Mary and her ludicrous suitor, but which she wore radiantly as she went to join her true love. The simplicity of her belief that God would smile on their union despite all that stood in its way, was a romantic ideal irresistible to my young mind. If I could play any part with true emotion, clarity and conviction, this was surely it.

However, a relatively simple role turned into a frightening ordeal, and the first night, although well received, left me tense and unhappy. Automatically, I had played Louis D'Alton's ending in accordance with his wishes, and while he was ecstatic, I did not sense approval from the company. The next night, Frank Dermody told me before the show that the board was furious, and that he had been blamed; I had better change my playing of the last scene or there would be trouble. The only concession I could make was to throw a bouquet to my (stage) mother.

The critics did not comment on the interpretation of the play's ending. They were favourable, for the most part, and there was no mention of the suicide scene other than that it was emotionally moving. But Maureen Delany, who was beginning to feel nervous of the board under Blythe's influence, was very worried and thought that my career at the Abbey had been endangered. 'You just can't give that fellow anything to hold against you,' she cautioned, knowing that Blythe would not have approved of my background. I knew from Green Room gossip that she feared for her own future as well, but her generous nature made her think first of other people's problems. I was very glad when the curtain came down on *Lovers' Meeting*, and always longed to get a second crack at the part in freer circumstances.

I began to experience again a curious dip in energy that was to dog me during certain periods of my acting career, when I would drop below performance level without knowing why. The fact was that I suffered from a form of anaemia for most of my childhood, and had periodic fainting fits which the doctors put down to lack of iron. A diet of vitamin pills and a pretty ghastly mixture of milk-and-Guinness did little to cure the ailment, which much later in my life was conquered by advances in medical techniques. But the major factor in my low-key delivery was uncertainty, and lack of a director in whom I could have placed my trust.

This production of *Lovers' Meeting* brought to an end Louis D'Alton's period as manager of the Abbey. Shortly after the play closed, he was asked to take a tour of the Abbey Players around the provinces of Ireland, which he had previously toured extensively in his 'fit-up' days. Louis and his wife Annie (later to become a popular TV figure in *The Riordans*) were to take charge of a troupe of senior and junior players, including Fred Johnson, Gerard Healy, Eithne Dunne, Brian O'Higgins, myself and – to everyone's amazement – Maureen Delany. The plan was to leave some of the main company to hold the home fort, with a few additional, bilingual players chosen by Blythe.

Maureen was in shock. Being parted from most of her contemporary acting friends was bad enough, but travelling with a five-play repertoire, for a period of months under less than ideal conditions, was a serious ordeal for a lady in her middle years. I went to her dressing-room when the news was announced, and found her in tears. Although I could see that a big name was needed to sell the Abbey wares in the provinces, she was the only one of the top four – the others were F J McCormick, May Craig and Eileen Crowe – to be sent out. She was aware that refusal to go might finish her with the new managing director, just as those left behind were conscious of some loss of identity in the influx of new Gaelic-speaking performers.

Some, like Cyril Cusack, had no problems. He was young, outstandingly gifted and had excellent Irish. His Gethsemane with the Abbey was to come much later, and there were many shining experiences ahead of him before he lost heart and patience with his beloved 'Theatre of Inspiration'. We all, young and old, had thought of the Abbey in similar terms, and it seemed impossible that one man could bring disillusion to so many.

There was a notion abroad that Siobhán McKenna was discovered by Blythe around this time; not so. Her mesmeric presence and interpretative gifts came from a higher source altogether, and were discovered in the Taibhdhearc in Galway before she was called to an Abbey audition. She did not choose to spend her career there, going over to the Gate for the earth-shaking *St Joan*, and then on to international triumphs which brought credit and pride to her country. Cyril Cusack took the same route, and Ray McAnally undoubtedly would have also, had he left the Abbey a little earlier and lived a little longer.

# 12

# *Exile and After*

There was a sense of great change in the Abbey. The company now contained many new names, all in their Irish version. All who were co-opted into the Abbey by Blythe had to have their names in Irish in all programmes and publicity; the older players were exempted, presumably because they were so well established in the public mind that a change of names would be confusing. Blythe set about forming a Gaelic-speaking company, so that plays in Irish could be produced without having to look outside for actors. He had already been influential in bringing Frank Dermody from the Taibhdhearc in 1940, even before he became managing director in 1941.

I was cast in very few plays on my return from touring, and one day in 1943 knocked on the door of the little office upstairs, and asked to see Mr Blythe. He sat at a table, smiling his Buddha smile that never seemed to grow warm. I was nervous, but I had to know the worst, and the worst was what I heard that morning. I can hear him now, explaining how I did not fit in with the new policies of the Abbey; how I would need to become versed in Irish history and language and how I could come back when I had a fluent knowledge of the language. He added that the board were delighted with my progress as an actress since I had come into the company. He advised a lengthy sojourn in the Gaeltacht.

I couldn't let him see me put down, although it seemed as if I might faint or, worse, cry. I had to earn my living; how could I afford to leave Dublin for such a long period? He stood up; the interview was over. 'Come back to us', he said, 'when you're better able to fit in.' I replied, 'No, Mr Blythe, I don't want to fit in.' From the Abbey I went to Stephen's Green, where I had gone so often with my joys and sorrows. I did not feel that anything was at an end, because I also thought that there were other things in life, other theatres and places to develop such gifts as I had been given. The last thing I resolved, before I went home to tell Mother, was that I would one day get even with Blythe.

Mother hugged me when I came home, and and told me to cry if I felt like it. She did not say meaningless things on the lines that everything would be all right. She did not even seem surprised, but she asked me if I really believed Blythe when he said I would be taken back if I had fluent Irish. I told her that I did not. I knew from the moment I told him my background that I would have no place in his plans, and that I would always dread him if I stayed at the Abbey. It was not necessary for me to know his history as a politician; I could *feel* his fanaticism and intolerance.

Mother said very little, except that I was better away from the Abbey for the time being. I lost my head and screamed that I would never go back, as long as the old bigot was there, and I would never forgive him. Of course that kind of scene had only one ending. Mother gently held me as I let the healing tears fall. I had been there nine years in total between the School of Acting and the Abbey Company, and I was not yet twenty-two.

Mother told me that the next step was up to me. She did not think that I would find life easy in a freelance situation. The easy option would have been to do what Blythe had said, and she would somehow have paid for the recommended stint in the Gaeltacht. But we both knew that I would never go back to the Abbey while he was there, so it simply didn't arise.

Next morning, I met Eithne Dunne for coffee in Roberts of Grafton Street, and told her the story. She was furious and consoling. On the one hand, she was glad that I was free from an unhappy situation; on the other, she felt Blythe was an absolute disaster, and she had to stay on because Gerard Healy had written a play (*Thy Dear Father*) for her, and it had been accepted by the Abbey board. Eithne felt sure the axe would fall on her, too, as soon as Blythe got round to it.

Gerard Healy was a most unusual young man who spoke beautifully and looked like a teenage academic. His hair had turned silver when he was nineteen, and he turned the heads of many women, young and old. He was courteous in an old-world way, and a very good actor who specialised in debonair and classical roles. There were many suitable parts for him when he came to the Abbey in the late 1930s, and I was always happy to be cast with him, as was Eithne, who eventually fell in love with him and he with her.

During the same period, Wilfred Brambell joined the Abbey, and we were great friends. He was a small, thin man with a huge comic gift, and, like so many comics I have met, wanted desperately to be taken seriously. We were once cast together in a play called *Pilgrims*, by Mary Rynne, and he was so sincere in our love scene – but the audience laughed at him, and Wilfred could not be consoled.

Wilfred had a wistful quality, and a great capacity for affection. He worshipped beautiful women, but was always afraid that they might laugh at him as the audience had done in that scene. It was no use reassuring him, telling him that he had other gifts besides his comic genius, that he was a very fine actor. His appearance was against him, and he was given to pulling funny faces when his back was to the audience, challenging the other actors not to 'corpse'. Thinking now of Wilf, and rejoicing in his enormous success in the TV series *Steptoe and Son*, I wonder if he ever managed to conquer his loneliness. He was only briefly the centre of attention in our group, when he rushed into marriage with a pretty divorcée whom he hardly knew; and, indeed, they did not stay together long enough to get to know each other. Poor Wilf, distracted by this experience, left the country to make his career elsewhere.

After my departure from the Abbey, I talked to actors I had worked with, often in the informal 'Green Room' of Roberts in Grafton Street, where we had coffee and passed around the current news. Gerard Healy, who had been with us on the provincial tour, gave me some really good advice, saying that I had nothing to worry about so far as getting work was concerned. He pointed out that I was well established through my years in the Abbey, but he knew I was not good at self-advertisement, and urged me to spread the word that I was now a free agent and available. Eithne agreed, and invited me to join a new company they hoped to form in the near future. Neither of them had any expectation of being kept by Blythe, nor did they want to stay after Gerard's play had been produced.

I did not go to see the senior members of the company, knowing they were aware of my departure. But to my delight and amazement, a beautiful bouquet arrived at our house with a card from 'Peter and Eileen' (F J McCormick and Eileen Crowe) wishing me luck and God's blessing. It was a generous farewell.

A real irony of my situation was that I did in fact love the Irish language, and longed to be able to speak it with native fluency. But I would never have conceded to Blythe that acquiring the language would have had any effect on my general ability, and anyway I would not be bullied into learning it. It was the beauty of Mícheál Mac Liammóir's voice, so rich in timbre, that enticed me when I first heard him speak in Irish. Blythe's voice was harsh, with a strong Northern accent, and made it sound discordant and guttural. His commitment to the language was certainly real, but he was not its most musical exponent.

Eithne had to fulfil her short contract with the Abbey, which she said was based on the unflattering premise that one of Blythe's bilingual protégées was not yet available to join up. The actress in question showed a maturity beyond her years, as did Eithne, who was rarely cast in mere juveniles. Like Siobhán McKenna, Eithne had that extra dimension in her playing that lifted her above average, a quality called stardom. Yet there could not have been two more dissimilar personalities. Their appearance, approach, presence and range moved them into different spheres of work, and it will always be arguable as to which of them had the greater talent.

Both, coincidentally, had major successes in playing Joan of Arc; Siobhán in Shaw's play and Eithne in Jean Anouilh's *The Lark*. Eithne could play Shaw superbly, and her Candida was a triumph at home, in England and in France. Siobhán's St Joan brought her fame in the West End and on Broadway. Siobhán was a magnificent Pegeen Mike in Synge's *Playboy*, and so was Eithne, each vividly memorable and utterly distinctive. And both of them, nurtured for a short time in the Abbey, moved on to a wider world of artistic acclaim via the Gate Theatre.

During the war, companies from Britain and Europe ceased to be regular visitors at our two largest 'commercial' theatres, the Olympia and the Gaiety. Edwards/Mac Liammóir moved their company into the Gaiety for the greater part of each year, and audiences revelled in performances such as Mícheál's acclaimed Hamlet, his brother-in-law Anew McMaster's Othello and Dame Sybil Thorndike's tragic interpretation of Mrs Alving in Ibsen's *Ghosts*.

At that time I was pursuing my own career as a freelance actress, and finding to my surprise and relief that I was rarely out of work. Mícheál had no opening for me when at last I was free but plays were being produced all over the place. Also there were radio broadcasts which sometimes took me to the BBC in Belfast, where I worked with some wonderful Northern actors such as Harold Goldblatt and Jimmy McGee. One of my most memorable experiences was in a version of *Shadow and Substance*, playing Brigid to Harold's Canon.

As I found myself constantly working in one-off plays presented by enterprising managements which sprang up at this time, I began to lose the sense of of exclusion that I felt for a time after I left the Abbey. All actors know the fearful state of disembodiment that comes with being out of work. It takes just a few weeks with no firm job in view to make one feel like a wraith, having no substance. Then the phone rings, the sun reappears and you are alive once more.

Fortunately, I did not have much time to think about all that. I took everything that I was offered and enjoyed it all, happy in my new-found independence, being now in my twenties and old enough to go to the North, or anywhere else, without parental permission. Mother did oppose my wish to go to London in 1945, because of the bombing, and prevailed for a while. I joined ENSA, the organisation set up to provide entertainment for the troops, and went to the North for a few months. Ian Priestly Mitchell, still remembered as a broadcaster and the radio voice of the Irish Sweepstakes programme, was asked to direct some plays for ENSA, usually slight comedies of the bedroom farce variety. He invited me to join three other Irish performers in a play called *Why Not Tonight*, a title which speaks for itself. Ian, whom I remember as an exceedingly courteous gentleman, thought I might acquire a degree of versatility, and learn the difficult art of playing farce.

I remember little about this piece, except that a young actress named Charmian Winwood gave a stunning comedy performance as a man-hating liberated type, and I was a willowy, rather stupid juvenile with arty notions. Of the two actors, one was named Joe Reid, and the other has disappeared from memory with the plot of this small gem. The dialogue was probably considered daring then, but the little I recall would not cause a ripple in a school play today.

Most of the places we went to were not named, for security reasons. We stayed in guesthouses in key centres like Belfast, and travelled nightly by coach to military bases where we entertained troops in halls and makeshift auditoriums, and afterwards went to the officers' mess for drinks, sandwiches and chat. What I now remember is a blur of such venues, and the heartrending sight of blinded and burn-scarred young men. Some had plastic surgery on their damaged faces, others wore gloves to hide their mutilated hands. We four entertainers were pressed into a close-up view of the horror of war. In the officers' mess, dining with the maimed and disfigured among their more fortunate, uninjured comrades, conversation was often far from easy. We had been warned not to discuss politics or the war at all, so there were awkward pauses while we waited for cues.

The officers questioned us about where we lived and how we came to join ENSA. I forget what the others said, but I chickened out and replied that it had seemed the right thing to do, when so many southern Irish had joined the British forces. There was a somewhat bitter reaction from some officers, who referred to the loss of life they were incurring because they could not use our ports, barred to them because of Ireland's neutrality. But mostly they were cheerful, enjoying the play while recognising its frivolous nature, and complimentary to us for performing for them, indeed for coming at all. There were no incidents, no amorous advances, nothing except a desire to make us welcome, and to talk about wives, families and home. We had not come for any grandiose purpose, being just actors who wanted to work, but it all proved to be a really valuable experience of the theatre and life. Although I did not take up Ian Priestly Mitchell's offer to go abroad with our little offering, *Why Not Tonight*, I was indebted to him for an unforgettable few months which changed my whole perception of the war.

In Dublin, theatre people, particularly the young crowd, were always giving parties. None of us had any money to speak of, so everyone brought something, and very little would set us off, in a flat, an attic, someone's home, a kitchen. One gin-and-lime could be nursed all night, and a few bottles of stout or ale, a few sandwiches or cheese and biscuits, could fuel such fun and laughter and gossip. I was able to lose my shyness after a drink or two, and we sang and, if there was a piano, danced. A fortunate host might have a gramophone, a square cabinet which produced a magical sound, but nothing was essential.

At one of these parties, I met the stage manager of the Gate Theatre. Seán Colleary was handsome and charming, and sang that night in a deep baritone. I was captivated by the song, apparently the only one he knew in English. It was 'The Old House', one of the most wistful of all Irish ballads. He did not sing it in perfect pitch, but it was already a classic for me, always hyper-sensitive to voices. Seán had a rich texture of voice, with overtones of his native Sligo.

He had green eyes, and was as dark in skin and hair as a gypsy. When he approached me, he said little except to congratulate me on some performance. I later heard that he was much liked, efficient at his work and very hard to know. There was, it was said, a wall around him, and nobody could get through.

I determined to be the one to breach that wall, although I still don't know why. It was a month or two before we met again, at another party, one which would now be called a reception. I was there because I had been an Abbey Player, and other theatre people were present amidst a sea of business people seeking to open or close something. Eventually the theatre people, managements excepted, left to go to some pub where we could talk freely. Seán moved over to me, and eventually we left and went walking. He began to talk as though he was starved of conversation, pouring out his thoughts and ambitions; why he was in the Gate to learn, how he wanted to direct plays in English and Irish, and how he planned to have his own company.

When he paused for breath, I was able to say that Eithne Dunne and Gerard Healy were forming a company, and if he wanted help I would form one with him. If we worked hard and saved, it could all come true. Then I suddenly became embarrassed, and almost shouted that if we became good friends, we might do it. He also became self-conscious, and said we ought to think about getting home, and that he would see me to a bus. We walked in an awkward silence, unbroken until I boarded the bus and he shouted goodnight after me. But somehow Seán kept turning up at parties or places I would go to with friends, and one night when we lacked money for coffee or a drink, I brought him home to meet Mother.

Although Seán was reticent, he was well able to cope with older people, and was very charming. He got on well with Mother, and passed muster with Doris, who made a brief appearance to have a look. But Mother had one reservation which she mentioned when he had gone. She felt there was something hidden about him, some mystery she could not put a finger on, and asked if I were fond of him. I said that I hardly knew him, but that we had the same plans and hopes. We talked the same language as far as the theatre went – and what else was there?

From that time, Seán and I were regarded as a twosome. We were asked out together, after his show or mine, and saw each other so often that I altogether forgot about Gerry Kiernan, a student actor who had been my 'steady', even though he spent most of his free time dancing with Doris. I was addicted to classical music and Seán to Irish airs, and although we had a mutual love of jazz, we generally differed in our tastes.

One evening, when we were alone in front of a roaring fire in the drawing-room, he mentioned that he was allergic to certain foods and required a special diet. He did not know the nature of his allergy, only that it caused him to have giddy attacks, but with the right diet, he had no problems. He just thought that I should know, as he assumed that I would be cooking for him if we married. I had never cooked for anyone, and indeed Mother thought that I should keep away from kitchens. But this was the first time that Seán had mentioned marriage, and I was anxious to do or learn anything that would keep him healthy, so I gladly promised to help, to seek advice and to keep our show on the road.

It was not so much a proposal of marriage as an assumption that we could not fulfil our destiny together unless we were married. We embraced, since we were now engaged in a way, and committed to a partnership in life and theatre. Seán made a frantic attempt at romantic passion, which resulted in both of us rolling and thrashing about on the carpet in front of the fire, getting too hot and untidy. Hearing a door open upstairs, we sat up with clothes in disarray, frantically trying to close buttons and tidy hair, then falling into separate armchairs with cigarettes in hand for extra composure.

Doris came in; she had been reading, and felt the need for a cigarette. She sat there smoking until we just had to tell her that we had become engaged. She burst out laughing, and said 'Idiots, you don't even know each other.' Seán rose to go, warning me to say nothing until Mother had been consulted. We did not even kiss at the hall door – and still I did not see the danger signs.

# 13

# *A Marriage in Haste*

Seán was very busy, and both of us spent a lot of time observing the Gate's company structures, learning as much as we could so that we would be fit for our joint venture. With stars in our eyes, and marriage in prospect sooner rather than later, we did not give much thought to finance. Nobody earned very much, anyway, and Hilton and Mícheál were a shining example of what could be accomplished without money.

Some of our friends had taken the nuptial plunge without looking beyond their immediate employment. In our case, the idea of marrying came about because, in some inchoate way, it seemed to fit the picture of a theatre partnership. I cannot recall any formal proposal, although Seán had long talks with Mother. There was a romantic aura about him, in the sense that he had a quiet strength and authority that did not require him to raise his voice. His dark features and long green eyes became animated only when he was reciting poetry to me, or going over the finer points of a script. He recited love poems to me in English and Irish; Yeats, Shakespeare and translations of ancient Gaelic verse. Yet we spoke little of love, and sometimes it seemed that we expected it to happen because we were engaged, rather than the other way round.

I always liked Seán an awful lot; most people did. But I found that he had a stubborn streak as strong as my own, unbending when it came to questions of what he believed to be justice and fair play. Mother was really fond of him, but thought that we were mad to be thinking of marriage without some financial security and no place to live. We spent our spare time looking at flats or even rooms. But as time went by, with the Gate preparing to go on tour and I being contracted to go north for another BBC play, we decided to get married first and find a flat afterwards. We found a cheapish room in Rathmines, and that was to be our base.

We didn't want anyone but our two families at the wedding.

I would buy a new outfit from my savings, and Doris was asked to be bridesmaid. Mother was distracted, and even poor mild Uncle Joe was enjoined to talk to me, as they felt that I must be really crazy. Doris stormed out of the house whenever we came in, thinking that it was humiliating for her to have her kid sister marry first. Aunt Lena warned me that marriage was not what it was cracked up to be, and that 'the other thing' was something to be put off as long as possible. How this was to be done without the co-operation of the bridegroom she didn't explain, muttering 'you'll find out.'

There was such pandemonium that Seán kept away until Mother demanded to know what his family thought, if he had one. I told her that I didn't know, never having met them. So she sent for Seán, and told him that he had better put that straight immediately. He invited me to tea at his home in Marlborough Place, where I first met his sister Eibhlín, a fair-haired, stout and pleasant-looking lady who seemed more auntish than sister-like. I was amazed at his parents, who really were elderly and white-haired, more like grandparents. Eibhlín told me that Seán was a child of their late years, totally unexpected but very welcome. They were a kindly but very bewildered pair. Old Mr Colleary stayed to welcome me, and then went out to the pub.

The rest of us had afternoon tea and Eibhlín expressed certainty that God had ordained our union, and would bless it. She was, Seán said, very religious, to which their mother added that she had a very important position in the civil service, and was a great promoter of the Irish language. I told her of my clash with Blythe, and to my chagrin she agreed with him, offering to help me become proficient in the language to please him and perhaps be reinstated. That produced such a furious reaction from me that Seán hastened to change the subject. Eibhlín opined that time was on our side, with both of us in present employment, and that she was happy about the whole thing.

After that, Eibhlín came to meet Mother, and it was decided that we should go ahead and get married with family consent, rather than make a defiant gesture which would upset everybody. But Mother was not happy, and Doris was so enraged that at first she threatened to boycott the ceremony; but her naturally affectionate nature overcame her reservations. Finally, there we all were on a late May morning in 1943, chilly at the unearthly hour of 8 am at the Church of the Holy Name in Beechwood Avenue, Ranelagh. The happy couple were stiff with cold and fright, never looking at each other and hardly hearing the vows – but like true professionals, responding when the priest gave the cue. Doris looked typically glamorous, Seán's best man produced the ring as required and everything else became a blur. There was a family reception at the Gresham Hotel, with Mother and Joe, Aunt Lena and Cecil, Doris and the Colleary family.

Mother put her arm around me and told me to eat something. Thinking that I might be about to faint, she gave me a glass of sherry. I wanted to be a child again, to beg her to make these grown-up people go away. Seán sat down beside me and whispered how much he loved me. I looked at him. He was such a gentle person, and he was my friend; it would be all right. The priest looked as though I were somehow in the wrong place; he kept staring at me, then at my sister. Mother told me later that he had asked her if I were really old enough to be married.

At the reception, photographs were taken, people drank toasts and made speeches. My uncle Cecil, a giant of a man who had a love affair with Irish whiskey, spoke at length about his own wedding. The only effect drink had on Cecil was that he became over-sentimental and lachrymose. He rambled on about his lovely wife Lena, called her lovey and said that she was his best pal, then referred to Mother as his best pal, too, while quite forgetting Seán and me.

At last it was time to go. As we had only three or four days before returning to work – Seán at the Gate and I in Belfast – Eibhlín suggested a quiet hotel she knew of in Greystones. We both loved the sea, and nobody from the theatre world was likely to stumble across us there. Mother said that we could have all our theatre friends to a party the night we returned. We were thrilled with this suggestion, and gave her lists of people to telephone. Then we said our goodbyes and were driven to the train.

Sitting opposite each other in the first-class carriage, I looked at Seán, thinking that everyone I really knew had returned to their lives, leaving me to cope with a complete stranger. I did not know this man with whom I now had to share a room for three days and nights. I saw him looking at me, and wondered was he thinking the same? After a while, he spoke politely about the reception, and how well it had turned out. I responded in similar vein, saying that I hoped it would be warm in the hotel; and he moved closer, asking if

I was cold. I did not allow him to embrace me, thinking that perhaps I could make some excuse, and nothing would happen in the night.

We lapsed into silence until we reached Greystones, where we took a taxi to the hotel. The lady at the desk was friendly, telling us when dinner would be served, and we went upstairs to unpack, and showers of coloured confetti fell from our luggage. We did laugh at that, and decided to leave it – the manageress would understand. Then we went for a walk by the sea, and everything was lovely again. It was very cold, but I had to take off my shoes and paddle. I could not make a stone skim over the water, but Seán could, and I loved watching them. We looked for shells, and splashed each other; then went back to the hotel ravenously hungry, and I thought, it may yet be all right.

We had a bottle of wine with dinner, and Seán had more drinks after that in the bar, while I went up to our room. I undressed quickly, had a quick wash and went to bed, thinking that I could pretend to be asleep, and nothing would happen. Seán came up, and I could hear him undressing and singing his off-key 'Old House'. He turned off all the lights except the one beside the bed, then got in and shook me gently, saying that he wanted to talk. He said that he loved me, that we were now man and wife, and were going to make love for the first time. I asked him to wait until tomorrow, a while, maybe a week, saying that we weren't ready, did not really know each other, yet. But suddenly he said, quite firmly, 'You're my wife and I'm your husband, and it's our duty to consummate our marriage.' He turned out the light, and with many endearments and no idea in the world how to handle this most important night of our lives, we did our duty; and I cried in the darkness to think that love could hold such terror and pain.

I think I knew then that the marriage was over. I lay watching the light come up in the sky, and when the clock said 7.30 am I got up, put on some clothes and went quietly out of the hotel, to walk by the sea. I was in quite a bit of physical pain, and it was not diminishing. A little later, when Seán was just waking, I told him that I had been walking on the beach, thinking about our future. He reached out for me, but I resisted, telling him that it was impossible to make love like that for quite some time, and that if he insisted, I would leave him. He was terribly upset that I had been hurt to such an extent; but although he agreed to wait until I was well again, he made it clear that he would not tolerate a prolonged abstinence. His

Irish Catholic upbringing would not let him accept the idea that a wife might refuse her spouse.

I could not believe that this intelligent, well-read young man could be so unwittingly tyrannical. I told Seán that we were friends or nothing, adding that I did not blame him for his views but that we had to find a compromise or our relationship would fall apart. Little more was said, but at night I was untroubled, and began to hope. In the evenings, I would read or study my radio script, and Seán would go to the bar and drink with some people he had met. We did not talk again about our problems until we got home.

Mother had arranged a great party in our house, and relations and theatre friends turned up in great numbers. Mrs Broughal, Mother's old friend and sometime nanny to us, came to help out, and Lizzie came up from the kitchen for a glass of port wine. Uncle Joe stayed only for a half-hour, really out of courtesy. As a recovered alcoholic, it was hard for him to be around all that drinking jollity. Doris, with Patty Broughal and a couple of beaux in tow, dazzled the company as always. Seán and I went into the hall while the party was at its height, and hugged each other, as we were parting for a few weeks next morning. He was such a kind and sweet-natured person that I felt a familiar surge of affection for him, and a sense that maybe we really were suited to each other. Mother was glad to see us so obviously close. Afterwards, she said that she had been worried when we were in Greystones. I told her that we had managed fine. It was a long time before she got the true story.

I went to the North for two weeks and did the broadcast, another play lost to memory in the blur of the many in which I performed. The Gate also went north to tour the towns after their Gaiety season, playing Shaw's *Arms and the Man*, Wilde's *The Importance of being Earnest*, Patrick Hamilton's *Gaslight*, Ibsen's *Ghosts* and Coward's *Blithe Spirit*. Seán was away with them for over two months. When he came home, I was sick, and Mother suggested that we put off the search for a flat until I was better. Of course she suspected correctly that I was pregnant, but what was described to me as 'only morning sickness' was an indescribable feeling of nausea and discomfort that went on non-stop for about three months.

Despite that, I went to work at the Olympia in two plays directed by an actor named John Stevenson, who was very much of the old school. He had an aggressive Dublin voice until he was on-stage, when it was transformed into one of rich beauty and impeccable tone. John was producing comedies, and engaged me to play the juveniles in two quite silly farces, but he was alarmed to learn that I was pregnant. We took a chance, and it worked, and I concluded my season after six months, as the baby had by then begun to make its presence known.

Shelah Richards begged me to play in her forthcoming production of *The White Steed*, by Paul Vincent Carroll. Although she swore that my condition could be camouflaged, I declined. I was fully convinced that I was bearing at least twins, and would be twice as large within a week. Seán was so thrilled that he assumed that I, too, must be euphoric; he had difficulty in understanding how irritating it was to for me to hear about his work at the Gate, when I felt so useless. I became preoccupied with health, taking long walks every day and smoking very little.

I was too restless to read much, and followed Mother around in the evenings asking what giving birth was like. My gynaecologist, Eamon de Valera, was not at all cheery, reminding me that the Bible said that 'we would bring forth our children in pain and suffering.'

Then, one night, I went into labour. After hours of calling for Mother and contemplating death I had the first of my best reasons for living. We called the baby Jacqueline after Seán, which is, of course, John or Jack. I was in the Baggot Street nursing home for some three weeks with a number of complications. Going home with Jacqueline, I still had various pains and aches, but it was wonderful to be back with Mother – Seán was on tour again, and we still had no flat. The whole household went wild over the new arrival, and Mother naturally behaved as if it were hers. Joe was more tentative; he liked children who could walk and talk, and retreated at the slightest wail from the cradle.

After I had been home a little while, I learned from a friend that Seán had collapsed on the tour, but had refused treatment and continued to work. This frightened me, and I took the first opportunity to tackle him and ask what had happened. He told me that he had seen a doctor, who found his symptoms puzzling; there were some days when his limbs would go numb for a time, and others when he had no control of them at all. Mother coerced him into going to a specialist, who diagnosed a progressive disease affecting his nervous system. The specialist said that it might be many years before it became disabling, and that there was a possibility that this might never happen. He would have to be treated, and alcohol was forbidden.

We were all greatly worried, and when Eibhlín next came to see us, Mother asked her about Seán's medical history. She told us that there had been symptoms when he was very young, but that the doctors had said that there was nothing to worry about. Coming so soon after the birth of our daughter, this put us all into reverse gear. We were all more than a little afraid, because no name had been put to the condition, and there was a vagueness about the diagnosis, and what the future might hold. But the gloom did last for long. There was Jacqueline to preoccupy us; Seán himself believed there was nothing seriously wrong with him, and I began to believe it too. I would not go back to the theatre until Jacqueline was old enough to have a child nurse, and we would soon move to the new flat we had found.

Within a month I was back in hospital with an appendix about to explode, plus a dropped womb – hence all the pains. Home again after three weeks, I was still shaky, and Elizabeth Broughal and Lizzie had taken over the baby. Slowly I got stronger and we were almost ready to move to the flat. It was a garden flat in Rathmines, quite near and just within our means, and I expected to be earning again soon.

Seán came home late one night, drunkenly staggering. I gave him coffee and got him up to our room, afraid that he would wake everybody. When he had sobered up, he said that he had a bad row with Hilton Edwards, and had handed in his notice. Of course I protested that he could not do that, we had no money. He replied that he had been unjustly accused of some stage-management blunder, and had upbraided Hilton who, in turn, had a lot to say. Seán had a pride that would not tolerate injustice, but what would we do now?

The next day Seán said that he would go to stay with his sister for a short while, until he found work again. Jacquie and I were to stay with Mother for just a few days. His credentials were excellent, and he was sure he would easily get a job, but when he went around the theatres, he found that they were all fully staffed. He had a friend in London who could get him temporary work, and while I was unhappy about this, I could see no other way to cope.

Then I got a letter from a man named Ronald McDonald Douglas, who was putting on a play at the Olympia called *Damaged Goods,* by Eugene Brieux, which had been a great success in England and abroad. It dealt with the evils of venereal disease and its effects on a young family. Ronald saw this as a cause as well as a theatrical venture. He was a Scot and always wore a kilt, a most attractive man in his forties, with a small moustache and steel grey lights in his wavy hair. He engaged me for the part of the innocent wife – and then asked me if I knew of a good stage manager!

Seán went to see Ronald and got the job, and there we were, both working in the same show for the first time. Mother hired a temporary nurse to take care of Jacquie when we were all out working. Things began to look good. Ronald was delighted to have someone of Seán's experience, and the newspapers were full of publicity for and against this play about the unspeakable disease never mentioned in respectable homes. Ronald McDonald played the main part of a sympathetic medical counsellor, and the play set out to demonstrate how ignorance and silence about sexual disease can ruin marriages, and, in some cases, doom families to blindness and death. In it a young husband has contracted venereal disease from a prostitute and has transmitted it to his innocent young wife, who is pregnant. The play was a sensation in Dublin, packing out the Olympia for several weeks, and grabbing the headlines in the daily newspapers. The merits of the play as such were not overly discussed; the subject was the focus, and reactions were red-hot for and against the staging of such a brazenly outspoken work in holy Ireland.

Ronald revelled in the controversy. He took on all comers in debate, and gave a short speech from the stage each night, informing an enthralled audience about casual sex, and how to combat the dread diseases that might follow such indulgence. So there were nightly queues outside the Olympia, waiting to hear Ronald, kilted for the curtain-call. He always maintained that he wore nothing under the kilt, and I dared to question this one cold night at a cast party. In silent rebuttal, he pulled my hand up under his kilt, and proved his veracity to my mortification. Everyone roared with laughter as I jumped away like a scalded cat. It seemed that I was not the only one to fall into his mischievous trap, and he was delighted that I had been caught.

Ronald was a nice man, a good employer, and he had a lovely girlfriend named Roisin, who was to be his next wife. He was very attractive, and lots of women found him irresistible. During the play and at rehearsals, he would often entrust the running of the show to Seán, who had a flair for direction and often advised on lighting and performance. Ronald did not want to continue as a theatre producer full-time, although he loved the theatre and was in every way the complete showman. *Damaged Goods* had been a special project, and he had an estate to manage in Scotland, and was anxious to get back to his real roots.

Seán could not face being out of work again, and one night, he told me that he was going to England. He had friends there, and could work and save until we could join him. I did not like this prospect. I wanted to work in the Irish theatre, and to bring Jacquie up here, but he replied that we could talk again about all that; his first priority was a steady job. He would come home frequently, and we would be together often. A few days later, he left.

# 14

# *Separations*

So I was home again with Mother, Doris and Lizzie and a beautiful daughter. We had told Ronald about our situation, and he felt that we were young enough to conquer it. He invited me to play the young girl in Strindberg's *The Father*, which he wanted to produce before disappearing into his Scottish mists. I could not believe that I was still being cast as fragile or fourteen-years-old, but it was a strong play, and I was glad to be working.

I really missed and was worried about Seán. His bouts of illness had never been accurately diagnosed, and I had no reassurance that they would not recur. I just hoped that he would not be too lonely and turn to drink. We wrote, at first weekly, but then one or other of us was too busy, and the intervals grew longer and the letters shorter. *The Father* was a hit, and I got some really good reviews. Then it was over and Ronald was gone, and we never saw him again.

Mother and I engaged a student nurse to look after Jacquie, who was given to temper-tantrums, sometimes screaming herself blue in the face, which alarmed me terribly. I sent so often for our charming and efficient child specialist, Dr Kidney, that Mother said he might as well take up residence with us. The nurse, tall and brawny, burst into tears and gave notice one day when her angelic charge threw a pottie, with contents, at her. As I was about to go into another play, I answered an ad in the paper and found not only a child-minding treasure, but a lifelong friend. Etta Freehill was from Cavan, and had left the family farm because she wanted independence and a chance to study to be a children's nurse.

We explained that we had a very temperamental child who had already defeated one brawny nurse, but Etta was not deterred. When she met Jacquie, who crouched in her playpen and screamed at her, Etta simply turned her back, ignoring the screams, and asked if she might see her room. As we left, I noted a golden head rising above the bars of the pen, and two astonished blue eyes following us. A few days of being cuddled when she was well-behaved, and ignored when she threw herself on the floor in ear-splitting rages, and Etta had won. She was unflappable, the most placid person I had ever met, and had a miraculous effect on Jacquie. Now I was free to work, and could help pull my weight at home.

I did not miss Seán sexually. We had never really recovered from our bad start, but I did not grudge him that small comfort on the rare occasions he got home. When the war was over, I was offered work in England. Denis Johnston brought me over to play in Teresa Deevy's plays on radio and in the experimental TV studios. Sadly, Denis and Shelah had split up by then. Denis had fallen in love with Betty Chancellor, a lovely Gate actress who had borne his child. This caused such consternation in pious Dublin that Betty was booed when she went on-stage after the birth, and received abusive and threatening letters.

Shelah Richards was heartbroken. She had two children, Jennifer and Michael, and could not easily divorce Denis without giving him a chance somehow to put things right, and keep the family together. Eventually, however, they divorced, and Denis married Betty. I met Shelah many times during those years, and while she was naturally embittered by the experience, she always loved Denis Johnston. She produced some excellent shows herself, and was the first to bring the great mime artist Marcel Marceau to Dublin. Later on I was to work with her again, in circumstances neither of us could have foreseen. Her charm and appearance, with blonde hair framing her attractively uneven features, grew ever more magnetic as she got older. I was at her eightieth birthday party in the Abbey Theatre bar shortly before she died, and there was still youth in her spirit and movement, although she was then terminally ill.

It was good that work brought me over to see Seán now and then, because his visits were increasingly infrequent. It was money, he said; he could not save if he came home too often. He was working as a department head in a packaging factory, and hated the job. The firm knew of his health problems, but his work was generally so good that they turned a blind eye to his occasional absences.

About that time I heard with deep regret that Eithne Dunne's marriage to Gerard Healy was over. She was now based in London, and heading for stardom. I met Gerard in Dublin, and he told me that he and Eithne remained friends, and intended always to give their daughter Ann a sense of family when work and circumstance permitted. He said, rather sadly, that Eithne and he had not known each other long or well enough before they rushed into marriage. The theatre company they had set up had failed, and they had, like Seán and me, been forced to abandon their plans and find work when and where they could. Our stories were, indeed, almost identical. Eithne had done some fine work at the Gate, and had then gone to London, while Gerard was, like me, freelancing in Ireland.

In the late 1940s, I was summoned to London's Mercury Theatre to play Pegeen Mike in *The Playboy of the Western World*. An actor-producer called Raymond Chandos was producing it, and also playing the role of Christy Mahon. He wanted me to take over the role for a few weeks, as the leading lady had gone to fulfil another contract for that duration. I was the antithesis of Pegeen Mike and could not understand why this man wanted me in the part. He said that he had seen me at the Abbey in a variety of roles, and thought that I was versatile enough to take it on. I had played other parts in the *Playboy* – Sarah Tansey and the other 'stranger' girls – but Pegeen Mike! Still, the man thought that I could do it, and that in itself was a challenge.

In the cast, playing one of the stranger girls, was an actress named Anna Manahan, who seemed destined to be one of the greats of Irish theatre, and was also to be one of my greatest and most enduring friends. This production was an incredible experience. As I came in to the Mercury *Playboy*, I learned that Elspeth March, then married to Stewart Grainger and a most accomplished English actress, had vacated the part of the 'Widow Quin', and not happily. Mr Chandos, who was quite awful in his lead role, seemed to have a habit of having second thoughts about his casting, and I wondered who had been his original Pegeen. Anna thought that it might have been Eithne Dunne, and that her passage had been a stormy one.

I came in innocently enough, to find the legendary Máire O'Neill (sweetheart of author J M Synge, who wrote the play for her when she was a vivacious, red-haired beauty) playing Widow Quin, and the sinfully handsome Breffni O'Rourke, Cyril Cusack's stepfather, playing Old Mahon. He was getting on in years, silver-haired, with a a gamey eye and penchant for drink, as well as a lethal supply of Irish blarney.

Máire instantly adopted me, directing me through the rushed rehearsals. She complained about how thin and pale I was, urging me to drink a lot of red wine to build me up. She herself had aged more, I feared, than she should have because of her own partiality to alcohol. It made her a sad caricature of what she must once have been, now with dyed red hair, ringed eyes and a slurred voice that affected her performances. She was also afflicted with a permanent nasal sniffle which she used in character parts, she told me, to good effect.

For all those drawbacks, the richness of voice that all the old Abbey players seemed to possess lingered on among the ruins of former qualities. Breffni also had a natural rich, resonant voice. Both were kindness itself towards me, knowing that I had a really tough assignment. I missed my baby, and Seán was having a bad spell, and couldn't be there. He had said that he would not come into rehearsals, but did not make the first night, either. He had warned that the odds were against me, but also said that I would deliver a different performance from the usual one and it was, indeed, different.

Fortunately, the play had already been reviewed, so that I did not have to run the gamut of the critics. Chandos gave me one paper which had missed the Mercury opening, and it said complimentary things about me on the lines of my performance not lacking fire or passion, despite frailty of appearance. It also said that Chandos was a romantic and plausible Playboy, which left me less than elated. It was a patchy production, but it at least had a good run and full houses.

Seán never did come. I went to see him, and he said that he was a bit depressed. I tried to persuade him to come home and try again, but he said that he could not let his employer down, and that something better was on the horizon. It didn't strike me then that he was drinking to keep his spirits up, the worst thing for him, and that his only friends there were fellow exiles, caught with him in a lonely trap of misery and drink.

Chandos hoped to bring the *Playboy* into the West End, but I signed off, being too lonely for Jacquie, Mother and home. Before the play had ended at the Mercury, I had cemented my friendship with Anna, and we promised to meet in Dublin. She told me that she also was a victim of Ernest Blythe's approach. She had been auditioned for the Abbey, but was dismissed out of hand for having only English.

On the last night of the show, Máire O'Neill took me aside during the farewell drinks party, and made an awesome request. She had all Synge's love-letters to her in her dressing room, and wanted me to bring them home to Ireland, then give them into the care of some solicitor who would guard them until she was gone. I was the only one she would trust with them. I wanted to do it, but was terrified of the responsibility, and told her the truth. I was too afraid something might happen to letters of such value, and she really did understand my almost superstitious fears.

I asked her would she not come back herself, that I would look after her and her letters, but she was very bitter about Ireland, and had sworn that she would never return. I think Synge's death must have broken her heart. She had a very brief and bitter marriage to Arthur Sinclair, a leading member of the very first Abbey company, and I think that she could not forget Synge, who had worshipped her until his untimely death. So I embraced her, promising to come and see her in London when next I was over but I never saw her again. A few years later, she grew sleepy in front of the fire, fell into it and died quite alone.

The day after the show, I was on the boat home with toys and dresses for Jacquie, and some gifts for Mother and Doris, too. But there was no word from Seán, who did not see me off, and would not come home. He was not earning enough to support us, but at least he had his independence; he was too proud ever to have become a dependant on anyone else. Jacquie was old enough to miss me as I came and went into plays, broadcasts – whatever would pay the rent. Mother was taking too much of the burden, and I could not have worked at all but for her goodness and Etta's loving care. I played in *Kind Lady* by Edward Chodorov in the Gaiety and *The Man with a Load of Mischief*, by Ashley Dukes, I think in the same theatre. Tom St John Barry produced that, but he lost a lot of money and did not try again. He was an actor with Edwards/Mac Liammóir before that venture, and did not stay long in Ireland after his first and last incursion into management.

When Jacquie was five years old, she developed a bad cough, and I took her to a health resort in the Black Mountains in Wales, courtesy of my friends and relatives. Although she frolicked and dipped naked in the sunshine, she grew thin and pale, and coughed throughout the night. I brought her home, where our doctor diagnosed tuberculosis; a small spot on her lungs, he said, but I would not be reassured. Seán came over and had a long talk with the doctors and specialists I had roped in; then went back to London, convinced that I was being hysterical, and that Jacquie was in no danger. She was lucky to have been diagnosed at an early stage, and the slight spread of infection was largely due to my having exposed her to the sunshine and swimming pools, and generally doing all the wrong things. So now the cure was to confine her to bed for a few months, and I stayed with her. There was no way I would have gone away anywhere, as I had acquired a neurotic conviction that she would die if I left her alone.

The news about Seán was good, however. When home, he had been his old buoyant self, full of plans. Following treatment in England, his dizzy attacks and the numbness they brought with them had vanished, and the doctors had concluded that he did not, after all, suffer from petit mal epilepsy, as they had originally suspected, although they would not commit themselves to a precise diagnosis. The main thing was that he was fit, and ready to start theatre work again soon as Jacquie was well enough to begin school. We would have our company; meantime he would save every possible penny in England to pay back Mother. Jacquie's room was soon piled up with soft toys and books and rainbow-coloured paints and crayons, and with fruit and flowers and chocolates. All our friends in theatre dropped in to see her and encourage me, while others, away from Ireland, sent well-wishing cards. Ria Mooney, who had taken over as Artistic Director of the Abbey in 1948, sent a postal order. I learned that Ria had brought with her to the Abbey her star pupils, (bilingual, of course) from the Gaiety Acting School, which she had founded in 1944, and that the Abbey company was again growing in strength. Nobody had thought that it could survive the premature death of F J McCormick in 1947. But now the company was being revitalised by actors infused with the old dedication such as Geoff and Edward Golden, Máire Ní Dhomhnaill, Philip O'Flynn, Angela Newman, Bill Foley and many more.

Jacquie had been in bed only a few weeks when, during one of our reading sessions, she asked if I would listen to her reciting extracts from two books. They were *Alice Through the Looking Glass*, which I had not read to her, and Agatha Christie's *Ten Little Niggers*, since retitled *Ten Little Indians*. To my amazement she read them both perfectly, not stopping even to ask the meaning of a word. I kept bringing her more and more difficult books, all of which she read aided only by a pocket dictionary. In a few weeks the reading process had almost outpaced my ability to feed it. After about four months she had an X-ray, which brought more disappointment. The little puncture was almost, but not fully, healed; it was to be three months more before recovery was complete, and another two until she could walk and run again.

I began to accept radio work, but nothing that would keep me away for long. Generous Uncle Joe offered me the fare to go to London to see Seán, who had not written since the good news of Jacquie's recovery. I gratefully accepted. Doris, who had also been attentive, told me that I had to get out and start living again. So off I went to see Seán, hopeful also of finding work and renewing our life and plans together, and I did get into a play almost immediately. It was Donagh McDonagh's *Happy as Larry* starring Sheila Manahan, which had three new roles built in to lengthen it. These were the Three Fates, equipped with Irish accents, and I got the part of one of them just by asking the director, Denis Carey. His mother May Carey had been an actress and drama teacher in Dublin, and his brother Brian was also in the business.

At last I could send some money home to Mother to help with Jacquie's expenses. Seán had moved to a single-room lodging for reasons of economy, so I took up an offer to share a room in Dee Halligan's flat in Woburn Square, and spent as much time as I could with Seán after work. I often stayed with Dee when I came to London after that, and with her great friend singer-actor Dermot McDowell. They always had a corner for homeless actors, in or out of work. Milo O'Shea and Donal Donnelly, both now famous in America, were often there in the crowded two rooms plus kitchen. When Milo was there, we would all stay up laughing until our ribs ached. Donal had one prolonged period of idleness, having refused a leading role in the famous *Z-Cars* TV series. He believed that his talent could not develop in such a context, and said that he would prefer to starve first.

We had such good times then, except for my deep pain and guilt at being separated from Jacquie and home. I had seen her little white face pressed against too many station railings on the way to the boat, as I left yet again, hoping that she would not cry, but in floods of tears myself. But later I would have the utter joy of returning, by boat or train, with a panda or huge pink Nellie the Elephant.

Back home, unhappy things were happening at the Gate. Mícheál and Hilton had rowed with Lord Longford, who had been their patron, and they had no money to continue their work. I had not been in touch with Mícheál about Jacquie's illness, because while he genuinely adored children, Hilton did not and also found illness repellent. The great duo went through a bad time in the 1950s, and lost more than money in their split with Longford. Top overseas companies were now taking up residence in the Gaiety again, and they were virtually homeless. As Mícheál subsequently wrote in *Theatre in Ireland*, 'Our own Gate Theatre Productions, for reasons that have nothing to do with lack of public support, but rather with the economic stress of soaring prices in everything but the price of a seat in the stalls...have ceased to function in the theatre that Hilton and I built in the late twenties, with all the God-sent if short-sighted enthusiasm of youth.'

Their two or three productions yearly took place from then on in the Gaiety or Olympia theatres, and the partners had to go abroad to seek work. I met Mícheál in the summer of 1950 strolling through Stephen's Green. I had Jacqueline by the hand, and had been recently told that I was pregnant again. This was a great joy despite the uncertainty of work prospects. It must have been a lean period, because we were going to feed the ducks and watch the fountains – but not to tea at Bewleys afterwards. Tea and cakes at Bewleys was 'only when Mummy was rich'. Jacquie would inform people, 'When Mummy gets a good part in a play, we always have cakes.'

Mícheál did not look as if food would have revived his spirits. Although he kissed us on the cheeks in his usual greeting, he didn't clown the way he used to when children were present. He wore his melancholy expression, and although I told him that I believed everything would come right for him and the Gate, he just looked away and murmured – 'such a beautiful country, such trees and mountains, and such uncaring people.' I assured him frantically that Ireland would never let him or Hilton down, that we needed them and their wonderful theatre. But Mícheál said 'Ah, but they are not all like you, Phyllis dear. We are in the minority.' Then he drifted gracefully away.

# 15

# *Home and Away*

In 1951, on 18 July after a performance of *The Plough and the Stars*, the Abbey went up in flames. Fortunately all the staff and players had left the building. The cause of the fire was never established, but not all of the building was destroyed. The vestibule and some of the offices survived, and with the help of willing passers-by, all the pictures were saved. Sympathy and offers of help poured in from all over the country, prompting Lennox Robinson to write 'It only needed this little tragedy to make one realise how deeply rooted is the Abbey Theatre in the national life of Ireland.' The directors of Guinness instantly put their small new theatre at the disposal of the Abbey until they moved to the more spacious Queen's Theatre, famous for many years as the home of variety shows.

The loss of the old Abbey saddened me. F J McCormick had died in 1947, shaking the theatrical community with his untimely passing at the age of fifty-eight. Ria Mooney had been artistic director of the theatre since 1948, and it was no secret that she dreaded the change to the vast Queen's Theatre, but at least the Abbey was not threatened with extinction. After fifty years, it was now truly our national theatre, politically protected, and accepted by the public.

Also in 1951, my son Graham was born, large and lusty. If it had not been for money worries, I would have been the happiest mother-to-be in the world. I had an absolute conviction that I was carrying a boy, and it seemed so right to have one of each, and enough years between them to give Jacquie charge of something better than a toy panda. Shuttling backwards and forwards, I had begun to feel a lot like a dandelion seed blowing in the wind. Moving around on trains and boats, between plays and parts I scarcely remember, played havoc with my sense of identity. And there was the guilt of leaving home and the guilt of leaving a husband in London, although this passed quickly as soon as I settled into home life again, where I could sometimes pretend that I was not married at all.

Graham arrived home in state to the great delight of Jacquie, Mother, Joe and the minders. Jacquie accepted Graham as her proper toy, to be wheeled outdoors and shown to everyone. He was a great smiler, as amiable as she had been tempestuous. Etta was charmed, and Mother adored him and obstinately called him Gregory, the name she favoured, and in time he came to be known as Gregg, except on official documents. Shortly after I brought him home, a house became vacant on Palmerston Road, and Mother's dream came true. She could just afford it, so we all moved; Mother, Joe, Etta and Lizzie, two children, two cats, a dog and me.

The house was big enough to have separate flats, and Joe took over the basement one to have privacy for his newspaper work, and because the garden area was more accessible for his pets. It seemed so right, moving to that gracious house with its high ceilings and long driveway. The steps up to the front door were a bit steep, but we were all sturdy enough, and as the house was a corner one, there was a delicious sense of privacy. The street was wide, and there was a park at the top of the long road, running across from left to right.

Doris had married her fiancé Ben the year before, a mixed marriage which provoked stern clerical disapproval. Doris was informed that the ceremony, if permitted, must take place in the little sacristy behind the altar of the church in Edenvale Road. Another requirement was a sworn promise to bring up any children as Catholics, and she must try to convert Ben. She exploded, threatening the parish priest with a registry office wedding instead. She was determined to have her bridal gown, a proper reception with guests, and would not allow Ben and his family to be humiliated, skulking behind the altar. At last Mother called a halt to the arguments. 'We'll all go to London,' she said, 'where you can be married in Brompton Oratory with all the trimmings.'

So Doris was married in Brompton Oratory, resplendent in oyster satin, with myself as matron-of-honour. Most of the relations and some English friends of both families attended. Joe cried off, as his work schedule would not allow him to come. It was a wonderful day, with Doris and Ben radiantly happy. Ben was a lovely man, as restrained as Doris was gregarious, quiet and kind and responsible. You could see that it would be forever with Ben and Doris.

It seemed now as though Seán was stuck like a limpet in London.

I began to think of him with a certain amount of exasperation. I had not known him well before we were married, and now there was a huge chasm opening up between us, despite all my efforts to the contrary. Whether I was really making efforts or becoming contented with the way things were was questionable.

Out of the blue came an offer of an American tour which would take me away from home for several months. The money was good, and I was to play some tempting roles, including my original part as Brigid in *Shadow and Substance*. Mother and I talked it over. I could not bear to leave the children, but I had to work, and they were lucky to have Mother, the minders and the new house. I needed the work for other reasons, too; I was becoming aimless about my career, taking anything and everything in order to make ends meet. Here there were good conditions; a splendid company run by Maureen Halligan and the English actor Ronald Ibbs, both of whom I knew from their excellent performances at the Gate in Lord Longford's seasons. They had formed a company called The Irish Players, and had been booked to tour universities in America.

Also in the company was a very fine actress named Gervaise Matthews, whom I had also seen in Lord Longford's productions, and the English actor Ken Huxley. A young actress from London was being tried out as Eliza Doolittle (in *Pygmalion*), and the handsome and talented James Neylin, the impish Brian Vincent, and Teddy Byrne, a subtle and versatile actor, completed the company. We were to leave from Cobh on a Cunard liner, the last word in floating luxury, and Maureen told us that we would have a few rehearsals on the ship, as the voyage took about six days.

I longed to go; to see so much of America while playing really good roles would almost be too good to be true. Seán had to be told, and I wrote to say that I was going to America and would be away for a few months. He replied briefly, saying that I was doing the right thing, and that we could talk when I came home. Logically, I should have welcomed such a patient, understanding reply, but was instead livid with rage and frustration. Something was going very wrong, but I was changing, and had ceased to blame myself. Soon it was time to say goodbye to the children, knowing that it would be months before I would see them again.

I soon made friends with Gervaise, and of course already knew Teddy Byrne and Ken Huxley and Maureen, who was the sister of my dear friend Dee Halligan of Woburn Street in London. Ronald

Ibbs could not join us for the first month or so, as he had been ill with tuberculosis some years before, and had to have extensive tests before he could be cleared for entry to the States. We were a motley crew, but infused with vitality and a sense of adventure. We had a special area on the ship for rehearsals, and had a lot of spare time to watch the ship cut through the waves, taking us from grey chill into tropical ocean. Soon we were lying on the decks in bathing costumes. Meals were first-rate, and since few of us were at all sea-sick, we enjoyed them hugely.

The day came when we sailed into New York harbour. The decks were lined with passengers waiting to see the famous coastline. The sun-lit buildings seemed to be full of colour, like a Disney cartoon, and some of the shapes towered up into the clouds. It was all so breath-taking that I forgot to brood, lost in the wonder of that first sighting. When our luggage had been brought ashore, we were introduced to our touring manager, Josie McAvin, a cousin of the Halligans and a woman of strength and capability. Years later, in 1985, she won an Oscar for set dressing on *Out of Africa*, but her abilities were manifest even then.

We began rehearsals the next day, polishing what we had already done and beginning to feel nervous. I endured a nightmare of loss and homesickness during the entire trip, the like of which I have never experienced since. I felt that I had made a wrong decision, and bargained with God every night, to buy myself a little peace and to keep the hope alive of being home safe with the children again.

The tour took us into thirty-two states and lasted for ten months. There were beautiful theatres, large and small, in Connecticut, Chicago, Dallas, Georgia, Florida, Mexico, Dallas, San Francisco, Los Angeles, Tulsa, Texas, Ohio – the list seemed endless. We travelled like Flying Dutchmen, doomed to go on and on, by Greyhound Bus or cars laid on by the agency. In the cars, we were free to vary our routes, and to use our free time to see more sights. We went to Niagara Falls, stopped for a conducted tour at Boulder Dam, and saw the Painted Desert, which is indeed like a huge canvas spread over a thousand acres. In the changing sunlight and shadow, the landscape acquired an illusion of colours unusual in sandy dunes and wastes.

We drove for three days along the rim of the Grand Canyon, stopping at intervals to look down into its awesome depths, and buying beaded ornaments from the Apaches who had stalls along the way. Further on in our travels we encountered the Seminole Indians in their sad reservations, living in primitive conditions, cooking on flat stones as they had always done, the food obscured by clouds of flies. They did not trust or talk to white people, and refused to be assimilated into white society like other tribes. We crossed into New Mexico and bought cheap turquoise and silver jewellery; tried out tequila with salted palms, and got drunk on tiny quantities. We took photographs of the orange groves we passed as we drove along endless, glittering roads, where sometimes mirages shimmered in the distance.

In Dallas, a very rich city, we were booked to give a matinée for the Ladies' Culture Club. After lunch, an oppressive sun was beating down, but the ladies were resplendent in jewellery, glittery dresses and fur wraps. We were transfixed, and from the ornate little playhouse we peeped through the curtains to view the opulence. Dallas was quite extraordinary, although we saw very little of it after the Yeats programme, which seemed to stun the Culture Club into silence. I can still see the ladies thanking us for a 'wunnerful experience', and heading for the cocktail bar.

This was oil territory, where some people were billionaires. James Neylin and I were invited to the home of a local Midas, which had a beautifully lush garden. Suddenly we saw hens, plain ordinary hens, and were seized by laughter, as if the ordinary was here bizarre and incongruous. In Texas, everything was larger than life, and big was deemed beautiful, and although it all seemed part of a film fantasy, the Texans were kindly and generous people. They were delighted that we had come with our plays, which they hugely enjoyed.

Mother wrote frequently, saying that everyone was well and happy, which, somehow, I did not find reassuring. Christmas came, and we had a week off in Los Angeles, which was hot and smoggy. Dan O'Herlihy, a dear colleague from Dublin who had achieved some fame in Hollywood films, invited us to his lovely home for Christmas with his family and it was good to be with friends.

Florida was a brochure of vivid colours, waving palms, tropical heat, rain that drenched you and suddenly stopped, leaving you steaming. New Orleans was magnolia and old southern buildings. San Francisco, with its crooked quality and unexpected paths and the magnificent Golden Gate Bridge was a place I could have called home under other circumstances.

The day finally came when we were going home. I had saved

quite a lot of money, and my suitcase was crammed with clothes and gifts. Going back to my dearest ones, I was even in the mood to enjoy the voyage. Some of the younger actors stayed back, hoping to make a breakthrough in American theatre, but their seniors, and those with families, were as happy as I was.

The family gave me an overwhelming welcome, although Gregg looked at me dubiously as if I was someone he ought to know, and Jacquie was reserved; a reminder that it was too much to stay away for almost a year, and that I would have to win back full approval again. Mother and I hugged tearfully, and Joe congratulated me on having survived the murderous gangs in the States. Etta and Lizzie were smiling and offering tea, and when I opened my cases to reveal their cargo of gifts, the children jumped with excitement, and all inhibitions vanished. Later, I had a long chat with Mother, and we decided that, after a decent interval at home, I should go to see Seán and try to persuade him to come home.

At the first opportunity, I took a weekend trip to London, where he had found better accommodation with a nice landlady who liked Irish lads. Although he agreed that there was no serious prospect of further promotion in his present job, he was loath to leave it, or London. Our early plans to form a theatre company had, he said, been an immature dream, and he urged me to be more practical. I told him that I planned to continue my career in Ireland, and he did not object. He would visit, and so would I, and nothing had changed except that he missed the children. But, in reality, everything had changed.

My mother, May Ryan, aged about forty.

Myself, at the age of two or three, about to step out into the
unknown.

1938. Myself aged fifteen, seeing a vision of St Brigid in *Shadow and Substance* by Paul Vincent Carroll, at the Old Abbey Theatre.

1939. Denis O'Dea as Canon Skerritt and myself in a revival performance of *Shadow and Substance*. Denis took over the part of Canon Skerritt after Arthur Shields, the original Canon, left the Abbey for the USA. Denis later married Siobhán McKenna.

1939. My first 'grown-up' role, with Joseph Linnane in *Illumination* at the Abbey Theatre.

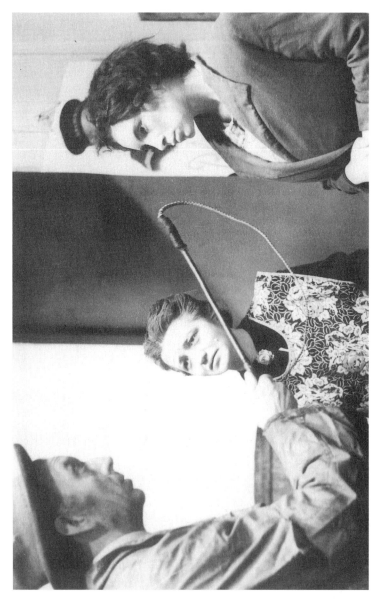

1942. FJ McCormick, Ria Mooney and myself in *The Fort Field* by George Shiels at the Abbey Theatre.

A scene from *The Whiteheaded Boy* by Lennox Robinson. *Left to right*: Ria Mooney, Eileen Crowe, Cyril Cusack, myself, FJ McCormick and Denis O'Dea. This was a typical set in those days. Recycling was the done thing.

Myself at twenty-something.

Confirmation Day for my daughter Jacqueline, pictured here with Gregg and myself. My fur coat was borrowed to give me an aura of respectability for the occasion.

1960. Maureen Toal in Tennessee Williams's *Cat on a Hot Tin Roof*.
In the 50s and 60s Maureen Toal was the epitome of glamour, often
compared to Marilyn Monroe. She was an accomplished actress in
revue and drama, and went on to win the Harvey Award twice.

1962. Norman Rodway, my business partner in Gemini Productions. Norman was a splendid actor with great charisma both on and off stage. His private life was said to greatly resemble that of Don Juan!

Jacquie as Rhoda Penmark and Eithne Dunne as her mother in a Globe production of *The Bad Seed* by Maxwell Anderson, at the Gaiety Theatre. Does this loving mother know that her little daughter has murder on her mind?

# 16

# *A New Discovery*

On the American tour, I had begun to formulate ideas for my own company. I looked at the casting, and made my own mental changes. The plays we performed were classics, but I had the old Abbey respect for new writers, and I wanted to discover playwrights, actors, and directors as well as having a core company of experienced senior players. I thought about personalities, how actors and writers might be catered for without the trauma inflicted by cold, unsympathetic management. I was eager to start, but still wanted more time to study the management scene.

On my return from the tour, a new theatre group called the Globe Company was the talk of the town. My friend Anna Manahan had joined them, and I asked her who they were, and how they had created their company. I got to know Anna better in the aftermath of her husband Colm's premature death. Naturally, she remained subdued by grief for a very long time, but she courageously got on with her life and career. I had long talks with her while she was with the Globe, and told her how much I longed to form a company. She told me that the Globe mainly comprised actors who had studied at the famous Brendan Smith Academy of Acting, and had rented the small Gas Company Theatre in Dun Laoghaire to present new plays from all over the world. She herself had joined them in the early 1950s, and explained that everyone was on a salary of £6 per week maximum, and that the rent was paid out of the weekly takings. The players devised their own settings, borrowed furniture from local firms, made their own costumes and generated their own publicity.

I went to see them as soon as I had settled, and became an instant fan. Productions like *Montserrat* by Lillian Hellman and *I am a Camera* by John Van Druten were not easily forgotten. The company included slim, blonde Genevieve Lyons, who contrasted perfectly with the lovely Pauline Delany, dark-eyed and enigmatic in her portrayals. The leading men were the robustly-built Godfrey

Quigley, equal to playing the Jester as well as Lear, and Norman Rodway, a magnet for the ladies in the stalls. They were joined in time by other fine actors, Milo O'Shea, Maureen Toal and Maurice Good.

The Globe had more than enthusiasm and innovation; it also had 'Fitz', the legendary Jim Fitzgerald, whose late father attributed to me a recommendation that opened the door for Jim to professional theatre. I would be proud to think that, as he is the only director I have ever encountered whom I could truly call a genius. His productions for the Globe in their small theatre, with no wing space whatever and a small, awkward stage, were revolutionary, bursting with energy and invention.

As the Globe company all knew my work, and I showed a degree of enthusiasm for theirs, we got along famously. Although I declined an offer to act with them because of my unsettled family situation, I learned by watching them how a group of actors becomes a team. I absorbed the elements that produced excellence against the odds, and how a whole theatrical enterprise could be launched with minimal financial investment.

Jacqueline, now nine years old, came with me to have tea with Madame Bannard Cogley, a petite French lady who had married an Irish Republican, and was totally sympathetic to the national aspiration to unity, and quite vociferous on the subject. Known to her friends as Toto, she was a founder member of the Gate Theatre, and despite her commitment to all things Irish, she remained quintessentially French to the end of her days. She was the first Women's Lib stalwart I ever met, and I wish the others had half of her persuasive charm. Toto was running a little theatre club in a basement in Mount Street, the Studio Theatre Club, staging occasional plays, and a talented group had formed around her tiny enterprise. She was so taken with Jacquie that she asked me if I would bring her to the Studio next evening to read for a part in *The Women*, by Claire Booth Luce. This was a controversial play about the divorce machine in America, which often left a trail of embittered adults and deprived children in its wake. It was satirical, but included a heart-rending scene in which a little girl pleads to have her parents and her trust restored.

There were other children reading for the part, and Toto proposed to arrange that each child would play for two nights only in the week, for reasons of school and sleep. Jacquie said she would like to

read, so we made our way down the next night, to find quite a
crowd of adults and children milling around in the little basement.
There I met, for the first time, Marie Conmee, one of our finest
comediennes, Claire Mullen, exuding glamour and Eithne O'Neill, a
redhead who showed an acid edge in her reading which she happily
did not possess outside the character. Jacquie read, and I thought
that she was made for the part. Toto's son Fergus was directing, and
he announced that four children would be used in the two-week
run, and that Jacquie would play on the opening night.

Jacquie was thrilled, and it was a happy arrangement to have all
the children involved in the show, so that no one felt rejected. Marie,
Claire and, most particularly, Eithne became life-long friends during
the run of *The Women*, although Eithne did not follow through to
become a professional actress. She became instead a source of
encouragement and affection for those she befriended in the theatre
throughout her lifetime. Many a time she took us out of depressions,
lent us money and clothes, and sought very little but our company in
return.

Jacquie was to perform twice weekly. It would do her no harm,
Mother said, and she obviously revelled in the rehearsals. Her
teachers in the school she attended in Pembroke Road were not so
sure, remarking in her presence that nothing good ever came out of
a basement. This made us all laugh outright, and the saying became
a catchphrase at home and in the Studio. On the first night, I was
more nervous than I had ever been. It is impossible to watch
someone you love performing without imagining all kinds of
disasters. But the play was a triumph, and people wept
unrestrainedly at Jacquie's scene. Next day there were rave reviews,
and praise for Jacquie that would turn the head of a seasoned actor.

Jacqueline was then a beautiful child, not at all like the fluffy
angel types used in advertisements for soap or hand creams. She had
chiselled features, straight blonde hair and bright blue eyes that
could smile or weep to order. Her photograph appeared in an
evening paper right after her debut in *The Women*. The picture was
spotted by producer George Brown and director Roy Baker, who
had come to Dublin dizzy from auditioning children for a film they
wanted to make starring John Gregson and Kathleen Ryan. Kathleen,
who had briefly been a student in the Abbey, had been discovered
by the Rank Organisation, and shot to stardom in Sir Carol Reed's
*Odd Man Out*. George and Roy were convinced that Jacquie was

perfect for their film, and also that I would be ideal as her coach for the duration; a salary for me, and more security for Jacquie. The newspapers were suddenly crammed with news of the Studio Theatre and its new child star. In the crazy way the theatre world swings round, I found myself employed to work for and with my little daughter.

Life at Pinewood Studios was a succession of magical experiences, and I was probably even more bewitched than Jacquie was. The first day on the set we were introduced to a little boy named Richard O'Sullivan, now a TV star, who was to play Jacquie's brother. He was about eleven years old, and was turning over the pages of his script with a sort of weary patience. I asked if this was his first film too, and he replied 'It's my tenth. I finished one yesterday, so I'll have to swot this one up rather quickly. There's not too many lines.'

Roy Baker was a gentle, patient man, and he introduced us to John Gregson, and to Kathleen whom I already knew. A succession of Irish actors arrived to play cameo roles such as Liam Redmond, Cyril Cusack, Noel Purcell, Jimmy Devlin, Marie Kean and others. Jacquie had lessons on the set each day for three hours, and spent three hours filming. Weekends and odd days off we were taken on publicity trips, to Kensington Gardens, to the London Zoo, where Jacquie was photographed hundreds of times. Other artists were filming in studios nearby. Bob, our very jolly PR man, managed to get us in to watch Dirk Bogarde filming, and afterwards he sat and chatted to us.

At lunch in the canteen, we would see the film stars at every table, as well as the impossibly beautiful starlets, who did not twinkle for much longer, because the Rank Organisation was soon to disintegrate, and different structures emerged in the film world. Talent came in instead of looks, and plain became beautiful. We were thrilled to see James Robertson Justice and Diana Dors, who was wearing a red tight-fitting dress covered with glittering sequins. At the time she was something of a sex symbol, larger than life. Margaret Lockwood was another big star, and catching a glimpse of such stellar favourites gave an extra thrill to an already exciting daily agenda.

Filming is hard work, and more so when children are involved, because their protective deadlines permit only a limited time to get results. There were a few other children playing minor roles, and Richard O'Sullivan had some family scenes as Jacquie's brother but mainly the film centred on on Jacquie's performance. Every night, after dinner, I would read over the following day's work with her. Then we would play board games, or read, until bedtime. Her school work was done in a room above the studio, but this study period was only a token gesture to child welfare.

I wrote to Mother every week and sent her money. I also wrote to Seán, telling him that we were currently filming at Pinewood and how it happened, but he did not reply. Jacquie had a birthday on the set, and they gave her a special cake and chocolates, and all the crew sang happy birthday; and then Roy Baker said 'Take your places, please.' Roy never lost a minute out of a working schedule.

While I can't recall now what the original title of our film was to be, I remember taking issue with George Brown about the new one. *Jacqueline*, I thought, was hardly an apt title for a film purportedly set in Belfast, with a mainly Irish cast and an Irish child star. But George was unperturbed. He thought it was a good marketable name, and considering the extraordinary success of that modest picture, he was proved right

From start to finish Roy Baker and George Brown had been ideal to work with, like kindly uncles to Jacquie, and friendly and accessible to their cast. George had another script which he hoped to develop for Jacquie, but he understood how anxious I was that she should have a recovery period from all the glamour that surrounded her on the set. She was eleven by the time the film had its première, and the reviews were so ecstatic that we were walking on air, proud that an Irish child with no real experience of stage or film had held down such a major role.

Our whole family was knocked for six by the crowds of people who mobbed Jacquie when she went out. Autograph hunters and mothers wanted to know how you went about putting your daughter on the stage or screen. Gregg did not quite understand all the fuss, and often Jacquie would only sign autographs if he was allowed to sign them too.

We decided to take Jacquie for a holiday before sending her to secondary school in the autumn so Mother took us to Lourdes and Spain. She had always wanted to visit Lourdes, and rightly said that we had a lot to be thankful for, with Jacquie's recovery from the long illness and her recent success. We were not religious in a pious way, but were believers, and the story of Lourdes had always appealed to Jacquie, although she had already acquired her own orthodoxy. We bathed in the contained waters of St Bernadette's stream, and gasped as the freezing waters engulfed us briefly. I was glad that we had brought Jacquie here, feeling that she would be stronger now.

Back home, Godfrey Quigley telephoned to ask if Jacqueline would play the Faery Child in a Yeats season which the Globe was presenting. As I had played this part under Hugh Hunt's unconventional direction, I felt that history was repeating itself, and that Hugh would be amused. Until, of course, having accepted on behalf of a delighted Jacquie, I found that the Globe director, Jim Fitzgerald, had ideas which made Hugh's approach seem antiquated. His faery child was an evil little piece who spat at the crucifix and menaced the priest and the older folk. It was a fascinating concept, and one which Jacquie really enjoyed. We had realised that she could only accept offers which could reasonably be fitted in with school studies and social activities. So we were really rather glad that creative opportunities were here on the spot, and that there were no momentous decisions to be made which might be disruptive.

One day the Globe directors were holding a rather noisy meeting in the little Gas Company Theatre when I walked in with Jacquie. Financially strapped as they were, their next play was of the utmost importance, but none of the suggested works had the right parts for the three directors and their wives. Maurice Good eventually rose to his feet and calmly denounced what he called the bizarre policies of the company. It was, he said, doomed to fall apart at the seams, not through financial strains, but because no company could survive by choosing only plays which suited the directors and their wives. There was a stunned silence. Maurice left to put on his make-up, and everyone else suddenly had somewhere else to go, very quickly. Jim Fitzgerald, who looked and sounded like a leprechaun, muttered gleefully 'And he's bloody right.'

I had started an academy with my actress friend Nora Lever, teaching speech through drama, while I managed Jacquie's career and schooling, and dreamed of my company. Nora also ran a company with actor and director Barry Cassin, called the 37 Theatre Club, but, like most gallant companies of the period, the effort perished for lack of cash. We had enrolled Jacquie at the St Louis Convent in Rathmines, when Godfrey telephoned to ask if she would be available to star in *The Bad Seed*, a play by Maxwell Anderson which had taken America by storm. It included a very good part which Godfrey wanted to offer to me, but Jacquie would need my support and I wanted to be free for her. At the heart of the grim story is an angelic child, Rhoda, who has inherited diabolical tendencies from her late grandmother, and who commits three murders. She has no moral sense or regrets, and displays an innocent charm which protects her from suspicion until her mother comes agonisingly to know her own history and her child's guilt.

This was to be the Globe's answer to its financial crisis. They brought Eithne Dunne, by now acclaimed in England and Europe, to play the mother, and Jacquie, whose star status was still high, to take on the lead as the child. Gerard Healy was chosen to direct (he and Eithne were still close friends, and loved working together). The cast included Anna Manahan, Norman Rodway, Donal Donnelly, Chris Curran and Genevieve Lyons, all exceptional talents.

Despite all expectations, *The Bad Seed* failed to fill the Gaiety. That, with other set-backs, caused the 'brave hearts' under the magnetic Godfrey, to give up the unequal struggle and disperse. I was heart-broken to see this talented company go to the wall. From approximately 1954 to 1960, under the inspired direction of Jim Fitzgerald, they had matured into fine artists, and enriched an impoverished theatrical scene.

# 17

# *A Company is Born*

In the fifties the Gate company was in a state of flux, although still capable of spell-binding productions. Another major excitement in the Irish theatre was the formation of the Pike Theatre in 1953, under the direction of Alan Simpson and his wife Carolyn Swift. They occupied a small premises in Herbert Lane, off Baggot Street, which seated about 50 people in sardine mode. At first they specialised in revues then thought daring, but which would hardly raise an eyebrow in a convent today. The Pike was certainly off-beat and had more of a reputation for so-called decadent parties than for what went on in its theatre.

The Pike then established an impressive reputation with the première of Brendan Behan's *The Quare Fellow* (which had been rejected by the Abbey), as well as the Irish première of Beckett's masterpiece, *Waiting for Godot*. Its reputation was further enhanced by the first European English language première of *The Rose Tattoo* by Tennessee Williams in 1957. In his tiny theatre, Alan Simpson worked magic with play, performers, lighting and music. Anna Manahan as Serafina shone like a beacon in a cast without a single weak link. The Simpsons had offered her the first real chance to show that, while she had great versatility in character roles, she could also carry off a part of towering dimensions. Unfortunately, despite glowing reviews at home and abroad, the production was halted by police because of alleged immorality. Alan Simpson then endured a lengthy and farcical trial for 'producing for gain an indecent and profane performance.' Some unnamed religious fanatic was so upset by an object dropped in the play that he or she complained to the gardaí. In those days, contraceptives were illegal in Ireland, and rarely talked about. Nevertheless, this guardian of our moral welfare correctly identified the tiny, offending object though in actuality a small paper disc was used. The case was thrown out of court when it became clear that two detectives sent to investigate the play's 'obscenity' were unable to find any. But the production was forced to close after two weeks, and many of the cast were subjected to a whispering campaign, as though they had all been caught in an orgy. The public remembered tales of the Pike night-life, and condemned the Simpsons and their works without further ado. At least the absurd court case ensured that no censorship of this kind would trouble Irish theatre again.

I cannot remember ever having been so angry as when *The Rose Tattoo* case broke. More than ever I longed to have, not just my own company and space, but a society in the theatre which would protect artistic people from being victimised. I talked to Godfrey Quigley about my ambition to create a company as fine as his although it was now acknowledged that the Globe was almost over as a group, and the Gas Company Theatre was soon to become vacant.

Godfrey, known as 'God', was a large, expansive man, kind and easy to talk to, but he thought that I might not have the strength to cope with the management side of the business. He outlined all the pitfalls, the financial and emotional stresses. The Globe directors had found that fellow-actors no longer regarded them as friends once they had assumed management responsibilities. Godfrey said that they had been accused of being miserly, of paying low wages when the reality was that they were risking bankruptcy. He thought it was madness for me to contemplate management unless I could find a wealthy backer.

When the Globe finally vacated the Gas Company Theatre, Godfrey gave a farewell party for all his 'dear hearts', and stayed sober long enough to warn me once more against naive dreams. Then, with a flourish, he bequeathed to me his business manager, Power O'Mara, his blessing and the Gas Company Theatre. Balancing a large glass of whisky precariously on his outstretched palm, he dared me to take on his 'cross and inspiration', Jim Fitzgerald.

The Gas Company Theatre was situated upstairs in a building on the main street of Dun Laoghaire. It seated a maximum of 200 people. The stage was too narrow and lacked depth, and when you walked off, you walked straight into the small lighting area and a very solid wall. Behind the stage was a long, communal dressing-room space, with a wash basin but no toilet. Once the audience came in, we had no access to the toilets, which were located off the stairs on the way to the auditorium. The cast and stage management were more or less sealed back-stage during the performance. The audience came in downstairs through the showroom and were greeted by an array of gleaming gas appliances, with a clearing near the stairs for them to ascend to the theatre. The Gas Company Board rented it out almost solely in the interest of sales, since the audience had little to do in the intervals but wander around inspecting their goods.

In those days there were very few theatres available to independent companies. Lord Longford had the Gate most of the time, and the Abbey was a closed shop. The Eblana Theatre, situated beneath the city-centre Busáras or bus station, was originally designed as a News Cinema, where people waiting for buses might spend an hour or so; these little cinemas had been quite successful in London. However, the idea was found less than useful here, and it was decided to change the half-constructed News Cinema into a theatre-cum-screen area, and lease it. The Eblana was, and is, a lovely little theatre, intimate and comfortable. But with the original chopping and changing, the stage area suffered by having a solid wall on stage right, with no exit space, and no wing-space on stage left either. There was just about enough room to squeeze a stage director on a stool so that cues could be whispered by telephone to the lighting box at the rear of the theatre. The most agile lighting man I know, Paddy Scanlon, used to climb over formidable railings in order to enter that box. For many years, he worked ancient lights and dimmers for which he really needed eight hands, sometimes with picturesque results, but mostly with accuracy and aplomb.

Despite Godfrey's warning, I still had the conviction that my company would always be happy and friendly, and, of course, successful. I would be in charge of our operations, and would never become a stranger to my colleagues. I would get a good business manager and PR, and we would all work happily as a team for the same money, hopefully a little more than the Globe paid.

I told Mother all about the Globe and the Gas Company, of course omitting any reference to Godfrey's advice. She was sympathetic, even though she knew well the dangers inherent in my impractical fantasies. Mother had to point out the painful truth; this could not be afforded. I was working on a radio series with Jacqueline; her schooling and Gregg's had to be paid for. Mother knew a great deal about what it took to start up and maintain a company. The bottom line was the welfare of the children, and I agreed to defer the idea of a special theatrical group until it was feasible.

At that time I was working with Jacquie on *The Adventures of Jacqueline*, a weekly radio programme sponsored by Clarke's shoes, which incidentally introduced me to a young up-and-coming writer called Hugh Leonard, who was one of the writing team. At the same time I was running my small school of acting from the house. Still dreaming of creating brilliant productions, I began to write and adapt, and an idea began to form. It may have been loosely based on the Christmas entertainments devised by Mícheál Mac Liammóir at the Gate some years before, but it was my own framework, and was to lead to my first ever production.

It was a chance meeting with Pan Collins and her husband Kevin which spurred me to action. She was a warm, friendly woman who had worked for the Gate, and Kevin was a journalist with the *Irish Times*. They invited me to tea, and I found myself talking about my plans, my dream company, and how I had conceived and adapted a Christmas revue. Pan suggested that I should form a co-operative company, and put the show on for a trial run. If the show did well the actors would make money, and I could use Jacqueline, as children would come to see her. Pan was so enthusiastic, so certain that anything was possible if you really wanted to do it. She offered to help with the publicity, being anxious herself to get into that end of theatre business.

That day in 1957, I left her house feeling light-hearted and light-headed. I had to find a small theatre, and remembered hearing that Ursula White-Lennon, who taught speech and drama, had acquired a little theatre called the Pocket in Ely Place. I resolved to see her with a view to renting the space for a few weeks. Pan had advised me to get a good title for the company and the show. Eventually 'Orion' productions suggested itself, both a play on my name and a contact with the stars, for luck. Pan liked it, and came up with *Guided Mistletoe* for the show, touching on recent publicity about guided missiles.

Ursula agreed to rent us the theatre, and we would now have to pray that the rent came 'through the door'. In our cast there were Anna Manahan and Jacquie, and a 'Paul Robeson' type bass named Charlie Byrne, who had achieved popularity in a radio show called

*Living with Lynch.* He was both to sing and stand in for various roles. Despite numerous offers from English managements, Charlie stayed in Dublin because he simply would not have been happy anywhere else, and fame meant nothing to him. Julie Hamilton, a gifted comedienne, played Queen in *Alice in Wonderland* excerpts and other snippets, and Ursula allowed her daughter Biddy and son Francis to play children's parts.

I had very much wanted Coralie Carmichael from the Gate company to take part as a guest artiste, but she was ill, with what proved to be cancer. Good friend that she was, she spoke to Mícheál Mac Liammóir, who offered whatever costumes would be useful to dress the show. It seemed that everywhere I turned, there were open hands and hearts willing the success of the first Orion show. Mother was secretly delighted that I had managed the 'test piece' without dropping my other commitments – although I did let the acting school die a natural death, since so few fees were being paid.

We found a gifted and sympathetic director in Brendan Cauldwell, not yet at the pinnacle of a career as a versatile stage and radio performer. We were also joined by comedian Eddie Bannon and by Eithne O'Neill, who had played brilliantly in *The Women* in the Studio Theatre, and who was to become a close friend. Other young people joined us, anxious to deliver posters, search for props, play small roles and stage-manage the show. Pan's husband Kevin devised additional linking dialogue. Fergus Cogley arranged the lighting with minimal spots, and made the giant 'book' out of which the characters appeared, as if the stories had suddenly come alive. Miracles were achieved. Anna Manahan and Julie Hamilton played the White and Red Queens, and Jacquie was the perfect Alice.

Anna had a special spot among her many roles. Oscar Wilde's stories for children had always been favourites in our family, and 'The Selfish Giant' was the current favourite. I had a vision of Anna in a white dress, alone in a spotlight, just telling this story. She liked the idea, but some of the others thought it wrong in the context of a revue-style show. The stubborn streak I hardly knew I possessed surfaced, and I said that it was definitely in; and, of course, it was one of the highlights, holding the audience spellbound.

We rehearsed in the front room at Palmerston Road. The piano was there, and we had found a young lady pianist mad or joyous enough to join the team. We were like a family, where everyone helped everyone else. Gregg would come into the rehearsals, and laugh and sing with the company; even at six years of age he could tell me that Anna was the best, and I had to warn him not to say that in front of the others. Jacquie was happy, with the White-Lennons for company. Charlie Byrne was often persuaded to sing after rehearsals, and everyone in the house came to listen to his rich, bass voice.

There was a wonderful gaiety about the Pocket enterprise, and a mysterious sense of some importance about this little show that carried us along like a friendly tide to unknown shores. Pan got a lot of mileage out of Anna and Jacquie in the papers. She also hinted that Phyllis Ryan might be changing direction in the near future, but she did not overplay that line; this was still a trial run. We sold tickets on the door during rehearsals. Anyone who was free took bookings, on cigarette packets, on the back of their hands. A friend of a friend turned up and offered to take charge of the booking and note down the proceeds.

The agreement with the cast was that, once the rent and the few ads we could afford had been paid for, the profits would be divided among the main workers, with special expenses for the juniors. Tea and biscuits for rehearsals would be supplied by management, which meant that I raided the kitchen in Palmerston Road, and put anything edible into a bag. Everyone brought their own cups or mugs, and we sent the kids out for milk. We had only a few days for to rehearse in the theatre, but this was valuable time, as we could try out the 'set' and the furniture which had come from our various houses. People found various ways to get the stuff there, by car or even by bus.

At last came the dress rehearsal, with a costume call followed by the first run-through of the show with lights, piano and everyone working at full pitch. Naturally, everything went wrong. The large 'book' structure fell down as soon as the first character walked through it; the few lights that we had failed, then came back without anyone knowing why. Charlie Byrne, unused to straight acting, constantly stepped on skirts, and created minor chaos by accidentally removing one.

It was so bad, it had to be good. Only the children survived, performing impeccably. Anna's lovely story seemed too long, and many of the songs too hackneyed. We noticed that a toilet flushing somewhere in the house sounded like Niagara, and drowned out dialogue. Nothing seemed witty or funny or imaginative – or even interesting. Only Pan Collins was optimistic.

On opening night scene followed scene to rapturous applause. Charlie Byrne sang like an angel, and acted with professional-seeming confidence. The children got a special welcome from the audience, and commendations in next day's reviews. Anna and Julie, in their many roles, convulsed even the critics, some of whom could be seen doubled up with laughter. Anna's reading was greeted by a respectful silence followed by loud, sustained applause, and even some cheering. Curtain call after curtain call confirmed the show's success.

No Broadway cast awaited the morning's verdicts any more eagerly than we did. They were all excellent, with many tributes to the cast and to Orion, and a few references to the influence of Mac Liammóir but no condemnation for that. Under such headlines as '*Guided Mistletoe* hits the target', they praised the show for being different, for featuring such diverse sources as Shakespeare, Dickens, Wilde and Lewis Carroll, to say nothing of Kevin Collins and Phyllis Ryan.

The Pocket was free for only two to three weeks, just enough time on full houses to pay rent and expenses, and divide the remainder between the cast. It was little enough, but a few pounds never went amiss, and could do wonders in the 1950s. The jubilant cast and I celebrated with tea and sandwiches. We were so high that we might have been drinking champagne instead of tea, and talk of further shows spurred me on. The Globe had started in the Gas Company Theatre, and I resolved to follow in their footsteps. I also determined to find out what were the real causes of the Globe's demise, so that I might avoid them.

In the aftermath of that first venture, I took stock of my public and private circumstances. Mother still thought of me rather as a child, who needed to be looked after but she and Joe listened as I outlined my plans. I would begin in the Gas Company Theatre. Then I would move into the recently-opened Eblana Theatre, under Busáras. When the company had really taken off, I would go into the bigger theatres – the Gate, Gaiety and Olympia. I had been busy sounding out the feelings of those actors I knew who were freelance, and had approached those of the Globe who had not gone to London to try their luck. I had no figures worked out, but had a hazy grasp of what might be needed to float one play. Mother and Joe decided to help: 'We're investing £100 in Orion Productions on one condition; if you make good, we'll accept the same sum back, and if you don't, we never want to hear about this investment again.'

# 18

# *Pioneers*

I re-opened the Gas Company Theatre with another revue, entitled *Caught in the Act*, on Easter Monday, 1957. I had taken the theatre for a trial period. The rent was reasonable, and Power O'Mara, Godfrey's former business manager, had arranged the box-office and agreed to stay on for a while. Back to the fold came Anna, fresh from her triumph in *The Rose Tattoo*, Julie Hamilton, and Jacquie, who begged to be in the first show. James Neylin, my old friend from the American tour, handsome and charming as ever, was also most welcome. An old and dear friend from the Madame Cogley Studio days, Dahna Davis also joined us, replacing Pan Collins in the PR department. Dahna had a good business head, and was also an asset in cameo acting roles.

We had £140 in the bank, as Andrew Flynn, a friend of Anna's and a successful publisher, had invested £40 in our project. It was a modest amount, but we managed quite happily and the show was well-received. Controversial and thought-provoking plays however, were what I really wanted to present, and most of all, new Irish plays. Godfrey had advised me to to do small-cast comedies in the off-seasons and to keep the big guns for the summer months, when the tourists streamed off the boats. I had been trying to get the rights of Tennessee Williams's *A Streetcar Named Desire*, which had caused a stir in London, and was considered highly controversial. In the meantime, I had to find suitable holding plays. There was no difficulty in casting, as actors had begun to come around Orion in throngs, hopeful of joining the company. Jim Fitgerald came to us tentatively at first, but soon understood exactly what I was up to. Among the plays we produced while waiting for *Streetcar* were some very worthy if light-hearted pieces including Noel Coward's *Blithe Spirit*, with Gerard Healy, Genevieve Lyons and Marie Conmee hilarious as Madame Arcati and *Return to Tyassi* by Benn W Levy, which Hilton Edwards described as a 'gray play'.

In the autumn of 1958 we found a witty English comedy called *A Lady Mislaid*, whose author I cannot recall, and invited Maurice O'Brien, a distinguished Gate actor and a master of farcical timing, to direct it. Maurice had just survived a cancer operation which left him facially disfigured. He had been handsome and suave, and was deeply traumatized by the change in his appearance. But his personal charm was immensely strong, and the real Maurice soon came through the scars. He had a sure touch with comedy, and guided the actors with authority. The production was excellent and a big success, giving me breathing space to think about our next offering, which was to be *Picnic*, by William Inge, an American who had recently won acclaim on Broadway and in Hollywood.

*Picnic* had a cast of twelve, and the Gas Company Theatre normally accommodated six to eight performers at most. Maurice could not see how it could be properly set, and knew it couldn't be cast. He became so agitated that I turned to Fitz, who thought it a fine play and a real challenge. He wanted Jacquie for the love-lorn fifteen-year-old, jealous of her sister who had won the heart of the handsome drifter. Claire Mullen was to play the female lead and Maurice Good the hero. All other parts were cast from actors we had already used in other plays; we were beginning to form an active pool from which to draw.

At rehearsal next day, Fitz brought along a tape of some musicians he had just discovered, not jazz, he explained, but nearly jazz. The music was by Dave Brubeck, and was different from anything I had heard before. There was a new rhythm and a strange, throbbing piano beating under an eloquent saxophone. The music was moody and vibrant, and Fitz used it to back a love scene, erotic in the extreme, and was dancing with glee at the effect. Fitz got the heat going all right with the Brubeck music, and I am still a fan of that musician. *Picnic* was a success, after which we filled in with light English comedies while I began to gear myself for more substantial work.

I eventually got the rights to *A Streetcar named Desire*, and found the casting problematic. Interpreters of Blanche and Stanley Kowalski were not easily found in our circles, but we knew of an actor of Canadian extraction, Laurence Bourne, for the latter role. Then I had the idea of asking Shelah Richards to return to the stage to take the tragic role of Blanche. She was too old for it, but was as slim and blonde as ever.

I browbeat Fitz into seeing it my way. In the end, he not only agreed, but came to believe that it had been his idea all along. The production was a huge success. Shelah was luminous, the cast worked heroically around her and Fitz put the magic in so that the weaker bits got by. There were some objectors to the play's stronger content, especially in the sexual sense. Letters were written by enraged parents to the directors of the Gas Company. A young critic named Fergus Linehan, writing in *The Sunday Review* accused me of mounting a decidedly blue entertainment, and I rang his editor, who was quietly amused at my fury.

*Streetcar* played to packed houses, but our finances were still precarious from play to play, and we had to keep an eye on all costs. Dahna Davis was well up to this task, ensuring that edible props like cakes and chocolates were removed after each show, so that hungry actors would not consume more than their stage allocation. There was a ludicrous row once when I was shown a box of chocolates, for use in the current show, in which the sweets were cut in halves, which certainly made the box last for the run of the play. I laughed so hard at this effort at good house-keeping that the actors saw the funny side.

We followed *Streetcar* with *The Tender Trap*, an American comedy by Max Shulman, which starred Milo O'Shea and was a runaway success. We were blessed in those early days with the talents of such as Milo, his wife Maureen Toal, Maurice Good, Gerard Healy, Genevieve Lyons, Charles Mitchel, (the famous RTE newsreader, who had spent many years with Lord Longford at the Gate) Gerry Alexander, Tony Doyle, (a fine actor now resident in England and prominent on stage and screen) Pauline Delany, Marie Conmee, Gerry Sullivan and Martin Dempsey, all names to conjure with. To this list many more illustrious names were to be added in the years ahead.

In 1959 we began to realise that while we had made an impact on the press and theatre-goers, we had very little capital after paying our way. Having heard about a play called *Lady Spider*, by Donagh McDonagh, I determined to get the rights. I went to Brendan Smith, Director of the Dublin Theatre Festival, and asked for a grant so that we could do justice to this intriguing new play. It was a realistic reworking of the Deirdre and Naoise legend with a most unexpected twist. Brendan knew me through my acting years, but this was the first time I applied to him as a director of a new company for grant-in-aid to produce a Festival show. He was very helpful, thought the choice of play excellent and managed to squeeze a few hundred pounds out of the budget for *Lady Spider*. It had a magnificent leading role, a Deirdre so different from the tragic figure of other epics that it posed an enormous challenge. This was a lady with steel in her make-up, and although the story followed the legend and the sons of Usnach were slain, the treacherous king's victory was undermined by the vengeful beauty he thought he had won. The lead was magnificently played by Maureen Toal, and the play proved to be the first of our many Festival successes.

Meantime Jacquie was working with the Globe in William Inge's *Bus Stop*, and Orion's next offering at the Gas Company was a light comedy by Kenneth Horne, *Trial and Error*. The following year, 1960, Orion presented at the Gas Company Peter Coke's classic comedy *Breath of Spring*, with a cast of top artists – Anna Manahan, Maureen Toal, Helen Robinson, Charles Mitchel, Maire Kinsella and Marie Conmee. Marie was the most formidable comic talent in the country with a lethally attractive smile which won her friends everywhere. The production bubbled and sparkled its way to packed houses and a long run. Even Fitz, apt to turn his nose up at light comedy, found this play worthy of his time and effort.

By some fluke of good fortune, we had acquired the designer Robert Heade for several of our shows, and what a bonus that was. Bob was in constant employment at the Gate, where he had designed many shows for Mícheál and Hilton, and for the Longfords. Bob wrought miracles with the meagre resources we could provide. He loved being asked to perform impossible tasks, and always managed to solve even the most intricate snares laid by the playwright. He was a one-man design team, often painting the set himself and helping with the carpentry. He always managed to fit us in whenever he was needed, often at both the Gas Company and the Eblana simultaneously.

Ideas for plays and programmes, including poetry readings, were crowding into my mind. Having fallen in love with *The Bespoke Overcoat*, a one-act play by Wolf Mankievicz, I compiled a set of three plays with the overall title of *Surprise Packet*, the other two being Sean O'Casey's *The End of the Beginning* and Chekhov's *The Bear*. The cast included Gerry Alexander, Milo O'Shea, Maureen Toal and Tony Doyle. This varied programme went down so well that we later had *Surprise Packet II*, but before that came

*The Reluctant Debutante* with Patrick Bedford (on leave from Edwards/Mac Liammóir), Charles Mitchel and Jacquie, happy in her first romantic lead.

# 19

# *Tennessee Williams and Other Victims*

In 1959, Norman Rodway had asked me if we could possibly form a partnership, and perhaps see a new company rise from the ashes of the Globe. At this time I had the rights of *Cat on a Hot Tin Roof*, by Tennessee Williams. After the resounding success of *A Streetcar Named Desire*, I really felt that *Cat* would draw even more people into the Gas Company Theatre. I also had very firm ideas on who should be in the cast, and, of course, I had to have Fitz. The part of Brick, played in America by Paul Newman, was generally considered to require a Greek-god kind of actor but I had my own ideas about this.

I had always admired Norman's talent, and liked him enormously. He was fun, naturally courteous and charming, and it was an open secret that he was usually embroiled in some sort of love affair. But in our close partnership there were no emotions tripping us up, and we could concentrate on being the best freelance company in Ireland. When he proposed 'Gemini' for our new title we knew that we were in for an avalanche of quips about terrible twins, and misunderstandings about the nature of our relationship. It was just impossible for people to accept what we took for granted, that we were simply close friends and working partners. We developed a remarkable rapport, knowing instinctively who was right, when to give way, when to talk things out. I knew what parts Norman should play, and he knew what everything cost – including actors with whom he was friendly. We ran the company from the bedroom of his Baggot Street flat, or from the auditorium of any theatre we happened to occupy. Norman had been an accountant with the Guinness group, and was marvellous with figures. Actors rarely looked for more than we could afford, because they knew that we had no real capital.

We decided to do *Cat on a Hot Tin Roof*, and Fitz was delighted. Almost simultaneously he and I put down Maureen Toal's name beside Maggie the Cat, Anna Manahan as Big Mama, John Cowley as Big Daddy and then we came to the part of Brick, Big Daddy's favourite son, married to Maggie. I said, 'You know that no one but Norman Rodway can come even close to it.'

When I invited Norman, he at first refused because he had little confidence in his ability to play what he termed a Greek god. Rehearsals commenced in the Gas Company, while we kept a low profile in case we might attract protests before we had a chance to earn them. John Cowley, nervous and known to fly off the handle, wrestled with Big Daddy; Anna Manahan simply took over Big Mama, and both were superb. After two days Norman threw down his script and said he was giving up, that he knew he was all wrong for this role.

I got Maureen to calm him while I looked for Fitz, who had gone out for a drink. He didn't return for two days, and, while we had search parties combing the pubs, we went on rehearsing. Norman was still sulking and unhappy, but Maureen's performance was beginning to give me goose-pimples. Norman began to use his underlying fear and resentment in his interpretation, while Anna and John were establishing some close links in their stage relationships. The onus of exploring the parts to the full began to bear heavily on the company's nerves. Fitz arrived at rehearsal the following day, and blew out all the rubbish; we were doing a damn fine play, and he wanted performances. The performances quietly mounted in power and energy; Norman was so absorbed that he had quite forgotten his earlier qualms.

*Cat on a Hot Tin Roof* exploded onto the Gas Company stage in June, 1960, and was a sensation. There were queues waiting to book, but there were also some ominous portents. Some incensed religious or concerned parent wrote to the Gas Company directors, and to the papers, complaining about this odious piece. One day Fitz and I were summoned to a meeting with the Chairman of the Gas Board. We had a meeting with the company first to brief them. They were flushed with the wonderful reviews, in love with the play, their roles and the packed houses. Fitz told them that we might be asked to take the play off, which made them very angry, and we discussed contingency plans.

The chairman was very polite, and had a copy of the play on his desk. He told Fitz that a colleague had taken his wife to the first night in Dun Laoghaire, and the good lady was so upset by the dreadful language that she fainted, and had to be taken home. He then read out random passages which, taken out of context, did sound a bit rancid; he concentrated on Fitz, apparently holding him responsible for mounting this terrible play. I found this amusing, but Fitz kept telling the chairman that I was the management and entirely responsible; he was the mere director. He did manage to say that the play was an acclaimed masterpiece in America.

The chairman declared that the play must be taken off now, or we would no longer be regarded as tenants of the Gas Company. As we left, I managed to explain that we had contracted people and could not stop the play in mid-week without being sued. He replied, 'Take it off at the weekend, then.' Quietly it was decided that we would stall as long as we could, confident that at least, after the *Rose Tattoo* debacle, there would be no more such court cases. We just had to concoct reasons to stall the closure until we had time to replace the show, but before then we had decided to transfer it to the Eblana Theatre.

I was heading for my first production with John B Keane, whose play *Sive* had swept the country, and who had not yet been featured in a Dublin Festival. We had met at a reception the previous year, and I had been bowled over by his soft Kerry accent and his sheer enthusiasm for living. He was a prodigious drinker then, and it was hard work pinning him down to deadlines, or getting him to discuss finance. Just when he was cornered into talking about the plot, or a date of opening, he would burst into a ballad or tell a hilarious story. Sometimes humble, at other times arrogant, as ready to start an argument as to reel off his latest poem, John must be one of the most complex characters I have ever known. Through our long years of collaboration and friendship, I have never been able to predict how he would react to any given circumstance. But we have weathered both tumult and calm, and nothing can dim the affection I feel for this gifted writer.

In the 1960s, getting a script from him was like prising pennies out of a miser. I would meet him at some pub in town, and end up, late at night, clutching a few pages of *The Highest House on the Mountain*. When Barry Cassin, due to direct it at the Festival, wanted to know what the plot was, I could not tell him – but John could, and as he outlined the story, we knew this was worth waiting for.

And we duly got it in time for rehearsals, although the odd page would still arrive in the post from Kerry. Barry, formerly a talented actor, had decided to concentrate on directing, and had done several plays for us before. We had, for a short while, been romantically involved, but decided that friendship was better.

Through directing John B's first Dublin Festival play, Barry formed a long and lasting relationship with the playwright that was more important to John's later development as a writer than any other factor in his career. Barry could understand John's characters, his beautiful and bawdy prose, and the constructional difficulties which arose from the way he worked. John wrote his plays at night, sometimes all through the night, in one constant stream of words and images, and found it difficult to go back and revise his work. Barry knew what was required, how to preserve the integrity of the work while making the necessary breaks in scenes and acts, and placing the intervals at the most effective points. John trusted him completely, and his trust was rewarded.

The plot of *The Highest House on the Mountain* concerned three old men living up in the hills of Kerry. One of them is a widower whose son is about to come home on a visit from England, bringing his bride to the old farm for the first time. The play deals with the sexual frustrations of these lonely men, to whom the sight of a woman is as scarce as the patchy grass from which they try to wrest a living. Their lives are dominated by lustful thoughts, bawdy conversations and drinking poteen. When the son arrives with his wife, his father tries to seduce her, and blackmails her by revealing that he believes she was a prostitute whom he met some years before in England. It all ends in the wreckage of the son's marriage, the flight of his bride and the renewed isolation of the old men. The production was well received; John was hailed as the Tennessee Williams of Ireland and John, Barry and I had launched a fruitful partnership.

Lord and Lady Longford were running the Gate, and it was rumoured that, if they met and approved of the managements of new companies and their proposed plays, they would let the theatre out for periods. We wanted to do a play called *Will Success Spoil Rock Hunter?* by George Axelrod, during the Christmas period, and needed a larger stage than the Gas Company. It was an American comedy, and we were casting Milo O'Shea and Maureen Toal in the leads. The Longfords favoured period, prettily costumed productions, so I brought in photos of Maureen, modern but glamorous, as the best I could do, aware of the risk involved. Norman had advised me that if Longford opened the sherry bottle kept in the office cabinet, all was well, but did not say that I would be obliged to match his Lordship glass for glass throughout the morning.

I held my sherry-soaked wits together by sheer will power until Lord Longford was called to another appointment. The door was held open for me, and I sailed graciously through, clutching the banisters for support when I was out of sight. I felt terrible, and had to take a taxi home to lie down and sleep it off. I was sure that Christine, Lady Longford, was smiling her wicked smile throughout the session; she never touched sherry herself, but had seen the ritual many times. While possessing a razor wit, she was also a kind, understanding woman, and a very gifted one. Some of her plays were brilliantly satirical of the times she lived in. She and Edward were an amazing couple, and seemingly very compatible. He had changed from a slim, handsome man to a walking health hazard, so obese that ordinary seats would no longer accommodate him. But they had helped Mícheál and Hilton to found the Gate, and funded their own theatre themselves.

Norman laughed long and loudly when I told him what had happened and promised to take his turn with the sherry – he swore it was the cooking variety – and go in to sign the contract. So we were on our way to the Gate, still in the Gas Company, and in and out of the Eblana when we had a spare play or an irresistible idea. Our days at the Gas Company were numbered; there was a rumour about that we would be required to submit scripts for vetting in future, which we could never have countenanced.

In that year, 1960, we asked Hugh Leonard if we might revive *A Walk on the Water* for the Theatre Festival. I think that this was the first new Irish play to introduce a homosexual character, beautifully played by David Kelly. We prevailed upon the author himself to take a role in this revival, and while his performance was quite acceptable, it was clear that his real talent lay in writing. He cycled everywhere, and often joined us in Mooney's pub for one for the road. I remember him then as warm, impulsive, unsure and very generous. It was not easy for young writers, but he was rapidly making his mark. The Abbey had accepted two of his early plays, but refused *Madigan's Lock*, which then went to the Globe, who had a huge success with it.

I don't know when I began to think seriously about love again. Maybe it was the presence around me of so many others who had partners or lovers which highlighted my loneliness or perhaps it was the passion that raged through the first performance of *Cat on a Hot Tin Roof*, engulfing Maureen Toal and Norman Rodway. They were obsessed with each other, and all I could do was pray that it would all have cooled down when the play was over. Naturally, the play was even more exciting to watch; the air seemed so charged that I wondered why there were not sparks visible. But when the play ended, the affair continued, and it was in full bloom when we went into the Gate, with everyone being careful to shelter her husband, Milo, from any awareness of the truth.

Discretion had to be observed if *Will Success Spoil Rock Hunter?* was to go ahead with any degree of sanity so nobody talked or even hinted that all was not as it seemed to be. The show went so well, with everyone apparently normal and friendly, that it appeared that the grand passion might have been quenched. Milo was in wonderful form, and the show, Gemini's first in the Gate, was an immediate success. The Longfords were delighted with both play and players, and asked me if we could come again with another production. Rodway was thrilled; Gemini was moving upwards. All the same, I knew him well enough to note the distracted look on his face as we talked about shows. Maureen carried it all off so well that I was convinced she was free of the mid-summer madness induced by the play. I never mentioned the matter to her, but I did tell Norman that I thought they were both heading for trouble.

After the Gate play, Milo, much in demand, had to leave for a contract elsewhere, and the torrid romance resumed. They now threw discretion to the wind, the grapevines hummed and people began to take sides. A disaster worthy of Greek tragedy seemed imminent. Christmas that year was less enjoyable than previous ones. I should have become accustomed to the frenzied rush for cards and gifts, snatched shopping interludes between discussions, rehearsals and the sorting out of actors' problems. These were beginning to surface as I fought to sustain Orion at the Gas Company, and Norman and I planned how to raise money for Gemini. We were going to phase out Orion but, in the event, this took longer than we had intended, mainly because we were both so busy that we hadn't time to set up Gemini as a limited company with a registered office. (We never did have an office, but used our accountant's address when necessary.)

In the Gas Company, after the Christmas play, I devised a second 'Surprise Packet'. I found a wonderful Tennessee Williams play called *Something Unspoken*, and proved to the theatre community that Marie Conmee had as much tragic power as she had comic facility. We included Synge's *The Tinker's Wedding*, with Maureen Toal and Anna Manahan wonderful in the key roles of the wife and tinker woman. An American play by William Gibson called *Two for the Seesaw* arrived, demanding to be presented in the Eblana. It featured two lonely people getting together to salve their marital bruises, and finding out that it's not that easy. It was a two-hander, a hit in London and America, and custom-built for our star-crossed lovers.

*Two for the Seesaw*, impeccably directed by Barry Cassin and beautifully played by Norman and Maureen, in a delightful set by Robert Heade, fitted the Eblana like an elegant glove. The glowing reviews, the intimacy created by the two-hander and the rapturous response from the audiences brought a new intensity to the off-stage romance. One morning Norman touched on the subject, and I ventured to ask if he was serious enough to consider marrying again. He said that he would not break up Maureen's marriage and that time would sort things out. I told him that he was fooling himself and all too soon the inevitable happened. Someone told Milo, who demanded to know the truth, and got an honest and sorrowful account from Maureen. Fortunately, Norman was not in the line of fire when the news broke. Milo demanded to know why I, a friend, had not told him what had been happening. Well, there was no way that I could have, caught as I was between the three of them, each a friend and dear to me. Somehow I knew that this was a break-up that could not be mended.

Norman did not re-establish his friendship or his affair. He had a short shelf-life when it came to sexual relationships and, apart from his friendship with me, these were the only kind he had. It was all a long time ago, and Milo and Maureen both survived, different but perhaps stronger. Milo is now happily married to a delightful actress, and they live in America where he is hugely successful on stage and screen. Maureen found love again with actor Eoin Ó Súilleabháin for a good span of years. When he became ill, she nursed and cared for him with courage and devotion, until he died in her arms. An ex-

Abbey actress, she has won many awards for her dramatic roles, and is now the queen of Ireland's high-quality TV soap, *Glenroe.*

That was the only time I tried to intervene in the private affairs of others, and the nearest Norman and I ever came to parting company.

We were invited to take over the running of the Eblana full-time, at a special rental. If we let the theatre, we were responsible for the rent. At last we had our own base, and freedom (we hoped) to present anything we thought worthwhile. Our previous productions at the Eblana had paid off handsomely. We dealt with Ed Kelleher, who was catering manager, a first-class man at his job who took charge of all theatre problems and enquiries. He had the toughest exterior and warmest heart imaginable, and we had many stormy passages through the years. He found it difficult to deal with airy-fairy artists, as we loftily asked him to put aside his catering duties and give all his attention to something more important – us. But we became the best of friends, and his help and know-how kept us going during the twenty-six years Gemini ran the Eblana.

Meanwhile, Mícheál and Hilton had been going through hard times since they lost their tenure at the Gate and they were forced to go abroad for work. During the years away, Mícheál began to put together his ideas for a one-man show on the life and times of Oscar Wilde, whose wit and personality he himself embodied for many of us. *The Importance of being Oscar,* directed by Hilton and performed by Mícheál, opened at the Gaiety in 1960. No one present at that first night will forget the experience. He was at once the narrator of Wilde's life and the interpreter of numerous excerpts from his works, with a brilliant linking script. In the second half, dealing with the court case and its aftermath, the audience was still. And yet, at the end, Mícheál lifted the show into a dimension of ultimate triumph over pain and loss which Wilde would surely have approved. Some time afterwards, Mícheál explained to me that one-man shows did not tire him; but playing with other actors did, never knowing what they were going to do and not daring to turn his back – 'dreadfully exhausting, darling!'

# 20

# *Hits and Misses*

In 1961, I noticed that Mother was limping rather badly. She suffered from arthritis, a family inheritance. She was not given to complaining, but she did hound doctors for the latest treatments, fearing that she might become incapacitated. Mother always came home from her long day's work with a leather bag full of things she said she needed. I never knew just what it contained, but it was always heavy, and she began to lean to her carrying side, when the limp was obvious. Joe was also worried, and took to meeting her at the bus-stop to carry the hated bag. I argued with him because he did not use his influence to prevail on her, while he told me that I should spend more time looking after her than I did minding a bunch of actors.

That year, at the Gas Company Theatre, Orion was presenting our second John B Keane offering *No More In Dust* for the October Theatre Festival, while as Gemini we were preparing to launch *The Passion of Peter Ginty*, by Hugh Leonard, at the Gate. This was an Irish epic based on Ibsen's *Peer Gynt*, and starred Milo O'Shea. The time needed for the meetings and discussions which preceded each Festival seemed endless; as a freelance company, we had to keep on producing viable plays to stay in business. I was never more torn between the two most important areas of my life than I was that year. Our family doctor urged me to get Mother to rest, an impossible task. We watched her soldier on, in really bad pain, taking this remedy and that, and steadily becoming more lame. I longed to snatch that heavy bag and throw it in the Liffey. Another me went about my work, discussing re-writes with John B, having more than one or two jars in his favourite dockside pubs. Then over to Norman and poring over the script of *Peter Ginty*, which was coming in more slowly than Hugh's previous work.

I raced around in Gemini and Orion, being the life and soul of the projects, but went home frightened and immature, unable to understand what was wrong with Mother, who had never been a day sick, yet now looked frail and feeble. She was having treatment to ease the pain. The doctors thought that she was right to remain active, if she could, until they arrived at a decision. All she would tell me was that she was in good hands, and that I was not to worry!

John B's play was set in a city bed-sitter, and featured two girls up from the country, naive enough to be played upon by city slickers. It had several good points, but set as it was in urban terrain, it lacked the usual poetic, racy language. It filled the Gas Company, but did not enjoy the long run of its fore-runner, *The Highest House on the Mountain*. Still, we were well pleased with its reception; it was another stepping stone on John's way to major works.

Mother was unable to come to the production, but I always gave her a detailed account of reactions to the show when I came home, if she was still awake. She mentioned to me that there was a new operation by which worn, painful hips could be replaced with artificial ones, and that she was considering this. It could give patients a new lease on life, without pain, and offered her the prospect of more years of work and activity. At first I was overjoyed, but then began to worry that the operation might be too dangerous for her. A decision on this vital matter was still some months away, and meantime the injections Mother was having seemed at least to alleviate the symptoms.

I plunged into the final rehearsals of *The Passion Of Peter Ginty* before its opening at the Gate, to find the last few pages of script arriving, and a tremendous sense of uncertainty prevailing. The first half was most entertaining, following the original tale only when necessary. Somewhere in the second half, however, what started out as a creative Irish satire changed into a close copy of the Ibsen play. This was so nearly a winner, with Leonard's wicked wit so abundant in the early sequences, that I have often wished that he would revise it. He was under a lot of pressure to deliver this play for the Festival, as he had TV and other commitments in London. As it was, it earned a fair enough critical assessment, and deserved its place in a Festival not overflowing with excitement.

During that Festival a section of Joyce's *Finnegans Wake*, adapted for the stage by Mary Manning, was presented at the Eblana by a company called Libra productions. This name cloaked the fact that Gemini was producing three plays simultaneously in the Festival, and Brendan Smith was justifiably worried that there might be an outcry from companies who had not succeeded in getting even one production approved. We went on with a cast headed by Patrick Bedford, Marie Kean, May Cluskey, Archie O'Sullivan, Martin Dempsey, Frank Kelly and others. Louis Lentin, the well-known theatre director, the only one of us who had genuinely studied *Finnegans Wake*, consented to direct. He had an understanding of that baffling work which none of his cast ever achieved. Only small sections of the book were dramatised, but they still added up to a cohesive whole. There was the Wake of Finnegan, the wonderful Washerwomen Sequence, the parable of the Ant and the Grace-hopper – and the great Anna Livia Plurabelle speech.

Marie Kean, splendid actress that she was, came closer to Louis in her ability to grasp the meaning of the text than anyone else, but I imagine that a lot of what she did was instinctive rather than cerebral. Archie O'Sullivan, a Dubliner to the core, had more than a few witticisms about his role as Finnegan, who was being 'waked' throughout the first part of the show. He had a nice, comfortable coffin to lie in, while the rest of the cast cavorted around him singing 'Finnegan's Wake', the song that had inspired Joyce. Paddy Bedford led an amazingly willing cast in scenes that changed magically as the director drained every drop of colour and meaning to be found in the piece. *The Voices of Shem* would make for a mesmerizing evening, whether or not the majority of its audience understood what they were hearing.

Archie muttered 'Jaysus, we'll be lynched,' but not within hearing of Louis, who was not a man to trifle with. If I had personal reservations about launching so difficult an entertainment, I kept quiet about them. Oddly enough, the show began to book heavily in advance of the opening, as though people knew there was something unusual going on in the Eblana. I told the cast we were likely to be booked out, to be assured by Archie that we were more likely to be thrown out!

Louis kept us up half the night at the dress rehearsal on Sunday, although we had to open on Monday. The electrician, dear Paddy Scanlan, got so furious, with over a hundred lighting cues and an impossible lighting board, that language as colourful as Joyce's flowed from his box until Louis was forced to quit for the night. Monday night arrived, and there were queues hoping for returned tickets. The early scenes were received in a stunned silence until the moment when Archie, as Finnegan, sat up from his coffin and said in vintage Dublinese, 'I don't understand. I fail to see. I daresay you too.' and promptly lay back again. This interjection exploded like a firecracker among in the audience, sending them and the cast into paroxysms of laughter. This set the tone for the rest of the evening. There was an atmosphere of high good humour, leading to a standing ovation at the curtain.

Louis Lentin and Marie Kean, who thought the hilarity was somehow disrespectful to Joyce, and suspected Archie and others of having manoeuvred the earlier laughs, were the only ones not overcome with relief at the enthusiastic response of the audience. Next day, there was great critical acclaim in the papers. A few days later we learned, in the witty ambience of the Festival Club, that the show had become known as *The Voices of Sham*. I always suspected Paddy Bedford of being the author of that witticism.

Archie O'Sullivan was, by his own account, born like O'Casey in a tenement; he was tall and thin, and not unlike O'Casey in voice and features. His best work was, indeed, done in O'Casey plays, but he had a wide enough range and gave some riveting performances. He had a huge capacity for whiskey, and only the pull of his professional career prevented him from becoming totally alcoholic. As it was, Archie almost never drank before or during a show or rehearsal but he made up for this when the work was done. An eccentric drunk, he had delusions of grandeur ranging from mere squiredom to monarchy to God Himself when he was really bad. When at the warming-up stage of drink, still sober enough to know exactly what he was saying, he would tell some unfortunate actor or director what he thought of them in luridly unflattering terms.

*The Voices of Shem* was such a hit that an English producer brought the whole company to Stratford East, then the home of Joan Littlewood. We were naturally thrilled to be brought to such a prestigious theatre, but were also worried about the impact of so difficult an entertainment.

I had difficulty persuading May Cluskey to travel with us. She was a lovely actress, warm and droll, and loved by all. She believed that any trip outside Ireland would land a person in an alien world where there would not be a strong cup of tea when it was needed, and where strange food was eaten. Cluskey also suffered from vertigo, and would not fly at that time, although many years later she did manage to get into a plane, well soaked in Scotch, her usual tipple; nothing else, she claimed, was safe. May had a round, innocent face (she called it a platter face) and straight brown hair, a disapproving Dublin mouth, pursed in anticipation of minor disappointments, and a plump, yet neat, figure. She had the driest sense of humour I've ever encountered outside of Moore Street, and a total inability to say anything unkind about anyone. We persuaded her that she would be safe on a boat, and made sure that several company members went with her to take her mind off her phobias. We had to replace Frank Kelly, who had other commitments, and were fortunate enough to get Kevin McHugh, who subsequently featured with distinction in many Gemini shows.

At that time Peter Ustinov's plays were very popular in Dublin, and he had starred in one them, *Photo Finish*, at the Gaiety Theatre, receiving a warm response from packed houses and a lot of hospitality during his visit. The show went on to the Saville Theatre in London, and we arrived just as the hundredth performance was due to be celebrated. He threw a party for the cast at the Savoy Hotel at which he also welcomed the Gemini Company. It was a splendid gesture and a wonderful evening. He made himself known to each of us personally, and wished us as happy and successful an experience as he had in Dublin. Champagne flowed like water, there was exquisite food, and we all tried to keep an eye on Archie O'Sullivan.

The reaction to *The Voices of Shem* at Stratford East was one of total disbelief. They did not understand a word of it. The critics thought the actors and the production were excellent, but there was no pretence by any of them to have understood the adaptation, nor did they conceal their bewilderment at anyone wanting to adapt such abstruse material. We did not get great attendances, and in a few weeks were on our way home again, not without honour but resolved henceforth to exclude plays from our repertoire which audiences simply could not understand.

Mother was surprisingly well at Christmas, and relatively free from pain. Aunt Lena and Uncle Cecil came in for their annual visit about a week before Christmas day. She had heard that the new operation was a great success, and advised that Mother should have it.

New Year, 1962, and we were all at Palmerston Road celebrating. The new show at the Eblana was set to run for weeks; like most of Fergus Linehan's revues it was packed with gentle satire, and rippled along with that delightful comedienne Rosaleen Linehan at the centre. As Norman and I pored over our plans for the year ahead,

Mother went quietly to her specialist, and arranged for the hip-replacement operation. She was to go into Jervis Street Hospital the first week in March. It was obvious that the pain from her hip was now intolerable. The surgeon had told her that she might have a slight limp afterwards, but no more pain. In those days, hip replacement was probably as much a pioneering technique as the first transplants, and as tough on the patients. I stormed heaven with prayers.

I left the affairs of the company in Norman's capable hands, helped by my friend and colleague, Dahna Davis, and took Mother to the hospital in a taxi. Joe waved us away miserably. Mother had never been ill before, and he was terrified. She was put into a semi-private room with four beds, cheerful with chintz curtains. A nurse told her not to worry; the surgeon Mr Brady was a genius, and had done lots of hip operations. A little later Mr Brady came in with the matron, told us both again not to worry and swept out.

Practical and cheerful as ever, Mother gave me all sorts of tasks to carry out, keep an eye on Joe, see that Lizzie and Etta were all right, not to tell Gregg until the operation was safely over, not to let Jacquie get upset. She held my hand tightly until the nurse gave me a final time-to-go; leaving, I looked back at her, red-gold hair on the pillow, sixty-eight years of age, looking like a girl. She waved, and I ran before she could see the terror in my eyes.

Orion was still producing at the Gas Company. We had a specially interesting play in rehearsal, an early Tennessee Williams work called *You Touched Me*, in which could be seen the beginning of his fragile Southern belles and an embryonic 'Big Daddy'. Louis Lentin, now well-established, was in charge of this production. Louis, socially a complete charmer, became transformed while directing. He was ruthless and tyrannical, open to no suggestions, and reduced some of our more sensitive actors to pulp. He would not allow tea-breaks, and gave lunch-breaks only because it was an Equity rule. But people worked for him, not only because work was scarce, but because he was very, very good at his job.

He could not bear an interruption during rehearsals, and on one occasion sent a stage manager to knock on the door of the ladies' toilet to ask an actress what was taking her so long. The reply from behind the door was not relayed by a now terrified messenger. Jacquie was cast in this production, but maybe because she was young and refused to take the intimidating side of Louis seriously, he made little adverse impact on her; in fact, she made him laugh. She would not discuss Mother's operation except in terms of total success, and I was grateful for the tonic.

The following day every time I phoned the hospital she was still on the operating table. When I tried again at 4 pm, and they said she was still there, I ran out and went straight into the hospital, incoherent with fear that she had died. My headlong rush was stopped by the matron, who told me that all had gone as well as could be expected – but I could not see Mother until the next day. I refused to leave, and sat in the waiting-room for hours, but finally, I had to surrender and go home.

As each day became a kaleidoscope of rehearsals and hospital visits, I began to see hope and to believe in miracles. It was a long, tough road to recovery, with severe pain from the leg still in traction. But Mother soon came home, and while it took time, the pain diminished. She walked with greater ease every day, and soon went back to work.

When I was starting theatre production, the *Rose Tattoo* case was winding up in the courts. I raged inwardly at the time, and swore to try to vindicate Alan Simpson and Carolyn Swift artistically in due course. Now I asked Alan and Carolyn to restage it at the Eblana exactly as it had been in the Pike. I had already alerted Anna Manahan, who was burning to play Serafina again, and I knew that, with these three, and maybe a few others from the original production, we could bring it off.

Since the end of the fifties and the slow demise of the Pike, the Simpsons had split up. Alan was working in France, and Carolyn was, naturally, not as enthusiastic about the revival as she might otherwise have been. She had been deeply hurt by the painful split, but gave me every help in tracking down Alan to ask him to return and direct this play again. Despite his harsh memories of it, he could see that the case would not be laid to rest until it had been seen by a much wider cross-section of the public than had been possible in the tiny Pike. The Eblana could seat 237, and we could rent the theatre for as long as we wished, giving an open-ended run. Alan eventually consented, we set a date for production discussions and casting, and the ball began to roll.

When Alan came home, he seemed to have gained a new enthusiasm for the project. We had a great casting session, and he worked with Carolyn as though they were still together, with no strain evident. Serafina's daughter was to be played by Eve Belton, an attractive newcomer who had recently made a name in Dublin in juvenile roles; and I persuaded a young Mike Murphy, fresh from Brendan Smith's acting academy, to play her boyfriend. Mike, today a television and radio personality, was then a very handsome young man, and a reasonably talented actor. He was courting his future wife Eileen at the time, and she almost ended their relationship when she heard that he was taking part in so infamous a play!

Claire Mullen's name was added to the cast, and the key part of the man who comes courting the widowed Serafina went to Gerry Sullivan, another very good-looking actor now prominent on TV, who later with Gemini gave some unforgettable portraits of John B Keane characters. Claire was a glamorous lady who liked good clothes and wore them well, but was a much better actress than her image suggested.

As rehearsals proceeded, Alan began to ask what arrangements had been made for the goat which, in one scene, Serafina has to pull across the stage. In the Pike, where there was a grassy place nearby, a goat had been brought and watched over by its owner until it was needed. But I did not expect to be asked seriously to have a goat brought through a busy bus station, down into a most confined backstage space teeming with actors and staff. To my horror, Alan said that he must withdraw if the goat was not provided, as he believed it represented fertility, good fortune and heaven knows what else – and he was not joking.

Carolyn supported his viewpoint absolutely. After many discussions with my stage staff and manager Dahna Davis, we learned that a goat had been seen grazing an some patchy land along the banks of an adjacent canal. Dahna was despatched to trace the owner. He found the notion of his goat appearing in a play hilarious, but agreed to walk her down every evening and collect her again for a small weekly sum. I was amazed at the reaction of the actors, who were willing to put up with any inconvenience so that Alan and the play could be vindicated.

The revival drew much publicity, and if I deplored the fact that much of this centred on the goat's debut, the point was truly made in the papers and on radio that this would be a historic occasion. Advance booking was extraordinary, and there was a virtual battle for first-night seats. The performance was lifted above my highest expectations, and when it came to the famous moment when something was dropped, there was an audible gasp from the audience, now familiar with the story. In fact, all that was dropped was a piece of twisted paper, serving as a condom. At the end, the cast received a standing ovation. Alan and Carolyn were cheered, flowers were presented and thrown. Anna stood proudly between them as the applause and cheering went on and on. Then Alan made a short, touching speech acknowledging all who had supported him; the cast, ourselves and, most of all, Carolyn, whose work and help had been unstinted. Next day all the reviews were ecstatic. We packed out the theatre for three months, and closed the show only because of a prior booking for the Dublin Theatre Festival. This was one of the achievements I was most happy with in my years with Gemini.

The run, however, was less than happy for the actors and stage staff because the goat was the cause of much general unrest and backstage discomfort. It hated its stage debut, and signalled its animus by leaving little piles of droppings everywhere. There were threats of resignation from those afflicted, and we had meetings with Equity about it. When it was realised that Alan had what amounted to a contract on the matter, and that either the goat was used or the play closed, the complainants decided to suffer on rather than lose their jobs. The goat itself got happier when it discovered that the ladies' hats had flowers on them, and proceeded to eat these as well as any detachable prop in sight. In the middle of the run, the goat's owner declared himself unwilling to walk it down to Busáras and back, saying that we would have to do it ourselves. No one wanted this job, so we advertised on radio, causing much public amusement and accusations of publicity-seeking. Two days before the owner's notice lapsed, a taxi firm offered to transport the animal for a weekly consideration. And so, for the last four weeks of the run, the goat travelled back and forth in the lap of luxury.

# 21

# *In Orbit with James Joyce*

H ugh Leonard had mentioned to me that he would like to write a one-man show for Cyril Cusack, based on the James Joyce autobiographical novels *Stephen Hero* and *Portrait of the Artist as a Young Man*. Norman and I thought that this was a fascinating idea. I was doubly delighted, as I had not had the chance of working with Cyril since the early Abbey days.

We decided to offer this play, called *Stephen D*, to the Dublin Theatre Festival, and we imagined the Festival Committee and poor Brendan Smith having collective apoplexy when we asked for at least treble our usual grant to produce a one-person show. We would have the biggest star name in the Festival, and would have to surround him with glorious settings, special lighting and so on. In those days the Festival budget was spent mainly in helping Irish companies to present high-quality, home-grown productions. Irish drama figured heavily in the division of spoils; then the rest of the money was used for international drama, dance and other imports of world interest.

Very little was left for the administration, which was always cut to the bone. Brendan worked for a pittance, and did most of the administrative and artistic work himself, with some secretarial assistance. Companies could bring their ideas to Brendan, and haggle for as much of the small cake as they could get. He was good at sharing out the rations, and a lot of excellent work got a showing when he was in charge. So Norman, Hugh and I felt reasonably sure of getting the backing for our one-man project. Some time later Norman and I were discussing a new comedy for the Gate, when Hugh Leonard rang from Manchester to say that he had begun work on *Stephen D* and had decided to add a few more characters. It worked better, he thought, with more voices, although Cyril's role would still be the raison d'être of the play. We didn't mind so long as it was still a small cast. Hugh was living in Manchester at this time, working on original TV plays and adaptations and making a name for himself.

We were not getting much in the way of new Irish writing at this stage, our main authors being Hugh Leonard and, to a lesser degree, John B Keane. Both had one thing in common; the power to draw audiences of all types and classes. They were always natural crowd-pullers, audiences could relate to their very different characters and styles; and both could mix poignancy with rich comedy.

I could tell that Hugh was completely obsessed with the idea of adapting the Joyce books and in love with the project more than was usual with him. He was not one to show his feelings easily. He would talk out his ideas, and hold nothing back about his plans and themes, but that is not the same thing. When he rang to say that he was coming home to see his father, and suggested that we have an early meeting to discuss production and casting for *Stephen D*, he sounded as eager and enthusiastic as a schoolboy. But he warned before he put down the phone that the cast had grown slightly since we last spoke, and I gathered that this was to be a one-man show with a difference. We met at a posh Dublin restaurant, and he bought us a most expensive dinner; he was very generous, and would pick up the tab for everything and everyone. During the meal he suddenly said, 'I don't think this play is really a good idea for Cyril Cusack, but it may be my best work so far, and I'm afraid it has got a very large cast.' This was stunning news. All I could think of was to thank God Cyril had not been approached.

That night we listened to the master-plan Hugh had devised for the adaptation, and it was so ingenious, so original and right, that neither of us would find any words except to marvel at his expertise. He was visibly delighted with our reactions, then grinned amiably and said he figured there would be twenty-seven actors needed, and that he would have the play finished in a few months. The main character was now Stephen (Joyce himself), and this part doubled with that of the Narrator of the action, so of course it had to be a young actor with experience and charisma – and then I knew. This would be the best part of Norman's life, and I would lose him once this very special ball started rolling.

The script arrived. I read the confirmation of our hopes and the total realisation of our expectations. *Stephen D* was brilliant. The director had to be Jim Fitzgerald, magical Fitz who not only had to be minded, but first had to be found so that he could be persuaded and pampered and put up with, not to mention being fought with and fired and reinstated.

I had given Fitz great shows to direct as well as what he called utter rubbish and he enhanced them all. But most of us aged visibly while working our way through what Godfrey Quigley called his Calvary, a pilgrimage through the occasional nightmares that Fitz could conjure up for those who wrestled with his genius. We felt that even he would be sufficiently impressed to stay close to us on this one. Norman was to play the central roles of Stephen and Narrator, and seldom have I seen an actor so resemble a tiger, tensed and quivering with prey in sight. I haven't seen many authors so genuinely pleased as Hugh was then. He was normally insecure about his scripts until they had won public acclaim, but he knew, as we did, that it really was that good.

It seemed no time at all until rehearsals were due to commence. We had been to see Brendan Smith, not with the script but with a synopsis of the play, a few casting details and a request for as much Festival money as we could prise out of him. By the time we confronted him with *Stephen D* and its requirements, Gemini had already had some solid Festival successes and quite a formidable reputation as a company with a varied and courageous artistic policy. Hugh's status as author and adapter was also well established. Brendan was too experienced an entrepreneur not to sense the excitement that charged our every word. His office was small, up several flights of stairs in South Great George's Street, and as we were all smokers, the place was soon blue and thick with our nervous puffing and Brendan's status cigar. There was no definite conclusion to our proposal and its costings, but that was normal; no one ever got a definite commitment on the first bid for Festival subsidy. However, we left the Festival office with a sense of victory. It was not hard to tell that Brendan was impressed, and knew that we had something special.

We had a fabulous cast in mind. There were Norman, Des Perry, Gerard Healy, Dominic Roche, Martin Dempsey, Sheila O'Sullivan and Ruth Durley. There was Fitz's protégé, Kevin McHugh, now an established actor and manager, then a prickly beginner. He had exactly the right quality for his role, a small but difficult part. After much searching, we cast an actor named Noel Ó Briain in the important part of Cranly. Noel had played with Hugh in the Land Commission dramatic society, (LANCOS) and subsequently went on to a distinguished career as a television producer and head of RTE's drama department. His work in *Stephen D* was exemplary, even though he was struggling with a part altogether at variance with his appearance and personality.

Back in the Festival office with Brendan Smith to discuss finances, I deliberately did not dwell on the extraordinary elation charging the Gate Theatre, but there was a hint of tension in the way Brendan questioned me. Would the play cause riots, run into trouble with the authorities? Was I sure that it was not offensive to Church or State? Of course I lulled his anxieties, although I really did suspect that there would be trouble from some quarters. I did not think the Church would be overly concerned. After all, Joyce was the most famous Jesuit student ever, and the Jesuits had kindly lent us a store of old cassocks, with black cloth wings coming from the shoulders. But I realised that Brendan was worried about losing his sponsorship, and that was serious. I believed that *Stephen D* would be a real turning point in Irish theatre, and was deeply certain that, whatever Brendan lost on swings he would recoup on roundabouts.

We were like an army, living on our nerves. As artistic director, I had to be there to do the soothing and the sorting. Fitz often fretted about management being present, particularly when a scene would not jell for him; but whenever I crept out for a cup of tea or some thinking time, he would let loose an enraged roar after me. He then would find a need for extra people, props, lights and other items he wanted me to conjure up for him. It was better to sit quietly and discuss the result of his work whenever he was ready, rather than to comment during the gestation process. He was off the booze during rehearsals, drinking large quantities of milk and chain-smoking, his nerves more ragged than any of ours coming into the home stretch.

Whenever I did get home, late and near-sick with fatigue, I fell into bed and prayed that never again would I get so involved in a theatre project that everything else was unreal and secondary. Mother was worried. She thought that my health would not hold up against such strain, but I explained that we were all in the same boat. I had never really believed before that I could make an adequate living from theatre production, but now I recognised a turning point. *Stephen D* held out hope for international recognition for the company, for Hugh Leonard and for Norman Rodway.

Fitz had told me little about the set, wanting to surprise and, no doubt, scare the daylights out of me. One day in the theatre he

announced to me gleefully 'We haven't got a set – don't need one!'
Aware from rehearsals how he got his effects, I did not panic,
although I knew there were seventeen locations in the script, and I
was a bit shaken to think that he might go for a completely bare
stage. Then he opened the curtains and showed me.

There was a rostrum right along the back of the stage, outlined
against a deep blue cyclorama. In its centre there was a square piece
like a large window, and at the sides flights of steps. Hanging in
front of these simple pieces was a yellow scrim curtain which looked
like gauze, and lifted away easily. The rest of the stage was bare. Fitz
explained that the actors, plus a few spot-lights and minimal props,
would create the illusion of all the other locations. Even after years
of knowing him I was mesmerised. Hugh did not see any of the
early hassles of dress rehearsal, being far too tense to appear. But, of
course, he had to have a look, and came late when nothing was
going on, and everyone was having a break. Seeing no activity
depressed him, and not even the whiskey he brought along lifted his
spirits until Fitz and the cast trooped back. We were, however, only
at the end of the first half, and he was persuaded to go home and
get some sleep. There was nothing he could do except worry.

On the opening night, complete confidence battled with
unreasoning terror, and I found it hard to reassure others when my
own hands were trembling so that I could not open my Good Luck
cards. Norman and I met for a moment in the scene-dock; I kissed
him and said 'This is it, Norman,' and he replied 'Let's go, Phyllie.' I
rushed to find Fitz superbly cool and totally aware of the
masterpiece waiting to open behind the curtain. Hugh was too
nervous to say anything. There were queues sitting on the Gate
steps, and stretching back past the Rotunda.

During the first half there was little in the way of active reaction
from the audience, and the applause at the interval was as contained
as the conversations at the coffee-bar were muted. Backstage the
actors worried, but I persuaded them that this play needed
concentration, not noise. Into the second half, Fitz's wizardry was
evident, permeating the script as it unfolded before a rapt gathering.
Then the audible gasp, as the nature of Joyce's arguments against
religious orthodoxy, delivered with icy clarity by Norman, hit home,
causing at least a dozen over-sensitive Catholics to vacate their seats
and make for the exit. They were hardly noticed. The audience
remained riveted. When the curtain fell, there was a silence, and

then pandemonium broke loose with cheers and countless curtain calls. On the following day, the reviews were favourable beyond our wildest dreams, and as the week wore on, foreign critics wrote eulogies about *Stephen D* and all associated with it.

During the months which followed Norman and I were in all the newspapers and on the radio, being interviewed almost daily and in the most flattering terms. But family life went on as though nothing had changed. True, Mother, Etta, Joe and even Lizzie, who still didn't really know 'what went on in them theatres', were aware that we had scored a hit, and that congratulations were in order.

The adulation we received during that Festival was quite phenomenal. Brendan Smith treated us differently, one might say almost deferentially. Hugh Leonard was certainly the writer of the year, and his brilliant adaptation had the critics reaching for their superlatives. We were mobbed in the Festival club – and although *Stephen D* was supposed to run for only the first week of the Festival, overflow audiences and the general excitement guaranteed that it would be back with bells on. Fitz, who seemed to hate his own success, went into a bacchanalian frenzy and drank the clubs dry – but that was normal. Norman gave me a lovely present, an amber brooch in an antique setting. From Hugh I got a beautiful amethyst cross on a gold chain. I have them still, but I cannot recall that I gave them anything in return; except, as Hugh said, the gift of believing in him, in the company, in my capacity to handle Fitz and in putting all the pieces together.

After the Festival and truly by public demand, *Stephen D* went back to the Gate for an extended run. The English reviews were even more enthusiastic than the Irish ones, so it was not surprising when offers came into the Festival office for a London production. Peter Bridge, a young entrepreneur, came over to see it and to discuss bringing it to the St Martin's Theatre in the West End in early 1963. Given the rave reviews, he was sure that his backers would come in enthusiastically. Everything seemed to be going smoothly until he became distraught about our set, or lack of it, and began to visualise a new, more lavish one for London. We had trouble convincing him that the way the play worked was partly dependent on the minimum of design and the clever lighting plot. Besides, we had got the reviews that excited him so much with *this* set, and any drastic change might lead to different reactions from the London press.

His next suggestion was more ominous; perhaps we needed a 'name' in the cast for London, say Peter O'Toole, instead of Norman. This caused a furore in the company, who were kept informed of every development, and total outrage on my part. As Norman, though terribly hurt, preferred to keep his distance from this new twist in the London saga, Brendan Smith, Hugh and myself met to exchange views and prepare to do battle for our star. Hugh, at the risk of losing out on a West End production of his play, stood solidly behind Gemini and Norman. He was prepared to tell Peter Bridge that the entire company, including Norman, travelled to London, or the show stopped here. That was a very courageous step for a writer whose dream of fame was now within reach, and it should not be forgotten that he willingly risked losing his chance. Eventually we confronted Peter Bridge. He took his time, consulted his backers and came back to us with a contract for the show to travel as it was, with the following reservations. He and his backers did not find Noel Ó Briain's Cranly the ideal choice, and Sheila O'Sullivan, who played Dante, would have to be replaced because of her strong Irish accent. It was no use arguing. He had given in on most things, but was adamant that these two must be replaced, and since they were not central to the show's appeal, it was up to us to concede, or the deal was off. We had to weigh the rights of the majority, more than twenty actors and our loyal author, but still felt that we were betraying the two unlucky people who had worked so hard.

We had signed and settled the deal, and were to open in February 1963, in St Martin's Theatre. Brendan Smith, on behalf of the Festival, was travelling to be with us and to take care of the business end of things, including salaries. Jacquie was already in London, staying with her cousins, and Etta, Lizzie and Joe would survive my absence, as they always had, and it was a plus that Jacquie was playing three or four small parts in *Stephen D*; perhaps Seán might come to see it, or me.

Norman and I set about finding the perfect Cranly. We knew that T P McKenna, currently an Abbey contract player, was the one who more than any other met all the requirements of the role. He was dark and handsome, and had some of that brooding quality which would have made him a perfect Heathcliff. Like the young James Mason, he could assume an aura of sophisticated cruelty which was at once provoking and fascinating. It certainly was an actor's 'cover', for there was no trace of it in his real nature.

T P was more than interested in this new opportunity, and approached Ernest Blythe for leave, with a total lack of success. He argued with Blythe that it was a terrific break for a young actor, and he would, of course, return to the Abbey to finish out his contract. Blythe wanted to know why he wanted to waste his time going to England when the Abbey was giving him good parts, and what more did he want, and so on. T P terminated the interview politely, then rang me to accept our offer. He never heard from Blythe again.

In Palmerston Road, Lizzie was getting feeble, and did only the lightest of tasks, and although our great friend Mrs Broughal came up to help as often as she could, someone more permanent was needed. Mother was working more from the house as a masseuse/chiropodist, but with her new hip, which was not as successful as modern replacements, she had to have a receptionist-cum-teamaker. Etta had her own little shop to look after, since her father had sent her the money to acquire one, but she always came home in the evenings laden with fruit and vegetables and other goodies, and took over the cooking and whatever else was necessary.

Gregg was promised a trip to London while we were there. He was then attending St Mary's School for Boys in Rathmines and beginning to show an extraordinary grasp of drama, poetry and writing. His drama teacher told me he was very gifted, and he had stolen the limelight in the school play *The Pied Piper*. He had also won medals at the Father Mathew Feis for singing. But he showed a masterly indifference to his natural talents, and much preferred visiting railway stations and old churches on his bike to practising drama.

All being well at home I was ready to take *Stephen D* to London. We had some extra rehearsals to work in our new Cranly and Dante, and Fitz had also to ensure that we had 'internal understudies' so small-part players were asked to learn the leading roles should any of the main players become ill. In England, understudies were essential to every production, but in Ireland we never seemed to appreciate their importance. Our actors went on whatever their physical condition.

The only thing we knew about St Martin's Theatre was that *The Playboy of the Western World* had run there in the previous year, 1962, and Peter Bridge had spoken scathingly about the Irish actors in that production, referring to them as drunk and aggressive in between shows, and offering to show us the porter stains on the walls of certain dressing-rooms. He warned us not to emulate this behaviour, as he was not prepared to tolerate it again. I told him grandly that Gemini had an absolutely clean record on that score. I was furious at the way people assumed that the Irish had no control, and that our actors lacked discipline, but I did admit that the alleged behaviour of some of the *Playboy* cast had been atrocious. I saw the stained walls, and solemnly promised that any actor found drunk in the theatre during our stay would be instantly replaced. That became a Gemini rule for future shows as well.

We rehearsed on the new stage, finding the theatre charming, neither too big nor small. Peter Bridge and some of his satellites attended rehearsals now and again, but left their verdict open until the final run-through. On the Saturday before the Monday opening, we gave a final dress-rehearsal, and Peter was inconsolable at the end. He thought the play was not, after all, suitable for London, that the minimal set and lack of colour, plus the Irish accents, would turn off the public. The play was, he moaned, too intellectual for commercial consumption. I thought that the production was even better in this lovely old theatre. T P was superb, and the cast knew exactly what they were doing, thanks to Jim Fitzgerald's patient drilling.

We were justly proud when the first night opened to a packed house and a standing ovation. It was a triumphant occasion, not just for Gemini and the company, but for Ireland. Afterwards we had drinks with Brendan Smith, Hugh and his wife Paule, and scores of Peter Bridge's friends, some who had money in the show and were beaming. Norman was undoubtedly the talking-point. He knocked them for six, giving a beautifully judged and entirely convincing performance, complemented by the equally superb T P McKenna. Des Perry scarified the audience as the sadistic Father Dolan; Dom Roche was the personification of priestly dignity and Gerard Healy held us spellbound with his marvellous rendering of Joyce's 'Hellfire' speech.

The following day we all went out to get the papers. There it was, just as vehement and ardent as it had been in Dublin; the justification for a London management to take a chance on a company hardly known to them. Rampant critical adulation, praise for the adaptation and for Joyce himself, for the director and the non-obtrusive set, and for Norman. They praised his appearance, voice, intellect, ability to create magic on the stage; they made him a star. T P also left them lost for adjectives, and the whole Dublin ensemble was praised to the skies. I went to the theatre to see Peter Bridge, who was actually smiling and told me that I had been right all along. There I phoned Mother, and learned that they had all read about the great success in the Irish papers, which carried photos of Norman and me, and of Brendan Smith. Mother was so happy, and promised to tell Gregg that his promised trip to London was assured. Jacquie met me at the theatre, and we were both delirious with the excitement of it all.

Later that evening, Norman and I hugged each other when I went into his dressing-room. I had been standing outside the theatre, my first time to see a play advertised in lights; there, lit up, was the name 'Norman Rodway' and the play *Stephen D*, which really brought a lump to my throat, because I knew that he would not be with Gemini much longer. Although he was reared and educated in Ireland, Norman's parents were English to the bone, and he was really coming home to the West End. There was no doubt that he would receive many attractive offers. Somewhere in England, Hugh Hunt was reading and realising that his 'little one' had kicked the stars. Somewhere else, Seán was drinking with his companions, blotting out what he could not accept. I would go to see him in a few days, when the dust had settled.

Agents, managements and influential TV people thronged the theatre. Norman and I had to meet them with Peter Bridge, to work out a TV production of the show before it ended and we all dispersed. One person sought by everyone was Jim Fitz. Managements and agents made appointments to meet him for lunch, dinner, any place and any time that would suit him – and he did not turn up for a single one. True to form, after his unnaturally good behaviour lasting up to the first night, he went on an unholy binge, and could not be found for several days. When he did turn up at the theatre one night, he was button-holed by some exquisite chap from the BBC, who was told to sod off and stuff his offer. I warned Peter Bridge not to let Fitz into the theatre or auditorium when he was drunk, and he was very irritating, insisting that he knew there would be alcoholic problems in an Irish company. I was so angry that I went home and prepared a list of famous and talented English drunks, brought it to his office the next day and recited it aloud to him; Robert Newton, Trevor Howard, Wilfred Lawson etc. Peter never mentioned it to me again.

It was such a delight when Easter finally came, and Gregg was free to spend a few days seeing London with me. At first I thought I might go home fleetingly and bring him back with me – I really was homesick for all at Palmerston Road. But I could not leave the show that particular weekend, and so phoned an amiable purser with whom I had become friendly on previous boat trips, asked him to keep an eye on Gregg and get him onto the train at Holyhead. He did so with great goodwill, and Gregg was something of a VIP on the trip. I was nervous until the train pulled into Euston and I saw his small figure emerge, and even though his self-esteem usually restrained him from kissing in public, he got the biggest hug I could muster. Luckily, Brendan Smith was able to extend his weekly visit, and he took over the theatre business, giving me freedom to show Gregg the sights of London.

# 22

# *Survival Courses*

It had been a lovely break, but as April and May turned the pavements into warm toasting blocks, and *Stephen D* continued to draw the crowds, the darker side of the success story began to unfold. First it was Jacquie, who got an infection in her thumb which rapidly spread into her right hand, and needed urgent hospital attention. She was in a lot of pain, but there was no way she was leaving the show. At the same time, a young actress with a larger role than Jacquie's became ill, and in a matter of days her family came to take her home, leaving Jacquie just about well enough to take over her role. Loretta Clarke, who had a small part in the show and who shared a flat with me, tripped over something backstage and bruised her face and back rather badly; we called a doctor and laid her off until she was quite healed. The others covered for her very well, and the show did not suffer.

I had not heard from Seán, and had not yet called to see him. Perhaps I felt that he might be hurt by all the success currently surrounding us, in which he had no part. Finally I made the journey to his digs, but he wasn't there. His landlady said he was gone away for a holiday, and I thought that he had probably gone home to Ireland. I rang Mother, but she had no news of him, and was sure that his sister Eibhlín would let her know if he was home. I began to feel really bad about the whole situation, especially about myself. I remember that I once asked Seán if, since we were living apart, we might consider getting an annulment; but he replied that there were no grounds, and no need since neither of us could marry again.

So I became immersed in the company again. Gerard Healy often asked me out for a drink after the show, and I really enjoyed talking to him about the similarities in our situations; he was separated and, in a real sense, so was I. We both adored our children. Gerard had more understanding than most men I met at that time. Maybe it was that we had known each other so long, and there was a deep fondness between us. I remember one night, the sun had been absent all day and there was a sharp chill in the breeze, and he told me to watch out for such changes in the weather; I was, he thought, too thin, and could easily catch cold. He himself, with his history of tuberculosis and heavy addiction to cigarettes, was developing a cough again. Next morning I got a message to say that he had 'flu, and that the doctor insisted on keeping him in hospital. We were not to worry; he would be back in the show in a couple of nights. Fitz rehearsed Kevin McHugh, who had been Gerard's understudy. To give Fitz his due, he also took over Kevin's original part so that the play would run as smoothly as possible.

The following day I called to see Gerard, but found that he was having tests and was not to be disturbed. I saw the specialist in charge, and he told me that there was no danger, and that they were conducting the tests because of Gerard's medical history. The doctor had seen and liked the show, and promised to return a fit Gerard Healy by the end of the week.

That evening Brendan Smith asked me to come up to the office in St Martin's, during the first act of the play, to go over some figures. The office was beside the dressing-rooms, and we could hear the actors' voices over the tannoy. Just as I was going upstairs, I was called to the phone near the stage door. It was the hospital. A woman's voice asked me if my name was Phyllis Ryan, and said that she was sorry to have to break the news that Gerard Healy had died suddenly. I left the phone swinging on its cord, unable to replace it on the hook. I couldn't answer or move. Brendan came down the stairs and saw me standing by the dangling phone, and knew that something was wrong. He asked me gently if I'd had bad news, and I said 'Gerry is dead, Brendan.' Then the floodgates threatened to open, and Brendan pushed me up the stairs and into the office, and locked the door.

He was weeping, but I couldn't yet let go. 'Brendan, the company – they mustn't be told until the show is over; I'll tell them when the show is over.' I was shaking, and he put his arms around me, telling me to keep the door locked during the performance, as actors often came in and out to chat and that one look at my face would tell them that something serious had happened. He kissed me and went out, and I locked the door.

I could hear the actors going by, running up the stairs to their rooms, laughing and joking. Norman and T P knocked on the door, calling my name, but I had turned off the lights, and they went away thinking that no one was there. Finally Brendan came back to say that he had notified Gerard's family – his wife Eithne Dunne and his aunt and cousins in Dublin – and asked me if I was up to telling the company after the last curtain-call. We went down and asked the stage management to keep the company on-stage at the end of the show. After several curtain-calls and thunderous applause, the company assembled for an announcement. I stood before them, with Brendan at my side, and told them, as gently as I could, that our beloved friend and colleague had died before the show that night. Norman and the whole company stood silently with tears in their eyes, shocked and bereaved.

Yet Brendan and I had so much work to do, and, unthinkably, an actor had to be found to replace Gerard. The show had to go on. Kevin was too young and, good though he was, it had been an unfair burden. Brendan, Fitz, Norman and I met in Peter's office, depressed even more by the drinks consumed the previous night in an attempt to dull the pain. Everything was gray and drab; London looked shabby, and the bleak, sunless sky bestowed no grace on spire or steeple. Brendan had a message for me from Eithne. Shocked beyond bearing, she had been put under sedation, but had first asked if I would go to the hospital to do and sign what was necessary, while Brendan made arrangements to bring Gerard home for burial. Of course I agreed, without knowing what might be involved, and I had a letter of authority signed by Eithne to take with me. First we discussed with a very shaken Peter Bridge the question of a suitable replacement for the role, and he suggested an actor called Joseph O'Connor, of Irish extraction, who looked right and had the required qualities.

I set off for the hospital where I met with friendly, helpful people who read my letter and asked me to sign a few papers. They gave me Gerard's possessions to be delivered to the next of kin. I told the registrar that the family would be in touch to arrange the removal, and saw Gerard for the last time. Brendan had taken charge of everything, and I do not know what we would have done without him. Eithne Dunne sailed home with her husband's coffin during the week. Joseph O'Connor took over with amazing speed; a likeable, gentle man, professional to his fingertips. But nothing could be the same again.

The run was nearing its end. I was getting reports from our Eblana

House Manager, Edna Shaw, that all was not well with the show there. I was lonely for Mother and Gregg, and for everyone at home. Jacquie said she was staying in London for a bit, as most of the cast had got themselves agents, and some had tentative or actual offers of work. Norman not only got himself an agent, but also a blonde casting director. He had not yet made a decision to break with Irish theatre, but there was huge interest in him both from England's National Theatre and the Royal Shakespeare Company.

It was so good to be back home again in Palmerston Road, to have cups of tea with Mother, Lizzie, Etta and Joe – and the cat, just one now, called Sheba. I suppose I knew then that no matter how much I might rail against double standards and injustices in Ireland, I had to live and be based there.

Shortly after my return, I was telephoned by Edna Shaw, a sturdy, hard-working woman who did not mince words. She managed the Eblana theatre and the box-office and front-of-house. She was sorry to trouble me, but the show at the Eblana, the beautiful *The Fantasticks*, by Harvey Schmidt and Tom Jones, was closing that week although we had booked it in for at least another fortnight. She gathered that there were unpaid bills, and that some of the cast who had been brought over from England had not been paid either salary or subsistence the previous week. The company had been formed by choreographer Patricia Ryan who had agreed to finance it. She was the first wife of the late Joycean scholar and writer, John Ryan. Unfortunately, although the theatre was packed for every performance, the show was costing about twice as much as the Eblana could take in, even at higher than usual prices. Edna informed me that Equity had been called in, Patricia Ryan was in hysterics and the rent had not been paid for two weeks.

I asked if I could speak to the business manager, and Edna said there were three or four of them, all representing Patricia or some other members of her 'company'. I sighed, told Mother I wouldn't be late, and went to view the scene of battle. Despite the wrangling and near-fisticuffs backstage, the show was excellent. It was sad that things had gone so badly wrong for the company and for Patricia, who would not have lost a penny had there been half a business head in her employ. I went backstage to tell them how good the show was, hoping to cheer them a little, but they all had grievances to which they wanted me to listen all night; so I withdrew, saying I would be at the meeting with Equity the next day. The legendary comic Cecil Sheridan was in the cast, and I remember how quiet he was, not joining in any recriminations or explanations. All he said to me was, 'I loved this show, you know. It's a shame.'

When I arrived at the theatre the next morning, many of the actors were intent on suing everyone connected with the management. Patricia Ryan couldn't come. Dermot Doolan, then secretary of Irish Actors Equity, reported that she was ill with the upset of it all, which aroused an unsympathetic response from the actors, who knew she was their only hope of getting paid. Dermot tried to explain that hurling abuse and writs about would not solve anything; they needed to get an accountant in to see what could be salvaged. I really had no input into this debacle, but had to mention that if the rent of the theatre had not been paid, I would have to make it good myself, and that simply was not on.

Dermot's idea was best, and I left it all in his hands. He found a good firm of accountants who went over the books quickly and accurately, but there was no joy in their report, and it seemed that Patricia had no more cash to invest. The English actors said they could not afford to pay their hotel, had not got the fare back to England and would sue through British Equity. Dermot promised to get them home safely, but hotel bills were still outstanding some months later. I was never paid the outstanding rent, and poor Edna Shaw was heart-broken, thinking she should have done more. The show closed the following night, and I was more angry than depressed that such an excellent production should have been so badly handled.

The Eblana Theatre had to be kept going. It was now dark, and Gemini could not get a show into it, because we were once more heading toward a Festival with Hugh Leonard's *Dublin One*, an adaptation of stories by James Joyce, who was beginning to seem like a relation who would not go away.

What would become of the Eblana? We did not want to lose our beloved little theatre, and there was no other company looking for a season there, since the wild tales about *The Fantasticks* had snowballed, with the theatre coming out of the false rumours badly. Mother and I talked the problem into the ground. Then one evening she said 'Ring Cecil Sheridan and ask him.'

Cecil Sheridan had been my ideal panto Dame as long as I could remember. With Jimmy O'Dea, Jack Cruise and Noel Purcell, he ranked among the immortals in the world of Irish variety. Maureen

Potter, perhaps the greatest of them all, was to take the mantle of high comedy from Jimmy O'Dea, but her time had not yet come. Cecil had been lured into *The Fantasticks* after a long association with the Gaiety and Olympia theatres; I was fortunate to find him in the Eblana. He was a slight man, of medium height with large soulful eyes, wisps of hair on a shining pate, surprisingly dainty hands and a stammer that I found painful until I got used to it. This impediment was so much a part of Cecil's persona that it was almost a trademark, and many of his friends echoed it affectionately when repeating a 'Cecil' story – and there was an unending flow of those.

He never stammered on-stage and was known as the fastest cross-talk comedian in the business. He could hold down a half-hour spot telling non-stop jokes without pausing for breath, and could obviously go on all night. He reduced audiences to such paroxysms of laughter that they were high for the whole night. Without question he was the best stand-up comedian I have ever seen and the funniest Dame. A meticulously authentic cross-dresser, he always insisted that the audience must know they were watching a man dressed as a woman. The boobs, costumes, earrings and tights had to be perfect, he said, and proved it with a stunning range of panto Dames, plus a few 'specials', such as Mae West or any other who took his fancy. His famous parodies, including Doris Day hits or other popular tunes, had lyrics which could be enchantingly droll or hysterically vulgar. I was privileged to come to know him as a friend, and to learn a great deal about the world of variety through our association.

Following Mother's brainwave, courtesy of her variety background, we both went into action. I rang Cecil, told him I was Maisie Ryan's daughter and a director of Gemini Productions – which he already knew – and asked to meet him the next morning for coffee. That proved one of the best moves I ever made.

We met at Busáras and had coffee in the bar. I murmured some polite banalities about the sudden closure of *The Fantasticks*, and then my voice died away. Cecil waited, spooning too much sugar into his tea, and then said, controlling his stammer with difficulty, 'What did you want to see me about?' Then the words came tumbling out, as I explained to him our position as custodians of the Eblana, my fear of losing the theatre if it went dark and the commitments Gemini had to the festival show at the Gate. I begged him to put a show in, starring himself; I would find the backing (God forgive me, we hadn't a penny), arrange the administration, design, costumes, anything. As I ran out of breath, he suddenly said he thought he knew the very show I wanted, and added that it would take him about ten days to rehearse. As he was scripting the show and taking the part of actor-manager, I arranged that the rent and expenses would come out of the box-office first, and that we would then go on a percentage, with Cecil taking the higher share.

He was on his way out of Busáras before I realised that I didn't know what the show was to be called. He replied 'The Good Old Days,' and added that it would include impersonations of old-time stars like Marie Lloyd, Sophie Tucker, Al Jolson and so on. He would require straight actors for the potted melodrama and the part of Master of Ceremonies. He would arrange piano and drums, and dancers and singers, and he knew where we could get costumes at a good rate. He had a strict rule about costumes. They must be fresh and regularly cleaned, and if he appeared in a ragged suit, they must be the cleanest rags ever worn. He had some famous costumes of his own, and knew a performer who had ladies' wigs.

We shook hands, and agreed to start rehearsals in the Eblana in two days! This conversation took a long time, as Cecil's stammer grew worse as we went on. He had never stammered on-stage, and although friends had evolved various explanations for this, no one knew for sure. Cecil was a very truthful person, and I asked him how he had conquered his stammer. This, he said, was due to prayer, and to a doctor to whom he had been sent by God. (Cecil was very religious, and had no doubt that God had directed him.) At the time, there was a pantomime being cast in the Father Mathew Hall (home of the Feiseanna), and Cecil was not being considered for the role of the Dame in *Mother Goose* but was offered a part in the chorus. His new doctor told him to go back and read the part for the producers, saying that Mother Goose, the Ugly Sisters, and other pantomime Dames – none of them stammered. Cecil Sheridan might stammer, but he was a different character on-stage, and that person did not. Cecil believed what he was told, and read for the part with perfect, rapid-fire speech. He got it, and never again had a problem professionally.

We assembled some very fine artists for *The Good Old Days* from both stage traditions. Cecil wrote a show-stopper for Anna Manahan, who could belt out 'Bill Bailey' with the best. Chris Curran featured in many songs throughout, and also got a solo spot near the end with his marvellous impersonation of Jimmy Durante, playing piano and tin whistle with equal facility. Cecil made brief appearances with old songs like 'Any Old Iron' and 'I Do Like To Be Beside the Seaside', but kept the best wine till the end, having made sure that all the other performers had a good innings. I have never seen such generosity from a star when the best numbers were being shared out; he always said that if an act died before you come on, you die too.

Just before the finale, he had a café scene with others seated at tables, and on he came as a blonde, busty Mae West inviting the audience to 'come up and see me sometime'. True to his conviction that a Dame must always signal the actor's masculinity, he would push up his false bosoms (designed to keep slipping down) and parade across the stage ad-libbing brilliantly.

Rehearsals for the show, with the stage manager (Rhona Woodcock, a lovely girl and a fine singer) handing out note-pads so that the artists could take notes, were a revelation. Most of us had never worked in variety, and had thought that they rehearsed as we did our plays. Anna Manahan, although thrilled with her star number and the whole experience, soon began to exhibit signs of panic. Nothing went into the note-pads! Cecil just went from one actor to the other and said 'You sing at no 9; you go off and rehearse that; you do this dance at no 5.' Even Beryl Fagan, who was equally good in plays or musicals, wondered where the script was! Chris Curran was not too fazed. Liam O'Callaghan, a masterly compère, looked startled, but said nothing.

I went to Cecil and explained that this was a new and scary way for drama people to work. He laughed at this, but told Anna that he would look after them all, and go over everything with them. The melodrama number, plotted by Cecil, was 'Sweeney Todd', and came after the interval. At the next rehearsal, true to his word, Cecil had not only a synopsis of the action, but an actual performance sheet, so that everyone knew precisely where they came on. He took Anna aside the following week, and they went over her number at the piano until she felt secure, and he did the same with the others. I pointed out to Cecil that Anna's number was really outstanding, and might steal the reviews, and, to my amazement, he was thrilled. 'You think it's good then,' he twinkled, adding 'I think they'll notice me too!' Mother was dying to hear every little thing, and I told her that Cecil thought the world of her, and said that she should never have left the profession.

The venture was financed on a wing and a prayer. 'Just a long run, Lord, to packed houses,' I prayed, but was not prepared for the avalanche of little miracles that rained down on us. The audiences queued to see the show; there were rave reviews in all the papers for Cecil and all his gifted company. There were standing ovations nightly, and there was an atmosphere of amazement and delight among the artists, almost like children who had not really expected Santa to deliver such wonderful goodies! Looking at the show on the first night, I saw a breath-taking pageant of old songs and stories, wonderful costumes, splendidly-timed dances, the whole varied and pacey entertainment backed by a clever and lustrous setting designed by Bob Heade. Eileen Studley, a pianist who had played for many Gemini shows, accompanied the singers; with the help of a drummer she also played silent-cinema music for the melodrama 'Sweeney Todd' in which John Molloy, famous mime artist and comedian, excelled.

*The Good Old Days* ran for seventeen weeks, a very long run in those days, and was still packing when we had to take it off for a prior Festival booking. I persuaded Mother and Joe to come to the show on the last night. I had arranged with Cecil that he would mention Mother's connection with variety during his curtain speech – and I saw the pixie look on his face that meant a plot was about to be hatched. At the interval I sent soft drinks to Mother and Joe, and my heart lightened when I saw their faces, filled with enjoyment like kids at a party. Mother sang along with all the numbers while Joe kept repeating jokes and chuckling. After Cecil's parody spot and his Mae West number, the applause was tremendous. Cecil eventually settled the audience down, and made his speech. He spoke of the wonderful, almost legendary lady May Ryan, who had helped and encouraged so many top variety performers when she was casting director in the Olympia. Suddenly the spotlights travelled from the stage down to Mother's seat, and an assistant stage manager presented her with a huge bouquet of flowers. There was so much applause that she had to stand to acknowledge it.

Then the curtains closed for the last time, and the audience filed out to the rhythmic beat of the piano and drums. Cecil wanted to see Mother. When we at last reached his dressing-room, he gave her a big hug, and thanked her again for all she had done. Even though she had not expected the flowers and praise, she was, I know, tremendously pleased.

# 23

# *Love, Friendships and Death*

I first met Liam Mac Gabhann, poet and journalist, on top of a
number 7 bus. He was very much in the news at the time, having
recently visited godless Russia with a select group of writers and
observers, and found some good things in the Communist regime.
Writing the truth as he saw it cost him dearly. He was
unceremoniously dropped from Radio Éireann programmes, and lost
other sources of income in Catholic papers, being deemed to be a
supporter of the Russian Antichrist, whereas all he had really done
was praise those aspects of Communism which upheld the rights of
the poor. I introduced myself, sat beside him in the bus and timidly
paid tribute to his integrity. We sat in silence until his stop came, and
when he got off the bus, I felt curiously lonely.

Liam was a man of average height, slight with high cheekbones
and thick, wavy gray hair. His eyes were gray-green under bushy
brows and, while he was not at all handsome, he attracted attention.
His voice was rich and resonant, quite unlike other Kerry voices I
was familiar with; his had a different music, perhaps something
peculiar to his native Valencia Island. I did not see him again for
quite a while. He was working for the *Irish Times*, and came into a
Fleet Street bar frequented by journalists. I was sitting with some
friends discussing James Joyce's only play *Exiles*, when Liam joined
us. I was suddenly tongue-tied, feeling a great sense of admiration
for this lean, silver-haired stranger. And again, when he left, I
experienced a sense of loss. I began to go to the same pub, hoping
to meet him again, and once he arrived when I was about to leave. It
was late, and he offered to drive me home. We spoke little on the
journey, and when we got to my door, he took my hand for a
moment and was gone.

I did not mention him at home, but a deep feeling had taken root.
I read everything he wrote, romanticised about his island ancestry
and incorporated him into my day-dreams. It was becoming an

obsession, a rather absurd and unsatisfactory one-way traffic. We next met at a press reception, which was so crowded that I had to manoeuvre to attract his attention. We left together, driving somewhere in his car, and I was suddenly warm and happy. We talked about our children, of our hopes and fears for them, and how they kept us sane. I rattled on about plays and some theatre friends I hoped he might know, but he said that he was not at home with actors, that he felt make-believe became part of their lives so that they forgot how to be real people. This made me feel a little down, as it might well apply to me, but when I was leaving, he took my hand and kissed it. I knew then that I had found a friend who would fill the empty space in my life.

Casting *Dublin One* and *The Poker Session* was then in progress. Hugh Leonard, with his feeling for the pulse of Joyce, had adapted the short stories for *Dublin One* with great skill. *The Poker Session*, an original play, was assigned to Fitz to direct, so we had to find the right person to direct the Joyce work, which was to open at the Gate in the first week of the Festival in September 1963. We were fortunate to find that Barry Cassin was free, and it was pleasant to contemplate at least one production free of the tensions generated by Fitz. Barry liked order, but tended to shy away from difficult situations such as actors coming late to rehearsal or tardy designers. These and other untidy little problems were mostly referred to me; but with Barry we were assured of a well-rehearsed, professional show.

Looking back, we mounted an extraordinary number of productions with scant resources, but those we did have were the best. Dahna Davis, who had combined the job of a manager of Orion in the Gas Company with everything from publicity to small parts, eventually left us – not our friendship, which I still treasure – to take up a prominent position on a fashion magazine. For domestic reasons, Dahna needed something more remunerative than theatre work. Later at the Eblana, she was replaced by Edna Shaw, an excellent manager and a great friend of Mother's. Norman managed the Gemini shows, and a part-time secretary typed whatever letters the two of us could not do ourselves. We were always aware of how much we depended on good stage management, and we always succeeded in getting the best – and they were all women.

Joan Huet was a wonderful stage manager to work with, able and courteous and strong enough to deal with awkward situations. She was the first lesbian I had met since Alice Delgarno and Babs de Monte, lead dancers and choreographers of the Theatre Royal, and she was altogether different from my preconceptions. She was extremely refined, and hated ill-mannered or boorish people. I became very fond of her and was sad when she decided to pursue her career in England. One night, when I was leaving her suburban house and waiting for a taxi, she spoke of her feelings for me and asked me to stay the night. I could only tell her that I loved her too, but that I was not part of her particular world, and never could be. An unbearable silence came over us both, and to compound my embarrassment I had to borrow money from her for the taxi. I had never felt so gauche and immature. But the next night when we met, Joan took my hand and squeezed it, to show there were no hard feelings.

Rhona Woodcock came next, a very different but equally capable stage director. When she eventually moved to the Abbey, we found an ideal replacement in Mai McFall. She happened to be free when we said goodbye to the lovable Rhona, and as the Abbey gained a treasure, so did we. Mai, a singularly attractive young woman, soon became a close and trusted friend of our family, and Mother almost adopted her on the spot. Her husband George was stage manager, set designer and painter of scenery at the Gaiety, and she had learned her trade, like so many others, at the Brendan Smith Academy. As she often said, not all of Brendan's babies were destined for the stars, but they were all trained in the true values of professional theatre.

At home, Lizzie had been most unwell, and the doctor had hinted at a need for regular nursing care in a hospital or home. Liam met me frequently for tea in Bewley's, and as usual I told him all my fears, rambling on until he took my hand and pointed out that nothing bad had yet happened. It had only been suggested that Lizzie might go into hospital, and Mother was a stronger force than I realised.

One day Liam called to the house with a book I needed, and, as I introduced him to Mother, I knew immediately that she liked him, but I also knew that explanations would be required. I told her that evening about my friendship with that remarkable man, and how much I needed it. She just said that such friendships could be dangerous when both parties were married. There was, I then thought, nothing between Liam and me to warrant such a wary reaction, and I was angry. I did not want anyone to question my friendship with him. Feeling let down, I told her that I would not invite him to the house again. All I succeeded in doing was to create a rift between us that took a few months to mend. It was Liam who sorted us out, quite innocently, by turning up with his dog on Christmas Day to wish us the compliments of the season. Mother brought him in for a drink, and suddenly everything was right again.

I had become accustomed to leaning on Liam in all kinds of emergencies, and it was inevitable that we should become lovers. It happened one night in a small flat in the Dartry area that I had taken for reasons of privacy. Home had become quite crowded, and I needed some space in which to read scripts, interview writers and actors and so on. Mother disapproved, thinking it extravagant and unnecessary. When I was moving in, Liam drove me there with a few items of personal belongings, and once installed, we embraced and it just happened. I loved him, and afterwards I felt relaxed and happy, as if it had been the most natural thing in the world. Liam was very quiet, and, while we drank tea, he asked me how I thought this would affect our relationship. I replied that it would only make us closer friends; we both had spouses and children, and could not be together in the normal way when other lives would be affected. He wondered if that kind of relationship would satisfy me, or any woman, but made no bones about his loyalties. His marriage was a contract that could not be broken, and his children, while almost adult, still needed his guidance.

I was prepared to accept the difficulties; after all, I could not leave my own children, either. All I wanted to know was the one thing that would make it possible for us to be together, even for short periods. And yes, he answered, he did love me; he said it over and over and, before he left, wrote it in a little book I kept for notes. I hugged him, feeling only a great joy that loneliness had been banished. That he was so direct, made no promises and had his priorities right were all part of my reason for loving him. I was, and would be, happy with what I could have of his company and affection, and was certain that I would never want more.

That evening, Mother knew everything as soon as I came home. She said nothing, but leaned more heavily on her stick and spent a long time looking out at the lights on Palmerston Road. We had a cup of tea together, but I was afraid to open up to her lest we should have disruptive words. I knew that she feared for me, and before I left to go into town, I managed to tell her that she and the children would always come first with me. She nodded, and I thought there were tears in her eyes.

Later in Groome's Hotel, with Norman and a few actor friends, I was on such a high that the first drink went to my head. Suddenly I felt part of the group, no longer the oddity without a lover. Liam and I remained lovers, discreetly and without hurt or harm to anyone, and fell back into deep friendship towards the end of his life. He was so good to Gregg, teaching him how to drive and listening to his problems. When Jacquie came home for a break, she found him fascinating, and advised me to hang on to him for the sake of the family.

Two other gifted men, both acclaimed today, moved into my orbit, and became part of my work and affections. I met both of them in a scene-dock, painting away at scenery, as each designed sets and often finished the paint-work on their designed sets and flats. Tomás Mac Anna, who had arrived at the Abbey after I had departed, had been a Customs and Excise official when brought there by Ernest Blythe. He was a fluent Irish speaker with highly idealistic republican views, more than enough to cause Blythe to take him to his bosom. Tomás could do no wrong in the eyes of his patron, and quite by accident, Blythe had for once done something superbly right. Tomás was a giant of a man when I first met him, with a slightly austere manner that was off-putting at first, until the shyness that caused it was revealed. He had no interest in clothes, and usually seemed too large for his suits, all wrists and ankles. His features were too strong to be called handsome, but his eyes were steady, reflecting his moods. I did not want to like any protégé of Blythe's, but I saw him direct a couple of plays in Irish at the Abbey, and a memorable production of Lorca's *Yerma* for which he designed a most evocative set. But it was much later, when he came to work for Orion/Gemini in his free periods, that I grew to know the exceptional nature of the man.

The other friend-to-be was also a designer of stage sets for musicals, plays, ballets or operas; all were grist to the mill of Patrick Murray, who hailed from Cork. He could, indeed, as easily design a building, or colourful interiors for homes, all with great panache and a tremendously inventive style. He could also, I believe, have been a talented director had he wished. I have listened to Pat carefully on aspects of every production we worked on together, and he is a prolific source of ideas, stimulating creative thinking in others. When I first met him, he was a handsome, well-dressed young man with thick, wavy hair and a mischievous grin which could explode into infectious laughter to disrupt the most solemn occasions. Today Pat is a much bigger version of himself, different only in the sense that there is, physically, much more of him; he has no interest in fighting the battle of the bulge. But his wit is as sharp as ever; Mícheál Mac Liammóir would have met his match here, and would have adored him in his own heyday. Pat was, and is, attractive to young and old, to women and even more so to men. The quality of friendship he offers is extremely rare.

As previously mentioned, another to become a great friend was John B Keane, who completely bowled me over when we met. He was tall and slim, with curiously hooded eyes which summed people up in an instant. A natural poet, he had a flair for earthy humour which left his listeners helpless with laughter, and he would sing ballads and recite verses at or without the asking. His Kerry charm and flattery were irresistible, but he could swing to being a hell-raiser and back again before you knew what caused the explosion. His wife Mary was quiet and attractive, and her presence was enough to quell any storm. If John was utterly magnetic to many women, Mary was his safe haven. I became devoted to them both and their family, a feeling that survived all the ups and downs to grow into a friendship I could not do without.

There is probably no playwright today so committed to a single company as for so many years, Hugh Leonard was to Gemini. He wrote eleven plays for us, original works or adaptations, and virtually every one was a Festival winner; some went on to success elsewhere, notably *Da*, which took Broadway by storm and won every major Tony Award. *The Poker Session* was a witty, unusual kind of thriller, containing some of the author's best writing. We had our wayward genius Fitz to direct it, and acquired a first-rate cast, crowned by the arrival from the West End of Marius Goring, a big name then in theatre and cinema. He loved the play, and was delighted to join Norman, Pauline Delany, Joe Lynch, Maureen Toal and Peggy Marshall in it. The casting did entail certain off-stage complications. Maureen had been involved romantically with Norman, who had been married to Pauline, who had subsequently had an affair with Fitz. 'That should bring an extra edge to the work,' said Fitz laughingly; but Norman was not amused, nor was I.

On the first day of rehearsals, Marius arrived punctually to find everyone assembled for introductions – except Fitz. We made all sorts of excuses to our guest star as we feverishly telephoned around in vain, until we had to abandon work for the day. Marius, making light of it all, brought us for drinks and regaled us with humorous theatre stories. The next day, Fitz was there, and I thought it best to make no fuss in public. We got started, but Fitz was strangely passive, with little to add to the exchange of ideas. A week later, I had become seriously worried. Fitz was turning up every day, but he wasn't bringing much with him; the actors were being gloriously inventive, but he was not there with the usual brilliant touches and suggestions.

The play, despite Fitz's passive role, was a Festival success. Although well received critically and well attended, it never had quite the audience appeal of some of Hugh Leonard's other work for us. Nevertheless, it opened at the Globe Theatre in London, under the auspices of Donald Albery, in February 1964, having already played in Brighton to packed houses and good reviews. It was all the more disappointing to encounter a mixed reception from the press and mediocre audiences after the London opening. Marius was furious, blaming the poor business on lack of publicity and indifferent London management. In any case, we were home within weeks, nothing daunted. Fitz, who had travelled with us to light and supervise the dress rehearsal, vanished after the opening night to drink his way through the run; heaven knows how he made it home again.

While in London, I noticed Seán was coughing badly, and looked dreadfully thin. I had gone to see him, to talk about Jacquie and her career, which then seemed set to be in theatre. She had met her father previously in London, on a getting-to-know-you expedition, but it was hopeless for both of them. They had been strangers too long, and it would have taken years for them to find each other. Seán had been home for the previous Christmas, but only briefly, and I had not then seen the signs of illness so clearly. I wanted him to see a specialist immediately, but he explained that he had already done so and, following tests, they had diagnosed chronic bronchitis. He was still smoking heavily, but denied that he felt any ill effects from this.

He added that he had been through a period of not eating, but that he had resolved to build himself up, and that I was not to worry. I asked him to go again to the specialist, and to write to me immediately he got a result, and he promised to do this. He thought Jacquie had grown into a lovely girl, but he had little to say to her, and wryly admitted that he could not understand young people any more. He still clung to the work-place he was so devoted to; they had been loyal and fair to him, and if he hadn't made a fortune, at least he had been enabled to keep his independence and self-respect. I went home the following day, full of misgivings about his well-being.

I never heard from him, or anything about him, until his sister Eibhlín telephoned us to say that he was in hospital with suspected tuberculosis. She said that all he needed was rest and care, and that he was in the right place for that. But Mother insisted that I ring the hospital and ask them to tell me the truth; she did not believe the illness was tuberculosis. I explained who I was and was put through to a lady doctor who told me that Seán had cancer in both lungs. It was of very long standing, and was terminal. I asked would I have time to reach him, and she said that there was no urgency, these things could drag on for months, unfortunately. I put the phone down, unable at first to grasp the meaning of what I had been told. There was a huge lump in my throat that stopped me from speaking or breathing. Above all, I could not cope with the thought of a long drawn-out dying.

Mother told me that I must go to London the very next morning. Jacquie was already there staying with a cousin, so she rang her, broke the news that her father was seriously ill and that I was on my way. Next, she telephoned friends, and arranged for them to book Jacquie and me into a guest-house near the hospital. Like a zombie, I began to pack. Next day Jacquie met me off the midday plane, from which we went straight to the guest-house and then to the hospital. I walked among the rows of beds looking for my husband, and found him sitting up in bed talking to a young priest. Such a smile came over his gaunt features when he saw us.

Seán was overjoyed that we would be constant visitors during his stay in hospital. It was obvious that he knew nothing of the cancer that was eating his life away. We stayed with him until evening, while he slept fitfully. Once he woke and held my hand, and said that he had been stupidly proud long enough; this time he was coming home. He whispered that all these years he had not wanted to spoil things for me, to be an invalid on my hands, but that it had been so lonely, so empty, no life at all. He dozed off again, and I told the nurse that we would go and get something to eat while he slept, and be right back. We went to a restaurant nearby, but neither of us had an appetite, and ate only to stave off exhaustion, knowing that we were facing a long night. Suddenly I felt that there was something wrong, that I had to see the chief doctor. If there were months left, why were we afraid that he would die if we left him for a minute?

We rushed back to the hospital, and I asked to see the senior consultant. It was the doctor who had spoken to me on the phone, and I asked her if someone as pale and emaciated as Seán could possibly survive for months, and she replied that there had indeed been a rapid deterioration. It tended to happen in relatively young people, and Seán was only forty-eight. They thought that the cancer had travelled to his brain, as he had been complaining of a numb feeling in his forehead. I begged her not to let him suffer any more, and she assured me that they did not permit unnecessary pain in that hospital; but she could not say how long he might live.

Jacquie was a tower of strength. She was facing the loss of a father she had not had time to know or love, but she blamed no one. She knew all the circumstances, and also sensed that Seán's stated wish to come home was a devastating emotional shock that I could not cope with, knowing the cruel truth. We went back to the hospital and sat with Seán, who was weak but very happy to see us. I had to keep talking as normally as possible, so chattered on about our company and the revue by Fergus Linehan that was packing them in at the Eblana, how the Abbey and the Gate were faring, the fortunes of his old employers Mícheál and Hilton with their wonderful one-man show *The Importance of being Oscar*. Whenever he slept, Jacquie and I would wander among the sea of white-quilted beds, smiling at the patients who had no visitors, hoping to cheer them in their loneliness.

Back at Seán's bedside, I noticed that his breathing had become erratic. Sometimes it seemed to stop; then, when panic set in and we were sure he was gone, he would sigh and appear to breathe normally again. I looked at the little locker beside his bed, and at his cigarettes, one half-smoked, in the ash-tray. The big scares had just begun to surface, and people had not yet understood or accepted that tobacco could kill.

It was very late, and Jacquie was looking so exhausted that I thought I would go and see if there was somewhere she could lie down for a while. Then I noticed that Seán, although not fully conscious, appeared to be in acute pain. I could see his face muscles tighten, and when I asked in a whisper if it was bad, he seemed to nod his head. I was out of my chair then, down the corridor calling for a doctor, a nurse, in such near-hysteria that I had to be restrained. I kept saying, 'He's in agony and you promised...' They brought me to his bedside, and administered an injection under the doctor's supervision. Jacquie looked at me. We both knew that this was the last treatment, that he would need no more and that his pain was over. The doctor told us that he would now sleep until the morning, and advised that we go to our hotel; they would ring us if there should be any change. I said that I could not go, that he had lived alone, and must not be left now. But Jacquie agreed with the doctors, saying that we were only around the corner, to be called at any time. I looked at Seán, sleeping peacefully with no sign of stress or discomfort. So I agreed to leave for a few hours.

We woke about eight the next morning, grabbed a cup of tea and hurried to the hospital. When we got to his bed, there was no one in it. I called the nurse, who said that Seán had died about six o'clock that morning. I did not believe her; no one had called us. I looked at his locker, and it was bare; his prayer book, watch and cigarettes were all gone. The senior doctor came and explained that he had died suddenly and peacefully before there was time to call us. I looked at her and accused her of keeping us from his death-bed, of knowing that he would, after that last injection, die within hours. 'Yes', she said; 'and so did you; you did not want him to suffer any more, did you?' I could not come to grips with what I had heard or seen, or what I might have contributed to my husband's last hours. Had he been needlessly alone in the end? It was too soon to pray. A nurse brought in Seán's prayer-book, but no watch, probably stolen. We learned in a daze that his body was now in the mortuary. We telephoned home, and Mother said that Eibhlín, who had been notified, was taking over the funeral arrangements if I had no objection. He was her beloved younger brother, and I did not demur. We were advised to come home and there await the arrival of the body.

We went to see Seán laid out in the chapel, and prayed. I don't know what prayers we said; it just seemed right to do it. Seán looked like all dead people look; stiff and endowed with sculptured features not his own. His hairline was his own, but nothing else. He didn't look as if he was asleep; he looked dead. We left that cheerless place and went back to the guest-house to collect our belongings. On the way Jacquie had to support me when I broke down, crying and clinging to some railings near the hospital.

I had not known what a good man Seán was. His reasons for not coming home were the essence of an unselfish, caring person who would not be a burden to any member of his family: who lived and worked in an environment unsuited to his temperament and ability and who suffered illness in solitude. That he drank latterly to subdue unbearable hurts does him no discredit. But I clung to the railings of a London street, and told Jacquie that I had never understood this good and gentle man, and that I hoped he, and she, would some day forgive me. She pondered all these things in her own time, but that day she kept me on my feet, doing whatever was necessary to get us on the flight home.

The day of Seán's funeral in Dublin the company from both Gemini plays turned out to lend support, and also many members of the acting profession who, until then, were unsure whether I was married or divorced. They came because they felt I would need company, and I did, more than they knew. My family, as always my main strength, kept my head high, and I can see the faces of Anna Manahan, Martin Dempsey, Gerry Sullivan, Jim Norton, Barry Cassin, all of them, to this day. I have no recollection of the actual burial, or of anything that happened after the coffin left the church, but I know that my dear company of friends bade me goodbye and went back to their rehearsals, and that I went home. I cried for Eibhlín, his older sister who had loved him most.

Life had to go on, and I fought against depression by working all the hours God gave. I had twice collapsed from exhaustion since taking on theatre management, once being hospitalised and having to work from a public bed, with furtive trips to a telephone in a corridor. Mother was terribly concerned that I would overdo it again, but I was beginning to notice signs of strain in her, which frightened me. If I mentioned it to her, however delicately, she would grow irritable and fractious, so I had quiet talks with Joe, who promised to try to get her to ease up. Many people called daily to get Mother to massage their limbs, but even more to soothe their minds. She would listen for hours to their troubles.

She spent the nights watching TV with Joe until bedtime, when she would come upstairs for a final cup of tea, a chat with Gregg if he was on holidays from school, and with me if I was home. Then she would do her accounts, so that it was quite late when she actually got to bed. She always rose early, and I noticed that she was becoming a bit breathless in the mornings. When I suggested, as tactfully as I could, that she go for a check-up, it caused such an outburst that I backed off. Mother had never been like this. She was the practical one, who normally went to the doctor at the first sign of anything wrong. Now the very mention of our much-loved family doctor sent her into a rage. Later she would apologise for this, and put it down to her annoyance at people (me in particular) with frail constitutions who ignored their own problems and fussed about her, who was never sick. I still worried about her, but said little.

Norman, a career in England before him, was preparing to move on, but not before he introduced me to Richard Hallinan, a businessman with a beautiful young wife, Susan, who had ambitions to become a professional actress. They were both born into money, and they were nice people, but just not on our wavelength. Richard was starting a theatrical agency, and also wanted to join Gemini as business manager in Norman's place. Norman felt this would be ideal for the continuance of Gemini, but it all depended on my reaction. I would still have full artistic control. Richard would cast each play with me and take over contracts, payments and so on, and he had an office and a secretary we could share. We all went out to dinner, and clinched the deal.

Richard was tall and handsome, with curly hair sandy in colour, and always well-groomed. Susan was petite and dark-haired, with expressive eyes like brown velvet set in a pale face, giving her appearance something close to beauty. Although it was not possible for me to warm to these two pleasant people immediately – I was, after all, losing Norman – Richard and I worked well together in the years that followed, and hung on in partnership until it was no longer possible. I grew fond of the Hallinans, although we did not have a close friendship.

As the Gemini plays poured in, and Richard and I began to work together and get used to each other, I had a new perspective on life. I had not fully recovered from Seán's death, and was still subject to nightmares caused by guilt, but I did not associate my life with Liam with any of that. I just sorrowed for Seán's wasted life, and my inability to make sense of our situation, and spoke very little about it. Liam and I met as often as possible, and walked in parks where he would quote verses about the nature of love, and I would long for the park gates to clang shut, leaving us in and everyone else out. He loved the hawthorn as I did, and one day wanted to make love under that tree, with petals falling on us like confetti. My life was rich and changed. I loved my family, Mother and my work, and now God had given me another love as deep as the others. I attributed my long years of loving Liam to the power of the Almighty, and saw no irony in two Catholic people in an extra-marital situation, giving thanks to the Lord for our happy state.

After Seán's burial, I had plunged into a work-load that would have tested an Amazon. John B Keane had asked me to produce a revised version of *The Year of the Hiker*, the cast of which included Anna Manahan, Martin Dempsey and other superb interpreters of Keane. They all excelled in the new version which de-sentimentalised the ending. The play was powerful enough to dispense with schmaltz, and Barry kept the mood of stark realism going to the end. The result was described as comparable to Ibsen by the senior critic of the *Irish Times*, Seamus Kelly, a powerful writer. He chose to deal in theatre criticism, and wrote so trenchantly that his often cantankerous reviews were almost forgiven. He could be devastating, and was probably the only critic in Ireland of whom the public took notice. A thin, red-headed Northerner with blue eyes and a thin mouth that rarely smiled, he drank more than was good for him or the theatre community.

I had a real admiration and even affection for Seamus, although we disagreed violently on many things. He had been very friendly and supportive when I was a young actress at the Abbey. I visited him as much as possible when he was dying, together with his friend and colleague David Nowlan, who inherited his position as senior critic. Seamus was deeply affected by the Keane play, and praised it highly; but later, when we tackled Eugene McCabe's *King of the Castle*, he was infuriated, saying that we had ruined a great playwright's career. I thought this seriously over the top, but had to wait for a revival of the play by the Abbey to realise that our version was nearer the mark. The Abbey production was heavy on symbolism, but lacked the earthy reality of the subject matter. Seamus then came and apologised for his earlier strictures. What he would have thought had he lived to see yet another Abbey production of the play, I cannot imagine. It defeated the play's premise by substituting an explicit sexual encounter for the original and powerful unresolved ending. It was such a travesty that I could not imagine what I had seen in the play, and went back to the script. There it was on the page, the rich and distinctive, almost brutal, dialogue that only Eugene McCabe could command.

One day, in 1965, I met the poet Brendan Kennelly outside the entrance to Trinity College, and he said that I should go to Listowel and try to get John B Keane to give me the bull! Brendan, a dedicated friend of John B, knew there was buried treasure among John B's discarded scripts, and as he spoke, I could sense that strange, almost mystical shiver down my spine that foretells a creative experience. Next day I drove to Listowel with Liam and we put the question to John B. 'We've come to look at the bull,' we said. 'Where is he?' John laughed and replied, 'In the field, but he's not for sale.' It took two days to get a promise that he would post the script of *The Field* to me. He had little confidence in it himself, but when I read it in its first draft, its power and beauty seemed to blaze from the pages and I knew that this was a great piece of writing. It was frightening too in its very truth, for it was based on a real murder in Kerry.

The rewriting of the play and the preparation for casting were unnerving times for John B and myself. John B was consciously depicting the actual murder case, in which the killer was known to everyone, but, of course, safe from the law. John B ran a public house in Listowel, which was his sole means of supporting his family while his writing skills were developing. There was always the threat that the murderer, hearing about John B's dramatic reconstruction of his crime, would retaliate, perhaps by burning down John B's premises. In Dublin, with rehearsals in progress, we felt the responsibility for the playwright's dilemma, and at one time even faced the possibility that it might be best to suppress the work. But the force of the play, plus John B's courage and that of his wife, kept us going.

One of the major difficulties facing director Barry Cassin was the transformation of the village bar-room set to the open countryside dominated by the 'field'. We had no resources to provide a revolving stage, to save crucial moments in the change-over, but we found a brilliant designer in Alan Pleass of RTE. The change was accomplished in a magical fifty seconds, noiselessly, behind closed tabs. The audience gasped when the tabs parted to disclose the countryside at night with the gate of the 'field' shining in the distance in moonlight that seemed to chill the blood. The 'Bull' McCabe and his son, Tadhg, huddled on a broken-down wall, discussing the 'antics of crows', while they waited for the man who was on his way to view the moonlit field that was to cost him his life.

The 'Bull' was not a one-dimensional villain. He could not be portrayed as merely an ignorant monster motivated by greed. He was all those things, but he was also a man who understood that the earth and grass of the fields were necessary for his survival and for that of his descendants. And he was capable of love, in his own way. A formidable challenge, indeed, for an actor. Then I heard that Ray McAnally was returning home from the West End, where he was playing the lead in *Who's Afraid of Virginia Woolf?* I sent the script to him via his wife, Ronnie Masterson, and next day Ray telephoned saying the play was wonderful, he was playing the 'Bull' and when would we start rehearsals! After that everything fell into place. We decided to open in the Olympia Theatre and then tour Ireland. The opening night was unforgettable. The hush at the end of the performance was as prolonged as the fearsome silence at the core of the play, and then was broken by the loudest ovation I have heard before or since in any theatre.

# 24

# *Myles, Flann and Brian*

Hugh Leonard revered Brian O'Nolan as a writer, and decided to contact him to ask for permission to adapt his novel *The Dalkey Archive* as a stage play. This is one of O'Nolan's funniest books, and I was enthusiastic about the project on two counts. I knew that Hugh would draw every ounce of Brian's manic humour from the book and give us a gem for the next Festival in September 1965 and I might get to know the great writer whose works I had enjoyed under the pen names of Flann O'Brien and Myles na gCopaleen. As he lived in the suburb of Stillorgan with his wife Evelyn, and was frequently seen in Dublin pubs with other literary figures, it was strange that neither Hugh nor I had met him before.

It was well-known that he had, in his time, put away more alcohol than his system could tolerate. He had been a civil servant, and it was reputed that he had tendered his resignation on the grounds that he was suffering from an incurable illness, alcoholism. Although he had rarely been seen at his desk for some time before that, he apparently received his full pension entitlement on leaving. Other stories suggested that he was accident prone, and when brought to hospital for minor injuries, could not be given anaesthetics because of his alcoholic history. This caused him to believe that the medical profession had fiendish designs on his health, and he was known for his attempts to sue any unfortunate doctor who had cause to treat him.

None of these stories encouraged admirers like Hugh and myself to force our acquaintance on the man in any social way, but *The Dalkey Archive* opened the door. Hugh's agent, a Londoner named Harvey Unna, made the first contact by letter, asking if he would be interested in having his book adapted by Hugh. The answer was quick; he was interested, and he invited Hugh, his wife Paule and myself to his home to discuss the matter. He mentioned that he had not been well, saying that it was feared that a nerve in his jaw had been damaged, causing him acute pain, but he looked forward to meeting us. We also looked forward, but with some trepidation. Not only was he a unique comic writer; he was also a brilliant scholar with a gift for languages. He had almost given Seamus Kelly a nervous breakdown by writing to his editor correcting spellings, phrases and punctuation in Kelly's daily column, especially if Irish, French or Latin had been used. Paule and I warned Hugh that we would say very little, and leave the academic stuff to him.

When we rang the bell that evening, and Evelyn answered it, we saw, sitting by the fire, a small neat man with a wax-white face and one hand pressed to his right cheek. As we came into the room Brian raised his head, two china-blue eyes regarded us and he waved us into his orbit. We intoned our names as if in the presence of divinity, and were seated beside him. He did not ask if we wanted any particular drink; just said, 'Gin all right?' and waved to Evelyn to do the honours. She, a quiet woman with great sadness in her eyes, came with a tray of crystal tumblers full to the brim with gin. Brian announced that he would have a drink with us later, and as we gazed miserably at our large drinks, said amiably, 'Drink up and then we can talk.' With his strange eyes like coloured glass boring into us, we began to sip, which provoked a further injunction to drink up.

The gin was neat, and as it burned its way down our throats, we began to talk, and to mention his books and columns. He did not deflect our praise, but gave back very little. I surmised that he was in some pain, and asked him if he was on medication for it. This galvanised him into describing his condition, which was like severe neuralgia, and he told us that he was to have further X-rays, but had no faith in any doctor's ability to diagnose or cure the complaint. The pain came and went at regular intervals, and the pills he had been given were useless. He urged us again to drink up, then gestured to Evelyn to refill our glasses, ignoring our protests. Then he began to tell us stories, mostly about people who were 'proper gobshites' who pretended they had read serious books on the best-selling lists. It was his malicious pleasure to invent book-names, and to induce a lot of right 'eejits' to claim to have read them. Pretentiousness enraged him, as did people who sneered at religion in his presence. He was, he said, a seeker after truth and an opponent of hypocrisy in all its forms; but I sensed, and found it to be true, that Brian O'Nolan was a most devout Christian.

After a while, he invited us to visit his local pub, where we could discuss the shape of the play and the proposed title – *The Saints Go Cycling In* – which I think he liked at once. The pain had abated, and he was feeling alive again so, bidding Evelyn goodbye, he marched us down to a nearby pub. He had a few drinks there and a chat with Hugh, after which we suggested that we should meet again when the play was more advanced, to discuss it and the cast. Surprisingly, he was quite willing to let Hugh forge ahead without input from himself; he knew of his reputation in theatre, and seemed to trust all of us. We left him home, thanked Evelyn for her hospitality and staggered into the night, Paule and myself falling into a flower-bed before we reached the car.

So the year began with a bang, and I had great work to look forward to. All was well with my world, with my children and the man who was only partly mine, but always there for me. I was getting on quite well with Richard Hallinan, my partner and director, although we were spiritual and mental opposites. We used his office in Aston Quay for Gemini business, and also for that of a theatrical company we started jointly, which was to bring us into conflict at a later stage. Because of their privileged background, Richard and his wife Susan had little conception of how the rest of us lived. She once told me that her weekly taxi bill equalled the salary of a freelance actor. Richard was similarly unable to grasp that the small wages we earned were what we lived on, and that many actors lived below the poverty line.

He had no instinctive love of the theatre, and it was no doubt Susan's interest that brought him to us. Gemini had, in the 1960s, an illustrious name in the business. Before he came, if any production had broken even with only the pre-production money back, and nothing to spare, I would dock my salary to make ends meet. Richard was aghast at this unbusinesslike approach. As long as he was manager, I always got my salary, and he his. If there was a loss, it went against tax. Gemini prospered, and Richard and I rubbed along fairly well. I still chose the plays and directors, and did most of the casting, withdrawing more and more from the business side. And, although it was nice to have a proper office, I worked mostly from home, as well as using pay-phones and every theatre we played in.

At home, Mother was increasingly worried about Lizzie. Our doctor had diagnosed heart disease, and she had a cancer which was not yet causing her pain; as is often the case with the elderly, it was slow to spread. Nonetheless she needed special nursing, and was taken temporarily into hospital. She did not like this one bit, but knew Mother was doing it for her health; there was always the chance that she could come back to us healthy enough to have a comfortable life in the only home she had known for most of her long years. But this was not to be. After a short time, we were told that she was dying. Lizzie went to her sleep peacefully and, as she told me on my last visit, with the sure expectation of waking up with God, and meeting her long-departed parents, brothers and sisters. She was almost radiant the last time I saw her, not at all afraid. We were all heartbroken to lose this simple, loving soul, as Dublin as the Liffey and as witty as the street sellers.

Mother had looked after our beloved minder as though she were her own flesh and blood, and her care had kept Lizzie alive long beyond the odds. I reminded her of this as she sorrowed for her lost companion, and brought her to her last resting place in Glasnevin cemetery, with all our family, the Broughals and a couple of Lizzie's nieces present. Such were the hardships of her early years that none of her immediate family, and few relatives, were alive to bid her farewell; consumption had killed off the majority of them. I can still see Lizzie's small coffin, surrounded by our flowers with our love and regret for her passing. She would never have expected that her life was so important and rich in giving; that was all she knew how to do, being without vanity. To this day Lizzie remains alive in my conversations with my children, and with their children.

Hugh was forging ahead with *The Saints*, and we were keeping in touch with Myles (as Brian was called), who was in and out of hospital. Having received a royal summons, we both went to visit him in St Anne's Nursing Home off Ranelagh Road. We pondered what to bring, and Hugh settled for whiskey while I chickened out and brought grapes and flowers. I arrived first to find him in his room reading; he put aside the book to thank me for coming and apologised that, because the doctors were trying to fry his guts, he was not in the best shape. Not wishing to get into that subject, I looked at the book, which was a scientific study by Teilhard de Chardin, the controversial Jesuit whose views and studies were considered by the Church to be so dangerous that he been forbidden to publish any more of them. Myles invited me to read and discuss the first page, but I could not understand a word of it, and said so, feeling that I was inviting dismissal. A big smile transformed his face, and I listened as he explained the text in words a child could grasp. He could have been a very great teacher.

Then he closed the book, and said with that gentleness I came to know so well, 'Most people pretend they know. You never do.' Hugh came in just then, produced the bottle of whiskey and enquired if Myles was allowed to have a nip in the hospital. Myles put the bottle under his quilt and rang the bell for the nurse. When she arrived, a fair young girl with a knowing grin, he asked her to get three clean tumblers. She returned with them immediately, and to our amazement, Myles, quite ignoring her presence, whisked out the bottle and poured out huge drinks for us and a wee one for himself. The nurse was quite unmoved by all this, and left the room briskly, laughing as she went. It transpired that she had already told Hugh on his way in that the drink would not harm Myles, but that he might not want it as he was having radiation treatment, which tended to make people feel sick. This time I ran to the wash-basin and topped up the tumbler with water, aware that Myles was watching with that mischievous grin that did not quite make it to his pain-filled eyes. We did not stay long. Hugh filled him in on the progress we had made with the play, after which we left, having stashed the bottle in his locker and promised to see him as soon as he had left hospital. Myles had cancer, but whether it was treatable remained to be discovered.

Casting *The Saints Go Cycling In*, which had parts for ten actors and one silent role for a 'mature' actress, was quite a difficult task. We had invited Denis Carey (one of the famous sons of May Carey, a well-known actress and producer who often worked for the Gate Theatre) to direct the play, and he had agreed. He had some solid West End hits to his credit, including *Salad Days*, a very successful musical. Denis left most of the casting to Hugh and me; he had been away from Ireland for a long time, and did not know the scene or what talents were available.

While all this was going on, we also had to find a cast for Tom Coffey's play *Gone Tomorrow*, due to open in the Gate a week before *The Saints*. It starred two remarkable men, Maurie Taylor and Jim Norton, who played teenagers to the manner born although they were both in their late twenties. We also had two great variety comedians, Mike Nolan and Cecil Sheridan, in leading roles; both could switch easily from pantomime to drama. To my great personal pleasure, we also acquired James Neylin, who had soldiered with us in the American tour of the 1940s. He was married now, with two children, and his English wife Joyce had given up her own acting career to be with him.

We had not seen much of him in recent years; he had a heart ailment, and rumour had it that he now preferred radio work to the more strenuous demands of the stage. According to his greatest friend, the actor Pat McLarnon, rumour had it wrong. Jim very much wanted to be back on-stage, and feared that managements were cold-shouldering him because of his illness. There was a suitable role for him in the Coffey play, and I encouraged him to take it, which he did with enthusiasm. He was handsome as ever, full of humour, and such a valuable company member that it soon dawned on me how greatly he had been missed during his absence from the theatre.

We cast *The Saints* quite easily except for the character of De Selby, a retired member of the long defunct Dublin Metropolitan Police. What was needed was a degree of knowledgeable insanity and a refined exterior, in a venerable but improbably agile body. All the other roles fell easily into place. Two young men at the centre of the action were played by Charlie Roberts as a semi-literate chancer whose brain-power was hilariously limited, and Bill Golding as his more intelligent but still gullible companion. Martin Dempsey was achingly funny as the policeman mortally afraid of riding his bicycle in case he should become one through an interchange of molecules and atoms.

Only a gifted writer could have created this comic nightmare with its demented logic, which infected the thousands of people who saw the superb adaptation. Denis Carey added a popular instrumental piece called 'A Walk in the Black Forest', which had nothing to do with anything except the lunatic ambience of the play. But we were still short of an actor to play the mad scientist, the retired DMP member now dabbling in other-world potions. Denis finally came up with the name of Newton Blick, an English actor old and young enough to meet our needs. He loved the script, and jumped at the chance to come to Ireland.

Newton was a gentleman of the old school, courteous, refined and a very good actor. Friendly and charming, he was obviously pleased to be part of a team bent on stage lunacy. The one worrying thing about him was that his only hobby was drinking, not during rehearsal or playing, but literally all the rest of the time. Denis, who knew a thing or two himself about drinking, said not to worry; Newt – so apt an abbreviation – was endangering his health, but would never threaten a show. Still, I invited Newt to come out of Dublin on Sundays and see some of our lovely countryside. He graciously declined, and countered by inviting me to his hotel bar, where he said we could discuss Irish scenery for hours without having to tire ourselves by travelling.

Both plays were now cast. Barry Cassin directed the Coffey work, in which it was good to see Jim Neylin joking and exchanging reminiscences in the old way. Tom Coffey had previously written a successful play for the Abbey called *Anyone Could Rob a Bank*, and another winner called *Them*, staged by Gemini at the Eblana, about a retarded youth who grows to manhood unaware of his sexuality until goaded by thugs into actions he does not comprehend. The injustice of his commitment to an institution, despite his manifest childlike innocence, was movingly drawn by the author, and Jim Norton's portrayal won him a wealth of critical accolades. *Gone Tomorrow* won an award in the Irish Life Drama Competition of 1965, but did not take fire. Deemed worthy and damned with faint praise, it soon sank without trace. Tom Coffey later decided that his successful business career had to come first, and ceased to write for the stage.

During this hectic time, I saw precious little of my family, and telephoned home more than I appeared there. I really tried to spend less time at rehearsals and more at home with Mother, but it was always when I wasn't there that the problems occurred at the theatre and minor rows developed. It was necessary for the companies to have somebody on the spot to refer to, and Richard was dealing with business matters in his office.

Both plays were going well. Alan Pleass, on loan from RTE, had designed an ingenious set for *The Saints*. Two revolving stages changed the setting from seascape to large rocks, De Selby's living room, and other locations by spinning the sets like giant turntables. *Gone Tomorrow* had a more ordinary setting of a village street and the interiors of comfortable houses, designed by Tomás Mac Anna, who was beginning to impinge on my consciousness in more ways than one. I had grown to admire this gentle giant of many talents who was not afraid to use words like love and magic when describing his experience of theatre. He had achieved some amazing results as director and designer, and was the only lighting designer I knew who could come even near to Hilton Edwards. I found Tomás to be a man of great kindness and compassion, and knew many actors who had benefited from his concern for his fellow workers. I always stayed close to a Mac Anna production; there was such an atmosphere of excitement, and so many ideas buzzing about. He never accepted that anything was impossible, and never panicked, so that no one else did either. He was obsessed with the Abbey and its history, and, although he was at liberty to do the occasional outside production, that was where his true loyalties always lay.

The revolving set for *The Saints* caused us some consternation during rehearsals before settling in. In contrast, the dress rehearsal of *Gone Tomorrow*, under Barry Cassin's orderly approach, was so sure and trouble-free that the cast made the usual predictions that no good would come of it on the night. The same superstition also decreed, of course, that a bad dress rehearsal meant a good show, in which case *The Saints* was clearly destined for greatness. I have never before or since seen such mayhem. The revolves did not work and special lighting effects went haywire. The actors, hitherto word perfect, began to dither and fluff their lines. Hugh Leonard, who had come to see a finished product, fled from the theatre and could not be pacified.

In the event, both shows had excellent first nights, with no hitches. There was a sense of enjoyment and achievement among the actors, and audience reactions were good, which made all the strains and stresses of the past weeks seem as nothing. Then, in the middle of the first week of the run of *Gone Tomorrow*, Jim Neylin died in his sleep. On top of that, two weeks after the opening of *The Saints Go Cycling In*, Newton Blick dropped dead while walking along a Dublin street. We were all devastated in our grief and disbelief that tragedy should strike at both shows. Replacements had to be made. Joe Lynch, always the biggest heart in the business, was free when Newton died, and came to offer his services as temporary replacement. He saved the day; the show was a smash hit, and booked out for weeks ahead. Rumours that the company was jinxed rapidly abated.

Jim Neylin had his family and all his friends to mourn him, but Newton was a loner, and it was hard to trace his relatives. Eventually a brother was located, who asked us to arrange that the burial, which he would attend, should take place in Ireland. Other actor friends of Newton's contacted us, and came from London; he was buried in Deansgrange cemetery. Curiously, he had a line in the play referring to that cemetery, and had asked where it was situated.

When the funerals were over, and *The Saints* was breaking records with a new De Selby, I went home to Mother to try to grieve properly. I couldn't cry. Liam came to see me, and talked to Mother. They both thought I should go away for a break, a notion I fiercely resisted. I knew I had to stay with the show, with the company who had carried on so bravely. Hugh and Denis had been shattered by Newt's death. Richard Hallinan had been a tower of strength, tracing Newt's relatives and friends. He and I had been called by the police to identify the body at the morgue, but that was not too terrible. Newt looked exactly the same, just dead. It seemed so sad that he should die in a strange place. James Neylin had told me that, whenever he was away from home, he rang his wife Joyce at least once a day. He was deeply devoted to her and their family, and he knew his unstable heart might let him down. He had been saying goodbye for a long time, and it was good that he died at home.

I sought the anaesthetic of more work, and I fear that, for a while, I was too frequent a visitor to Groome's hostelry. That period of drink-and-be-merry didn't last too long. I had neither the head nor stomach for such sustained drinking, and grew tired of being sick on a daily basis. Myles had been at the first night of *The Saints* and very pleased with the show, but afterwards he went back to hospital for more treatment. Now he was back home, very ill and disinclined to leave his bed, so I telephoned Evelyn and asked if I might call to see him. She said that I would be very welcome to call, but that he would see no one, nor would he attempt to get out of bed despite medical advice to make the effort. I replied that I would come if only that he might know that we missed him, and that he had our good wishes. That same afternoon I made the visit, and sat talking to Evelyn, who was depressed and under great strain. Then we heard noises from Myles's room, and Evelyn flew down the short corridor, coming back breathless to say that he was a donning a dressing gown. After a painfully long interval, he appeared, looking like a shrunken image of his former self, and barely made the short distance to the table, where he sat heavily into a chair.

He greeted me in a surprisingly strong voice, and I gave him a get well card signed by all the company, told him how much we missed him and how well the show was going. He was very still, hunched over the table, motioning to Evelyn to get me a drink. He said that he himself had no wish for food or drink, adding that his condition was due to his having offended St Augustine and one of the St Patricks by portraying them as figures of fun in book and play. They, he averred, were responsible for the medics having plotted to 'fry' him, and put him out of action. I smiled at first, thinking that he was being facetious, but realised in time that he was absolutely serious. Evelyn told me he had reached this conclusion after a particularly nasty bout of radiation sickness. I soon left, thinking as I looked at his paper-white face and wasted form that I had seen him for the last time. Incredibly, however, before the run at the Gate had ended, he telephoned to ask for seats for the final night. I sent him the tickets immediately, and got a brief note in reply saying, 'I'll be there on the last night, God willing – the bugger has let me down a lot lately.' He did come, very weak, and spoke from the stage after the performance, thanking every member of the cast and explaining to a rapt and astonished audience how the vengeance of Saints Augustine and Patrick had traumatised his life, and warning against ridiculing the saints and the unknown. He spoke so fervently and so wittily that it was impossible to believe he was dying.

A few months after the show, on 1 April 1966, Myles died. In the midst of the ceremonial grieving, I had an image of him squaring up to St Augustine, and ending the rift between them by making even God laugh.

# 25

# *Aiséirí*

In 1966 Tomás Mac Anna was commissioned by the Irish government to write and direct a pageant as part of the fiftieth-anniversary celebrations of the 1916 Easter Rising. The venue was to be Croke Park, provided free of charge by the GAA and eminently suited to Tomás's passion for big, expansive settings encompassing big, expansive themes. The aim was to represent the ideal of Irish republicanism from the French Revolution and Wolfe Tone to Cathal Brugha's reaffirmation of the Easter week proclamation to the first Dáil assembly in 1919.

I hadn't a notion that I would be involved in this massive undertaking, and already had a full year planned at the Gate and Eblana. But when Tomás phoned and asked me to do the casting, I accepted with indecorous haste. I was truly excited to be part of such an epic event, and it was unlikely that I would ever again work in Croke Park. The casting proved enjoyable; as I read the script, I put faces and voices on the many characters, sometimes assigning more than one role to gifted mimics among the acting fraternity. Tomás summoned me to a meeting involving the army and the FCA, who were needed to supply redcoats, insurgents, croppy boys, citizen armies and British Tommies. At the meeting, Tomás described each of our responsibilities on a blackboard. One colonel was responsible for 'blowing up the field', another would provide troops for both sides of each battle. I was to find twelve trained horses and riders accustomed to explosives and firearms, one hundred assorted boy scouts, thirty-two actors for speaking parts and a singer who could fill Croke Park with the help of special sound systems; the list seemed endless.

At the end of the session I approached Tomás, pointing out that I had never cast horses before, not to mention boy scouts and other extras. As usual, he simply beamed and assured me that I should have no problem. A few weeks later, I had tracked down the required number of non gun-shy horses and men, who had featured in a recently completed film, *The Blue Max*, and rang Tomás proudly to tell him the good news. 'Well done', he said, 'but we can't use them after all; the GAA won't allow horses in Croke Park, because of the damage to the ground.' He never realised how close I came to walking out on him.

That pageant was one of my greatest theatrical experiences. I engaged Mícheál Mac Liammóir to speak the linking dialogue without having to appear, and his magnificent voice soared across Croke Park, alternately in English and Irish. The army band provided stirring music, and searchlights swept the ground and sky with green, white and orange colours. Jimmy Bourke supplied excellent costumes. I cast my net wide, catching the many voices of Thomas Studley in seven different characters, Patricia Cahill singing beautifully, Dearbhla Molloy, John Kavanagh, Bernadette McKenna and many others starting to make a name on the Irish stage, all from the Brendan Smith Academy. Cecil Sheridan, playing a worker from the 1913 lockout, was removed by a burly military policeman, accused of being a layabout gatecrashing the show. He was eventually rescued, stammering and furious, using language that even the army found novel. Tomás handled the huge crowds, armies, actors and citizens with relish, the army entered into it all with enthusiasm and Croke Park was blown up twice nightly with tremendous realism. It was a mighty experience, and only the bitter cold and storms of that April kept audiences at bay, and almost blew the participants off the battle-field. RTE televised the spectacle, with poor results because of bad lighting and inadequate resources.

Only one casting I made was disputed by Tomás and, indeed, by everyone else. I wanted Ray McAnally for the role of Patrick Pearse. He was almost the opposite in appearance to that popular photo of Pearse, carefully posed so that his profile was cleanly etched and his badly turned eye was hidden. But I insisted, knowing that Ray would look more like Pearse than that photo before the show began and certainly no one doubted his ability to play the character. So I arranged that one evening Ray would knock on the door of the director's viewing box above the field, and enter in full Pearse regalia, with the face he had built from skin-masks sent from England and a totally changed hairline. When he walked into that box, Tomás and the army officials thought they were seeing a ghost,

the spirit of Pearse himself. It was a magnificent impersonation, and
a talking point in theatre for some time.

That pageant could have been staged only by Tomás Mac Anna,
and my admiration for him soared, even though the icy weather
eclipsed some of his more brilliant effects, blowing large props
about and dampening the splendid display of fireworks. Sadly, few
punters could brave the elements and freeze in the hard seats of
Croke Park. Despite everything, none of the actors involved would
have wished to be anywhere else.

Then it was back to the Eblana, where I had a Gemini
commemoration programme to open, directed by Barry Cassin. This
was to be an evening of poems, prose and mini-scenes strung
together by Eamon Keane, brother of John B, into an idealistic
appraisal of the 1916 Rising and titled *Victory Is Less Than Defeat*.
Eamon was a luminous actor, a gentle, sad personality who really
could not cope with the tribulations of life. The show's second half
was a one-act play by Eugene McCabe called *Pull Down a
Horseman*. This took the form of a discussion between Pearse and
Connolly about the Rising. Pearse wanted it so that the beauties of
Ireland, enhanced by freedom, should pass into the safe-keeping of
future generations. Connolly, hard-headed and realistic, cared for the
material welfare of the people and fought to alleviate their poverty.
The contrast between the two idealists was brought out with vivid
power by the author, who developed the play from an idea by Liam
Mac Gabhann. T P McKenna was a riveting Pearse, and Niall Toibin
brought such power to his portrayal of Connolly that I felt I knew
the hearts of these men for the first time.

I worked with Niall Toibin often in later years, in times of great
stress for that actor and even greater for me. Many times theatres
echoed to explosions of anger and frustration, and many times he
swore, or I did, that we would not work together ever again. But
since half that noise we engendered grew out of my lack of
tolerance, and Niall's inability to drink without turning into a hostile
alien, our mutual respect and affection won the day again and again.
He has always been so talented, a brilliant mimic and comedian, and
a powerful actor.

This was a year that held the best and worst in company
relationships. At least I was able to take my moods and frustrations
home to Mother and Joe, who was very canny about people, and
could always see the reason behind sometimes bizarre behaviour.

The two of them still went to the pictures every week, to the Stella in Rathmines. They really loved their night out, and when they came back the entire story of the film would be discussed in detail. I marvelled at how happy they were, and the first pangs of dissatisfaction with my situation began to stir. Liam was not a free agent, and no matter what I had said or thought in the first flush of our romantic involvement, I was beginning to suffer from symptoms common to any woman who falls in love with a married man.

There were worries too about Jacquie, who wished to marry a young actor she met in a TV show in London, a handsome, rebellious Romeo who seemed to spend more time tormenting his wealthy parents than in getting on with his own career. Mother and I knew that Jacquie was of an age to decide her own future; and who was I to remonstrate when my own impulsive union with Seán had caused such widespread unhappiness? I went over to London to meet the parents of Jacquie's amour, and had coffee, which I detest, served on a silver tray, with an optimistic, bemused English lady who thought that a girl as beautiful and talented as Jacquie must be the answer to her son's problems. I made a bid for time, for a year or so to pass so that the two could know each other better, but was swept aside in a torrent of accusations; how could anyone want to spoil the happiness of these young people? It was clear that she wished me back on the other side of the Irish Sea.

So they got married and had a couple of good years before the groom said goodbye to married bliss – but not to Jacquie, whom he adored – and joined a Buddhist community. Jacquie, when it came to the crunch, told him he could not have it both ways, and pushed him into his new calling. As celibacy was his undertaking and not hers, she felt divorce was inevitable. Mother and I were glad when the matter was legally settled without rancour. Since Jacquie only came home for brief visits at Christmas, we worried about her, but not on any financial score; she was very intelligent, and had a bewildering ability to find new jobs and challenges. She had thought of writing a book about her adventures in the work-place since her career as an actress had been cruelly ended by an allergy to certain kinds of lighting, perfume and make-up. This caused brief periods of unsightly eye inflammation and facial swelling. The best specialists in Ireland and England could not find a cure, and the allergy cut short what would certainly have been a distinctive acting career. It took Jacquie a long time to come to terms with her misfortune, but she did, and got on with her life.

Mother was unable to come with me to London to see Jacquie, as her own mobility was now limited, and telephoning did not seem enough. It was around then that Gregg came into his own. He grew very close to his beloved grandmother, who lived for the holidays when he was home from school. They became confidantes; despite his tender years, he had a rare understanding of older people. Ray McAnally, a frequent visitor to our home during our productions together, often engaged him in conversations about cars, trains and other mechanical inventions far removed from theatre. They both regretted the abandonment of steam vehicles and trams, and Ray found their exchanges refreshing. Like so many gifted people, he had disliked talking shop outside the job in hand.

Siobhán McKenna also loved to discuss a variety of subjects rather than engage in the incestuous theatre prattle which tended to leave non-practitioners out in the cold. She was now an international star, more likely to be in Europe or America than in the country she loved. Whenever Siobhán came home, I would meet her, always with the same gathering of friends around her like a queen with her courtiers. She had such a vivid personality and warmth of nature that she drew all eyes wherever she went. Like Mícheál Mac Liammóir, she was the centre of any gathering wherever she appeared; but she also gave freely of herself to those in the humblest of positions who sought her advice. Of all my friends, Siobhán was the one I felt most privileged to know well, not only because of the greatness of her talent, but also because she was such a lovely person. She was full of life and of love, and insisted that we should spread it around. Of course, she could also be tempestuous and formidable if her trust was betrayed, or if any of her friends was unjustly treated.

I loved the times when Siobhán was in town; she came in and out of my life like a vision, bringing colour and warmth and a sense of majesty. We always plotted *our* show, the play that we would do together; but those times were hectic for both of us, and our plans were thwarted by our heavy commitments. It was to be many years before we achieved our wish to work together on a play, although we did manage to arrange occasional poetry and play readings. In 1965 Siobhán went into management at the Gaiety, producing Shaw's *Captain Brassbound's Conversion*, and told me afterwards that this venture had been the most frightening of all her theatre activities.

In 1966, incredibly, Gemini again presented two plays at the Dublin Festival. At the Gaiety we had *Cemented With Love* by the recently deceased Belfast playwright Sam Thompson, which left me with some of the worst memories of my career. The other play, at the Gate, was *Mick and Mick*, by Hugh Leonard, by now a Festival/Gemini institution. It was developed from an original TV play by Hugh, and starred Maureen Toal and Joe Lynch in a larger-than-life portrayal of, I suppose, Irishness. It was directed by Guy Verney, a distinguished guest from English TV, who was a delightful person and easy to work with.

Barry Cassin was to direct *Cemented With Love*. We shared the same admiration for the late Sam Thompson, and regarded his plays as early prophecies about developments in Northern Ireland. This play explored the conflict between sectarianism and tolerance as played out between the generations. Ray McAnally and Jim Norton, the first at the peak of his profession and the other on his way there, took the roles of father and son. Ray played an ageing Orangeman who had raised his only son to inherit his tradition of bigotry and sectarian hatred. Jim played the sensitive and gentle offspring who had the strength to defy the corrupt system and even the father he loved.

Ray had a weakness in approaching unsympathetic roles, being reluctant to be saddled with the image of a cruel or unlikable character. Now he began subtly to soften up his hardline character. Barry Cassin, who had worked with Ray before, found himself up against a stone wall, and it gradually began to seem as if the son's rebellion was undermining his old dad's traditional faith and beliefs. At this point Barry called me into what was becoming a controversy. I pointed out to an adamant Ray that his interpretation was clearly against the author's intention. Sam's widow was sending her solicitor to see the rehearsals the following week, and, if he was dissatisfied, we might not have a play to argue about. Ray said he was acting for the good of the play. I responded that his part was so strong that even if the audience hated his character, they would never forget it. Jim contended that his role would become meaningless if the father were to emerge as the righteous one.

It was agreed that the outcome would depend on the powerful final scene, where the son tells his father that he can no longer live with the past, and must leave home to find his future. He tears an orange lily from his lapel, and throws it defiantly on the ground. This scene is clearly the son's, whose final words are moving and memorable. The playwright had given the father virtually nothing to say, and there was no way the situation could be reversed. We felt secure. Ray could have his moments, and play on the audience's emotions – no one could do that better – but at the finish, the son would triumph and so would the play.

The following morning Ray came to rehearsal with a slight change to his script, which sought to adjust what he called the emotional balance. The Orangeman now had a point, suddenly becoming a lonely old man, deserted by his turncoat son; and Ray left us in no doubt that this was how he would perform the last scene. Barry lost his temper and threw his cup of tea against the scenery. The screaming recriminations and name-calling abated only when it was announced that the solicitor had arrived to see a full rehearsal.

When it came to the final scene, Ray played it just as he had said he would in his new version. When the rehearsal ended, the solicitor approached Barry and myself, and bluntly informed us that the production was a travesty of Sam Thompson's intentions, and that he would get an injunction to prevent it appearing in the Festival the following week. I phoned Brendan Smith to arrange a meeting, and also bearded a white-faced Ray, told him that we had no play as a result of his changes, and summoned him to a meeting at the Festival offices.

Since *The Field* the previous year, I had been best friends with Ray and, while I had heard of mood-changes and difficulties from others, this was my first experience of his other side. Brendan Smith, at the meeting, tried to reason with Ray and with the solicitor, explaining how the withdrawal of the play would affect the Festival, the Gaiety, future fund-raising etc. The solicitor replied that he was there on behalf of Sam Thompson, and would see his wishes upheld, or else. I wearily suggested that Ray might drop the few lines that changed the final scene so drastically, and that he might sharpen the character enough to validate the author's clear intention. Finally, Ray said that he would not put Brendan Smith's plans in jeopardy; as to myself, Gemini, Barry and – glaring at the solicitor – others who knew damn-all about theatre, he would make sure that he did not make the mistake of involving himself and his reputation with such a bunch of insensitive incompetents again.

We went ahead with the dress rehearsal, the technicals and costume calls, while not a word was spoken by Ray to Barry or me.

Jim Norton, understandably apprehensive, told me he was dreading the opening night. He was not alone. Barry, despite the hostilities, directed the play superbly, showing his talents at their highest peak. *Cemented With Love* opened to audience acclaim and a rapturous press. Ray did not alter a line of the script in the final scene. When Jim threw the orange lily on the ground and left the old man alone on-stage, Ray swayed a little as though he had been struck, picked up the crushed flower with trembling hands, looked with misting eyes at the departing figure of his son and let his head sink slowly to his chest as the curtain fell. It was a consummate piece of acting which engaged the sympathy of everyone in the audience. The old blackguard on the stage made mincemeat of us all without stepping outside the agreement reached with the Thompson family. By heavens, I hated his guts that night, but somewhere inside a hallelujah sounded at the sheer audacity of that last, tragic gesture.

After all that trauma, I was in no mood to face another epic. The rights of a play which had swept America and the international scene, *Who's Afraid of Virginia Woolf?* by Edward Albee, became available at the same time as the Olympia Theatre announced that there were three weeks vacant there from the end of November, into December. It was perilously close to Christmas, a bad time for theatre. Still, it was tempting. I told Richard that I would take the chance if we could get T P McKenna to play the male lead. In a cast of four, a mature married couple and a younger pair, the senior roles were the more difficult and challenging. The play was something of a marathon, over three hours long, and physically and emotionally demanding. We were lucky, and got T P McKenna for the lead, joined by Susan Hallinan, ideally cast as the ingénue wife and an actor from Northern Ireland, Bill Morrison, as her husband. The female lead was harder to come by, but fortune smiled on us, and a beautiful Canadian actress, Katherine Blake, who had already had a huge hit in the role, accepted our offer to come and play it in Dublin.

With Barry Cassin directing, we opened as planned in the Olympia, with an early start at 7.30 pm because of the play's length, and packed the theatre for the three available weeks. The beautiful writing, with its merciless exposures of human frailties, put the audience through an emotional wringer. If we had the theatre for three months instead of weeks, Richard and I would have made a lot of money. As it was, we had to be content with ecstatic reviews, a tiny profit margin and the joy of putting on a near-masterpiece.

# 26

# *Swings and Roundabouts*

Although numb with the past year's activities, I had nevertheless propelled myself into a co-production with my friend Brendan Smith, affectionately known as Mr Theatre. We had chosen *The School for Wives,* by Molière, and had cast Godfrey Quigley in the main role, with Pat McLarnon in strong support. This gracefully amusing period piece proved to be an attractive holiday offering. I spent St Stephen's Day at the dress rehearsal, and that evening at the first night, and did not get home at all to partake of the usual festivities. When Jacquie was home, she went out with Gregg, visiting other young friends. I alone missed out on the relaxation of the day. I wondered why I persisted in overcrowding an already packed schedule with yet another play.

Some time later, when I was having a drink with Siobhán McKenna in Neary's of Chatham Street, she gave me part of the answer. 'Gemini is the chief employer of actors today, because of the amount of plays you produce. You feel guilty when actors approach you, and you have no work for them. That's part of it, and the rest is, you love doing it!' Siobhán usually managed to hit the nail on the head. I still see her so vividly, the broad face with its high cheekbones, devoid of make-up; her tall wide-hipped frame moving with long strides down a Dublin street. How often, as she walked down Grafton Street, she was accosted by flower sellers or buskers seeking autographs or just conversation. I never saw her refuse them, or be less than gracious. If I ever got angry with the more aggressive overtures, she would remind me that these were the people who paid our wages. When she was making a public appearance, launching an art exhibition or opening a fête, she could look incredibly glamorous.

Gemini began touring in the 1960s, and the Cork Opera House became almost a second home. More and more we were relying on Pat Murray's splendid designs for Festival and touring shows. We had our biggest theatrical disaster in Cork with Tom Coffey's *Anyone Can Solve A Crime*, due in great measure to the late arrival of the script, but we also had smash hits with *The Field*, Brian Friel's *Lovers* and other plays. Under the caring eye of Pat Murray, our worst experiences in Cork were almost as enjoyable as our successes. He introduced us to his friends in great numbers, and our time there was filled with invitations to private homes as well as public functions. How much Gemini appreciated our reception at the Cork Opera House is on record. We premiered three major plays there, and it was always the first date we booked when touring, followed by Limerick, Sligo, Tralee, Galway and anywhere else we could get in.

Hugh Leonard had a brilliant idea for our next Festival production. He wanted to adapt James Joyce's magnificent short story *The Dead* for the stage. It was to be preceded by his original one-act play *The Late Arrival of the Incoming Aircraft*, to form a complete contrast in styles. *The Dead* is so delicately crafted, so redolent of an earlier and more gracious era in Dublin society, and so heart-breakingly sad. I longed to see this come to life, trusting Hugh's ability to conjure from the page a version true to Joyce. Sound but uninspired, Barry Cassin once more was top of my list of directors. I saw this as a watershed for him. This time I would demand from him all the qualities I had seen him apply to his best work. The magnitude of the task ahead would, I felt, release him from the self-deprecation which had prevented him from reaching the peak of which I knew him to be capable. He was thrilled with the assignment, and we made a pact that there would be no holds barred. No ego would be permitted to dominate, or upset this applecart. As the exact location, and even the probable house in which the first scene took place, were well known, we had to have a top designer. The second scene moved to a room in the Gresham Hotel, and snow falling throughout the action was imperative. We both said 'Pat Murray' and 'snap', and went to fuel our excitement with a large pot of tea. Barry had some time earlier joined Ray McAnally on the wagon, believing that he, too, had developed a drink problem. Both these men dismissed drink from their lives, and went on to do better work than ever before.

Meantime, an Irish writer named Críostóir Ó Floinn, who wrote mainly in Irish, submitted an unusual play to the Festival called *The Order of Melchizedech*. It had a lot of promise, and featured a young girl named Mary who convinces a naive priest that she is pregnant without having had any male contact. He runs away with her as a protector, but is destroyed when she admits that she is no virgin, but a virago seeking vengeance on the Church for imaginary slights. The play needed cutting, and delicate handling if it were not to degenerate into melodrama. The author proved too sensitive about his own work, resisted any changes in the script and deplored the few cuts that were made. Melodrama ruled, and the plot lost whatever credibility it might have had. Ronnie Walsh, playing the priest, was often late for rehearsal, but the last straw was when he did not turn up at all for the dress rehearsal, unnerving his fellow performer and causing an unsteady first night that added to our difficulties.

The play was not successful. Ronnie Walsh was apparently working on another project when he went missing, something he had neglected to mention when he signed his contract. He was not, however, entirely responsible for the demise of the play after a week's run. There were the tensions caused by the author who was not in tune with what we were trying to achieve. In addition, our leading lady, the fine actress Aideen O'Kelly, was distracted by Ronnie's outrageous comings and goings. There was no way the play could build or survive.

Well, if one side of the seesaw was on the ground, the other was soaring as I watched *The Dead* unfold under Barry Cassin's sure direction. Mícheál Mac Liammóir, home from fresh triumphs abroad with his *Oscar* show, told me that he was looking forward to seeing it. He loved the story as I did, and promised to come on the first night. Mícheál often came to our shows, but I could never persuade Hilton Edwards to come. His excuses were often bizarre, and indeed he did not intend them to be convincing. Hilton always decided in advance that he would not see anything worthwhile, and thought the critics had lost their reason if they overly praised anything not from the Edwards/Mac Liammóir stable.

We had a wonderful cast, once again headed by Anna Manahan, with Helen Robinson as her sister, the two hostesses of the evening. In the story the lives of the characters are revealed with insight and clarity, so that we come to know them intimately. I had, in my own childhood, attended evenings so much like that one that I felt part of that vision of innocent pleasure. The cast loved every minute of rehearsals, except perhaps that fine actor, Jim Norton. He may have been too young to enter into the full complexity of the older Gabriel. His approach to the role was exceptionally honest, and he was emotionally perfect, but he was too young to be totally convincing.

Martin Dempsey, the actor-singer who had graced many Gemini plays and revues, played Mr Browne, described in the story as extremely talkative. At the first rehearsal, leafing through the script, Martin remarked that this garrulous man had only two short speeches in the entire play. This is the nature of adaptations; it is not possible to retain every speech, or indeed every character. Martin's comment was rewarded by Hugh Leonard, who added more lines to the role. Conor Evans was a brilliant, boozy Freddy, and Brenda Fricker, young and impossibly pretty, was a perfect maid-of-all-work. Pat Murray's set was superb, so much so that when the curtain went up there was a prolonged round of applause from an audience. It featured large windows with snow visibly falling, and lightly landing on the sills in soft piles. Inside, all was warmth and bustle, a marvellous impression of high ceilings with a chandelier in the main room. Behind a closed door music played and dancers moved, becoming visible as the doors opened to allow couples to come in for refreshments.

There were some problems with the set, as the final scene took place in a bedroom in the Gresham Hotel, 1907-style, and part of the set was built to revolve. The changes had to be rehearsed until the least possible time had elapsed between the end of the dance scene and the arrival of Gabriel and Gretta at the hotel. The lighting was complicated: there were no memory boards or other computerised aids at that time; changes were effected by stage directors cueing the lighting man by intercom. After the technical run-through came the dress rehearsal, the last chance to get it right before the night. The curtains opened to reveal the set at first dimly lit, then brightening to reveal the windows with snowflakes gliding down the panes – but such snow! The flakes hit the ground with a thump, followed by a flurry landing back-stage making a noise like bottles breaking. An enraged Pat Murray leapt onto the stage, while the cast, and myself, collapsed in helpless laughter. A well-intentioned stage hand had swept up the snow used in the previous rehearsal without noticing that pieces of wood, nails and other debris were also in the snowdrift.

The abiding memory I have of that production was born in a drab room half-way through rehearsals for the play. Barry Cassin stopped the actors during the dining-room scene and said: 'I think we'll just freeze this moment in time. Everyone must stop moving as if turned to stone, a cue will be given and the lights will change.' This became a perfect moment, an exquisite frieze framed by Pat Murray's evocative set. There was an audible gasp from the audience as time stopped; then everything came to life again as though nothing had happened. The transition to the Gresham Hotel worked smoothly, as did the last heart-breaking scene where Gretta (Maureen Toal) mourns the young man who, long ago, had died for love of her, and Gabriel realises that he can never awaken such a passion of feeling in his wife.

I am proud of this production in a special way. Mícheál Mac Liammóir wrote beautiful letters to us, full of warm praise, delighting in an artistic vision brought to full fruition. The critics quite lost the run of themselves, and raved about the show from start to finish. One again Hugh Leonard and James Joyce, a powerful alliance, spurred us on to the kind of luminous experience that theatre is, or should be.

I came home from the final night to find Mother in bed, refusing to see a doctor. Etta blurted out something about Mother fainting in the cinema. Joe shut the bedroom door gently behind us, and we went down to the front room. He told me that Mother had almost fallen on the way into the cinema, and an usher had got a chair for her. Her colour was bad, and she sounded as if she were snoring. After a few minutes, she opened her eyes, sipped a little water and insisted on going on into the cinema, not wanting Joe to miss it. They got a taxi home and, after Etta had made her some tea, she consented to go to bed. She was perfectly all right, she insisted, just a 'turn'; a word which could cover anything from a tummy-ache to a heart attack. I ran upstairs and demanded that she let me call Philip McMahon, her friend and doctor, but she begged me not to; it was too late, and she might see him in the morning. I told her there was no might about it, and stayed in her room that night, in the little bed that used to hold Jacquie in her teen years. I didn't sleep, but stayed awake and daydreamed about *The Dead*, and the snow falling on the young man's grave.

Dr McMahon lived ten minutes away, so I gave Mother a cup of tea and told her he was on his way. She was not pleased, saying that he had better be quick, as she had a day's work to do. The doctor came and went, and I had to follow him to the door to ask what was wrong. He just said, 'Your mother knows what to do,' and left abruptly. When I questioned her, she said that she had a tired heart, and that she was to take things easy and rest more; it was not serious. She was to avoid stairs as much as possible; no pills or alarm bells, and she wanted nobody to fuss over her and upset Joe. It was agreed that she would come downstairs in the mornings to work, and go up again at night, with no climbing in between. I went to the theatre with a heavy heart. I began telephoning Mother every day, wherever I was, to check on her and see if there was anything she wanted.

Christmas was almost upon us again, and no more scares. I wrote to my sister Doris, now in San Francisco, who was anxious but relieved. Jacquie was certain that I was, as usual, over-reacting. She had a theory that I was so conscious of how small the family unit was that I was in constant fear of it being diminished, and there may have been truth in that. Joe was restored to his usual quiet contentment. I began to plunge more and more into theatre activity, planning poetry readings, finding new plays and devising schemes for letting the Eblana theatre to other companies on a more extensive basis so that Gemini could tour more. I loved going into the country, and what reward there was when audiences flocked to our shows and invited us back. In between our major plays, we presented revues, sometimes made up of satirical songs and sketches by various authors, including Wesley Burrowes, and one-off contributions from journalists who specialised in humorous articles. But most of our successful revues came from the pen of Fergus Linehan, for many years unrivalled in the field. They generally starred his wife, Rosaleen Linehan, one of the most subtle and versatile comediennes in the business. Other members of this small but lucrative string to the Gemini bow were noted actors Niall Buggy, Des Keogh, Gerry Alexander, Frank Kelly, Angela Vale, Anna Manahan, Anita Reeves and Dearbhla Molloy, then the baby of the group, now an internationally renowned actress and unashamedly my favourite. Dearbhla is honest to the point of danger, caring and kind, and I cherish her almost as a second daughter.

Many other actors joined the Gemini/Linehan revue team from time to time. The young Brenda Fricker, now the winner of a Hollywood Oscar, took part in a show that brought her to the attention of a British TV casting director. Joe Pilkington, Martin

*Contd on p. 253*

John B Keane. His magic touch as a playwright and his appeal to audiences through his vivid characters and poetic dialogue helped to subsidise Gemini for many years. He remains a close and dear family friend.

1963. Mai McFall, Stage Director for Gemini Productions. Mai was a loyal and trusted friend, and stage director par excellence.

'Oh, I do like to be beside the seaside!'
1965. Cecil Sheridan in a Gemini production of *The Good Old Days* at the Eblana Theatre. This show was a joyous experience for me.

1965. A Gemini production of John B Keane's *The Field* at the Limerick Theatre Festival. Here the stranger, Robert Carrickford, is warned by the local publican not to bid for 'The Widow's Field'. *Left to right*: Cecil Sheehan, Robert Carlisle, Áine Ní Mhuirí, Geoff Golden, Arthur O'Sullivan, Ann Rowan and Robert Carrickford.

1966. Rosaleen Linehan and Des Keogh in *Funnybones*, by Fergus Linehan, at the Eblana Theatre.

1968. Ray McAnally was delighted with the moustache and beard he grew for some film or other, but he had to shave both off shortly after this photo was taken!

1969. Marie Kean as the first 'Big Maggie' in John B Keane's play of the same name, with Gerry O'Sullivan as the 'Commercial Traveller'.

December 1970. A Gemini production of Fergus Linehan's *Black Rosie*
at the Eblana. Niall Buggy and Brenda Fricker played young lovers in
this, perhaps Fergus Linehan's best revue. Niall recently won an
Olivier Award for comedy, and is also a leading actor in film and on
TV. Brenda made her career in England on stage and screen, and
won an Oscar for her performance as the Mother in the film *My Left
Foot* directed by Jim Sheridan. Both actors come back to Ireland
regularly to work.

1970. Myself as Artistic Director of the first Limerick Theatre Festival, at a presentation by the Mayor of Limerick, Councillor P Liddy.

1970. Dearbhla Molloy has progressed from sweet, pretty juvenile roles in the 70s to Gertrude in *Hamlet* in the Gaiety for the Renaissance Theatre Company, and Phaedra at the Gate in 1996. Some leap!

1971. Ray McAnally as Mr Barrett and Kate Flynn as Elizabeth in *The Barretts of Wimpole Street*. Here, Mr Barrett is telling his daughter to be careful who she trusts, and to follow his advice in all things.

1972. Maureen Toal and Anna Manahan in *Sweet and Sour*. After eight months in the longest-running revue in the history of Irish theatre, these two actresses veered decidedly towards the sour!

1973. Frank Kelly playing Oliver in the Gemini production of Hugh
Leonard's *Da*. Frank has a devastating wit, and caused as much
laughter off stage as on. He has a remarkable comic talent, with a
serious side to his nature that rarely shows.

1973. The Irish première of *Da* was directed by James Waring. John McGiver, shown here, gave a breathtaking performance, notable for stillness and economy of movement and gesture.

Gemini on tour with Neil Simon's play *The Gingerbread Lady*, directed by Ray McAnally. *Left to right:* Dearbhla Molloy, Anna Manahan, Philip O'Brien and Claire Mullen.

1974. Gemini on tour with *Da*. Edward Golden as Da with Kevin McHugh as Charlie Now.

Myself, Artistic Director of Gemini Productions.
Still dreaming...what's next?

Dr Conor Cruise O'Brien and I in 1975. There but for a quirk of fate goes — a playwright? He wrote some interesting works for theatre, including *King Herod Explains*, which starred Hilton Edwards at the Gate Theatre.

1975. The front cover of a programme for the first season of the
Irish Theatre Company.

1975. Des Keogh as Elyot and Deirdre Donnelly as Amanda in Gemini's production of Noel Coward's *Private Lives* at the Eblana Theatre. Directed by Robert Gillespie and co-starring Alan Stanford and Deirdra Morris, this production was critically acclaimed as the best in Europe.

1981. A gala tribute given for me by members of the theatrical profession.
*Left to right:* Denis Johnston, myself, Hilton Edwards and Brendan Smith. Hilton
Edwards, who was gravely ill at the time, left his hospital bed to attend the Gala
held in my honour. I will never have a greater tribute. Sadly, these three famous
men have passed on.

1983. Garrett Keogh, Jane Brennan and Ruth Hegarty in the Gemini production of *Play it again Sam* at the Belltable Arts Centre. The gifted Garrett gave a wonderful impersonation of Woody Allen in the play.

1985. Siobhán McKenna and Maureen Potter in *Arsenic and Old Lace* presented at the Gaiety Theatre by Gemini Productions and Gaietystage, and directed by William H Chappell, at the Dublin Theatre Festival. The two old ladies are alarmed at the antics of their weird nephew, who has had his face altered by plastic surgery to resemble Frankenstein's monster. Siobhán and Maureen were such fun to work with that this became one of the happiest companies and the happiest show ever staged by Gemini.

Hugh Leonard, a great and ever-loyal friend, gave Gemini eleven
wonderful years of Festival plays.

*Contd from p. 228*

Dempsey, Alan Stanford, David Kelly and Pat Leavy were also involved, and most of the players mentioned were also in many Gemini dramas. Versatility was the order of the day in revue, and this ability carried them with distinction into their future careers.

Vicious rumours often branded Richard Hallinan and myself as business moguls feeding upon a community of actors too poor to put up a fight for their just dues. As Richard had a decent office space on Essex Quay and ran an agency, it was assumed that we must be making fortunes. If a play had a long run to full houses, we were definitely in the millionaire bracket, and the plays that lost money were never entered into the equation. The truth was that we were paying for the losers with the winners, and often waited for our own salaries until the end of a run. The times were hard, for us as well as our companies. Richard was hurt and furious when he heard the uninformed criticisms of a minority, while I retreated more and more into my own phantom reality.

The Abbey staged Brian Friel's *The Loves of Cass Maguire* and Brendan Behan's *Borstal Boy* that year, both enormously successful. Siobhán came back to play the title role in *Cass Maguire*, and her portrayal seamlessly blended and heightened the tragedy and comedy with that extra power she alone possessed. She was unforgettable, like the play, for me one of Brian Friel's most lyrical and moving dramas. Brian, now an internationally recognised playwright, had become a dear friend as our lives in theatre criss-crossed. He is today as generous and warm-hearted as ever, having come through his own dark night of the soul, and wrestled with the demons of self-doubt and near-despair that seem to attend on greatness.

Christmas 1967, revue-time in the Eblana, and the family had gathered as usual. The toast was given as usual by Mother, that we should all be together in love and plenty this time next year, God willing. How heartily we applauded the sentiment, we who been scared stiff by her indisposition earlier in the year. Earlier that morning, Liam had called with his dog for his now customary drink with us, to wish us all prosperity and write secret words of love on my note-pad. We exchanged gifts on Christmas Eve, and bought each other elaborate cards on which we wrote tender messages to add to the printed ones, always ending with 'forever' or 'always'.

I was conscious that, whereas I kept his card on display for the season, he either hid mine or kept it in his office; certainly he could not bring it home.

The new year dawned, and it seemed set to be a good one. We always saw Hugh Leonard and his family at Christmas, and he always seemed to have half-a-dozen ideas for a play, from which he would eventually select the one he most wanted to write. This year, after the artistic triumph of his adaptation of *The Dead*, he was writing an original play with a devilishly subtle plot. Involved as he was in writing plays for TV, both here and in the UK, he had to make a start on his new work for the next Festival early in the year so as to have it ready no later than August.

Among other things, I wanted to mount *The Anniversary* by Bill Macilwraith for Marie Conmee. She had not played for us in a long time, mostly as a result of her partner, a most possessive lady who was extremely aggressive when drunk, which she often was. An offer of work to Marie was often construed by Mary Brady, her friend, to be an offer of something else. Most people in the theatre were terrified of her, and Marie's career suffered. She was aware of this, but she was a loyal and loving soul who would not desert her friend. While all I knew of Mary Brady was unattractive and threatening, perhaps there was another, softer side to her, the one which had made Marie her devoted friend and lover. Drink was a huge factor in both their lives.

It was during a row between the two, when Marie was on her own, that I approached her to play the role of the mother in *The Anniversary*, a larger-than-life character played originally in a film of the same name by Bette Davis. She was delighted, and I felt that the part might well restore her to her proper place of prominence in her profession.

Preparing for this show, with the revue *Darts* still running in the Gate, and Brendan Smith anxious for a Gemini production of Tom Murphy's new play *The Orphans*, I became more relaxed with regard to domestic worries. Then one evening in early April I went upstairs with a cup of tea for Mother, to find that she had collapsed near her bedside, half bent over the candlewick quilt. Her eyes were closed, and she was breathing in a dreadful, rasping manner. I tried to lift her on to the bed, but I could not; I screamed to Etta for help, and we both managed to lift her on to the pillows. As I put the quilt over her, she opened her eyes and said quietly, 'I feel sick, very sick.' I ran downstairs to summon Dr McMahon urgently. Etta had brought her a cup of water, and I noticed, as she sipped from it, that her lips were blue and her face was purple. After a time she grew pale. 'Dr Mac is coming,' I told her, and she sighed and said, 'You shouldn't have got the poor man out of bed.' She then seemed relaxed, and told us not to call Joe, not to worry him.

When the doctor arrived, he examined Mother and had a private word with her. I waylaid him on his way out, and begged him to say that she was all right, it was nothing serious. He stopped in the hall and said, 'Your mother must rest; her heart is not the best, and you must see to it that she doesn't climb stairs, or carry anything heavy. But don't treat her like an invalid, let her do what she can, or you'll aggravate her condition.' I told him I was going to have a bedroom made for her downstairs, and he was pleased about that. 'Live as normally as possible', he said, 'and I'll call again in a day or two.' Almost in tears, I asked him, 'Please tell me she won't die,' and he smiled and replied, 'We won't let her.' Tears of gratitude rolled down my cheeks.

That evening I began a new way of living. I worked as hard as ever, but made sure I was there to supervise the change of bedroom, to cancel people who wanted to come to see Mother early in the mornings, to advise Joe, to line up Etta and Mrs Broughal so that Mother was never alone. I phoned Jacquie, who said that she was in a new job, but would come home at once if needed. Gregg was at school, so I left him in peace; he would be her standby in the summer. I contacted Aunt Lena, who said she would come to visit whenever she could get away. And I handled Joe with as much care as I could. I told no one in the theatre, but I did tell John B Keane and his wife Mary, who were in Dublin for one of his plays. They were both compassionate and brimming with good sense. I went back to work with a calm certainty that the danger had passed, and a determination to be in several places at once if necessary.

Lena and her husband Cecil came to see Mother after her illness. She was resting on her bed, covered with a light quilt. They asked a lot of questions about insurance, and the cost of making a downstairs bedroom. They talked about the cost of everything, and how hard it was to manage nowadays. I thought a more light-hearted vein would be appropriate, and threw in some theatre stories which at least raised their eyebrows, and made Mother laugh.

Mother found their visit depressing, although she had asked me to phone Lena several times; I think she wanted to talk about private things. Lena had a pessimistic view of Mother's illness, which she thought might become debilitating and leave her bedridden. She scared me with talk like that.

All that was needed to convert our dining-room downstairs into a bedroom for Mother was to partition off part of it and add a wash-basin and a commode which also functioned as an armchair. She was not too happy about the move, but capitulated when she found that going upstairs caused her severe breathing difficulty. She had the same trouble in the mornings, although she slept, as directed, banked with pillows to keep her upright. I brought her tea before I left for the theatre, and made sure she was dressed smartly, hoping this would boost her spirits. Joe came to see her each morning, as deluded as I was, optimistic that she would be fine if only she took things easy for the present.

# 27

# *Death and Survival*

D r McMahon called one evening to find Mother in a state of near-collapse. He ordered her to bed and, when I arrived, took me aside and bluntly told me that her heart was very bad and that there was no treatment for it but rest. Next morning she was clearly no better, and I begged the doctor to come and help her. He sent an oxygen machine which I had to use at least every half hour throughout the day. I called Gregg, who was home for the holidays and he took over the air machine while I telephoned Aunt Lena, sent a telegram to Doris and another to Jacquie. I telephoned the Gate, leaving Mai McFall in charge, and all Mother's clients. Then I took over the machine again, and told her, while she was relaxed between applications, how much I loved her. Lena came and said that she would take turns sitting with Mother at night. It was almost evening when Dr McMahon arrived with a consultant. I knew there was no good news when they asked to see me alone. The consultant asked me how Mother would feel about seeing a priest, saying he thought that she should.

That night she was delirious, thinking that Gregg was waiting for her somewhere, and that she was being prevented from seeing him. I pacified her as best I could, but she talked about him through the night with a terrible urgency, trying at times to get out of bed. As the sun rose, she became lucid again. Joe came upstairs, looking forlorn and tired; Mother took his hands as he sat by the bed, and I saw the love between them.

The day was peaceful. A priest arrived. I told her that he had come to give her strength. She was really glad, and her eyes were shining as he left. Gregg spent a good part of the day sitting with her; Lena said that she would stay another night, and I was grateful. Mother was too tired and sleepy to eat, and when she did fall asleep with my arms around her, I was strangely happy.

I must have nodded off, for I heard Lena calling, 'Wake up, your mother's dying.' There was something different and wrong, and I rushed to the telephone, asking the doctor to come immediately. When I hurried back to the bedroom everything looked the same, but Mother had gone. Her face was peaceful and her eyes were open, but she had left me while I was telephoning the doctor. I got into the bed beside her and hugged her warm body, cradled her and whispered my love. Lena let the doctor in, and I heard myself saying unseemly things, saying she was not yet cold, give her an injection, anything. He replied without emotion, 'Your mother is dead, God rest her soul.' He gave me the telephone number of the Sisters of Mercy, who would lay her out.

I wanted to stay with Mother, alone. She hated people being laid out in brown habits. I knew what she would wear, and her auburn hair, which had defied her seventy-five years, would go so well with her blue dress. I would wait for dawn, my hand once more in hers, just the two of us. Then I would tell Joe, and Gregg, and Etta; they would have to cope with the reality. It was 27 July, 1968. The next day was my forty-fifth birthday and cheerful, coloured cards came through the post; Happy Birthday.

A young nun on a motor cycle arrived with a wonderful blue garment, its satin sheen exactly right. She asked me to leave her with Mother for a while, and, when she called me back, gave me Mother's wedding ring, which I put on immediately. She called out as she left about how happy Mother must be with Himself, up there in heaven. Jacquie and Gregg clung to each other with grief, desolate at their loss. They lent strength to me, helping with non-stop telephone calls, friends coming to the house, all the activities which break like a storm over a place of bereavement. People from the theatre, from every walk of life, filled the house and, later, crowded the church. Tributes flowed in from known and unexpected quarters. The priest who had anointed her said it was as though a bishop had died on the road. An avalanche of flowers came.

Mother's main estate was in the Palmerston Road house. Jacquie, Gregg and I huddled together, and made plans to move. We tried to think what Mother would have done, unable to speak coherently as the real impact of her death hit us. After a few days Gregg, unable to face the house, went with my blessing to the country to visit friends. Jacquie had to go back to her job in England. Etta and I were left to face the house.

At first I could not go back to the theatre, or go anywhere at all.

I opened Mother's black metal box with the key James Traynor, her solicitor, had given me, and found hospital receipts for operations, for trips to Lourdes, thank-you letters to Mother for paying for these, contributions to charities, to orphanages and more. These piles of receipts were evidence of a life given to compassionate deeds done quietly and secretly.

Mai McFall and others telephoned from the rehearsals, and I said that I could not attend, and they should contact Richard Hallinan. Tomás Mac Anna telephoned, wanting me to give a talk at some prestigious occasion in the near future, on freelance theatre. I declined. Eventually Dr McMahon called and decided that I was in shock. He gave me a prescription for tablets and some advice about getting back to work. I took the tablets and stayed put. It was Tomás Mac Anna who broke through the paralysis, arriving one day with the demand that I should go back to my actors, and do my job. I told him I had given up too much for theatre, and would never go back. He banged the table, roared things about cowardice and letting my mother down, and stormed out of the house. I was terribly shaken, and hated him for his harsh intrusion into my private despair. That evening Hugh Leonard arrived and took me to dinner to cheer me up, and I took wine, forgetting about the tablets, and passed out on the floor of the Trocadero. Much embarrassed, he advised me to get rid of the drugs and stand on my own feet, and that night I threw out the pills.

The next day I was back at rehearsals of *The Anniversary*, and the actors greeted me as though nothing had happened. Only our designer Bob Heade told me to change out of my dark clothes 'Your mother wore bright colours,' he said. He was right. Many, many good friends and a myriad theatre people gave me back the desire to go on living and achieving. My family and close friends gave me affection and support. And Liam Mac Gabhann stayed a little way apart, and gave me love.

Joe told me that he was leaving to go and live with his sister in Belfast. He could not endure the house and its memories; the loss of his beloved Maisie had left him with little to live for, except to spend his remaining years with his own people. I could not ask him to share pot luck with Gregg, Etta and me. All the savings were frozen in Mother's account, for I had never got around to opening a separate one of my own. I had to put a roof over our heads when the Palmerston Road house was sold. Gregg was determined to do his Leaving Certificate in Rathmines College of Technology. Liam had predicted that he would be a journalist, and it seemed as though this was the career he would follow.

Hugh Leonard telephoned one morning to talk about his new play for two actors, *The Au Pair Man*. He had the idea of casting Joan Greenwood, a distinguished figure on stage and screen. She had a throaty, sexy voice, adaptable to all sorts of roles. I had mentioned Donal McCann, an extraordinary young actor then soaring up the theatrical charts. He was based in the Abbey, where his talent shone with a difference that undermined that theatre's convention that all actors were equal. Negotiations were opened with Joan Greenwood's agent; she was reputed to be easy to work with. Donal was, compared to her, at the beginning of his career, but had been seen to effect in London in the Abbey's production of Dion Boucicault's *The Shaughraun*, splendidly directed by Hugh Hunt. His outstanding performance in Patrick Kavanagh's *Tarry Flynn* had also added to his stature.

The date for rehearsals of *The Au Pair Man* arrived, at which point Joan Greenwood's agent phoned to say that she had chicken pox, and could not travel for at least a week. We despatched Donal McCann and Mai McFall to London to begin rehearsals there. Ted Kotcheff, a Canadian director of repute, was to direct the play. There would be two weeks rehearsal in London, and one in Dublin, three weeks being the maximum, even for a spectacular, in those days. Pat Murray was our designer, and it was a tonic to me to have him around, demanding that I should keep the flag flying at top mast.

I had been approached by Anna Manahan and Helen Robinson with a plan to help promote Irish playwrights by giving rehearsed readings of new plays of merit. A professional director would work on the plays with the writer, and professional actors would take part in the readings, It would be run on a voluntary basis; any money that came in at the box-office would pay expenses for cast and director, and the rent of the venue where the reading would be staged. It was an inspired idea. I joined the group immediately, and we set a deadline for the first event. We would not exclude international dramas, but wanted primarily Irish plays, even from established playwrights who might have experimental works they wished to try out.

Among the plays submitted was one called *The Orphans* by Tom Murphy, which contained some really magnificent dialogue and rich characterisation. The theme, however, although profoundly moving, was maddeningly obscure to audiences on a first hearing. Had Tom not been there to explain it, even we would not have grasped its significance. Then again, as in all Tom Murphy's work, the sense of being caught up in something intrinsically life-enhancing outweighed the innate obscurity. Play Circle, as our group was called, invited managements to each reading, and built up a membership who came to all readings for a modest fee. Members of the public came too, for a lesser payment. Representatives of the Dublin Theatre Festival came, and invited Gemini to present *The Orphans* for the next Festival. It was to be directed at the Gate Theatre by Abbey actor Vincent Dowling, whose main job was to ensure that the play was clearly comprehensible to audiences; he professed to understand it fully.

Casting it was not difficult, as Tom Murphy's work was attractive to actors. Vincent asked me to search for an actor to fill the part of a father, a simple countryman, whose son has abandoned the priesthood. He cannot understand this, being from a time when such a breach of vows is as great an evil as murder. I had seen a very funny man impersonating Madam Butterfly in a revue at the Gas Company Theatre, a Cork comedian with a sad face. His name was Cecil Sheehan, and when I located and telephoned him, his first reaction was to say, in his gentle Cork voice, that I must be looking for Cecil Sheridan; they were, it seems, often mistaken for each other. I assured him that there was no mistake, and that he was the one we wished to interview about the play. Amazed, he agreed to see Vincent, after which he got the part. Even in rehearsals, he brought tears to everyone's eyes with the truth of his portrayal. In finding the actor, I also found a loyal and affectionate friend whom I loved and admired to the end of his days.

Lighting up the desolation of mind and spirit that afflicted me so often since the summer came Joan Greenwood, minus chicken pox, radiating glamour and goodwill, altogether irresistible. It was typical of her that, when she noticed a poster for *The Au Pair Man* starring herself above the title, and 'with Donal McCann' below it, she insisted that it be changed to give both of them equal billing. Unselfishness apart, she had a good point. The play was a two-hander, and she knew that Donal's talent was exceptional. They were marvellous together, and brought off a full realisation of the play's meaning and potential. Ted Kotcheff directed them with panache, and it was a pleasure to work with Joan; there was a sweetness in her nature, and her ready wit was never unkind. She was the only person I knew who, like myself, carried everything needed for the working day in a carrier bag, bringing it everywhere, including receptions and interviews. The play was successfully launched at the Gate, and went later to the Duchess Theatre in London. Pat Murray's set of a house tottering on its foundations, a metaphor for the British Empire, aroused such favourable comment that he could have made a lucrative career in the UK, but nothing could prise him out of Cork for long.

During all this, I was frantically searching for a house to live in after Palmerston Road was sold as part of Mother's estate. Etta and Gregg and I would have to move shortly after Christmas, as Uncle Cecil as executor had been advised – wrongly – that January was a good time for house sales. After viewing a few depressing dwellings, Mai McFall and I found a house in Braemor Road, Churchtown, as good as we were likely to find. The Dublin mountains were visible, there was a village atmosphere and it was not overlooked at the rear. The back garden was a manageable size with a hawthorn tree. I went to see James Traynor, the solicitor acting for the estate, and he advanced us enough money to clinch the purchase, with vacant possession set for January. We had been happy at Palmerston Road, but it was now empty of what had been most dear to us, and consequently easier to leave.

Jacquie informed us that she was bringing a friend for Christmas, an Indian barrister named Romy Patel. She thought we would not be able to deal with our grief in that house of memories on our own. A few days before Christmas, Jacquie arrived with Romy, who believed all mothers should be venerated. and particularly the mother of his fiancée who, incidentally, had not accepted this status. She did not wear jewellery, and resented Romy giving her expensive bracelets and watches, which she always returned. Having been briefed on my passion for smoked salmon and red wine, he filled our fridge with salmon and bought a case of wine. Our house was too cold for his comfort, so he installed an electric heater, which moved from room to room with him. He was a slender, sinewy man of medium height, intelligent and humorous, interested in politics and literature. I thought him far too indolent to shine in his profession; certainly he displayed no sign of ambition, and clearly enjoyed the good life.

John B Keane sent me his new play *Big Maggie* early in the new year. I already had two plays lined up for Gemini, but this one had a special impact, and I ached to see it on the stage. In the character of Maggie, John B had challenged the stereotype of the long-suffering mother and widow. He had written anti-heroine material before, and was way ahead of the feminist movement. Maggie had an appetite for vengeance as well as justice, and was bent on moulding her family into prototypes of her own liberated persona.

John B had thought of writing a play for Anna Manahan, and although *Big Maggie* was connected to that wish, the play that emerged was not the one he had originally planned, but Maggie was a role to covet. By the time the play had run its first course for Gemini, I had the privilege of engaging five major actresses for the part – Marie Kean, Joan O'Hara, Doreen Hepburn, Anna Manahan and Ronnie Masterson. Barry Cassin directed them all, and nothing could make him name his favourite among them.

Richard Hallinan and I discussed opening the play in Cork, and touring it to Dublin's Olympia via Limerick. Finding that Anna Manahan was not free, we approached Marie Kean, who had never appeared in John B Keane's work, and who was fascinated by the character. We assembled a memorable cast around her; Dearbhla Molloy, Robert Carlisle, Liz Davis, Gerry Sullivan, Archie O'Sullivan, Robert Carrickford and Eileen Lemass. Eileen was married to Seán Lemass's son, Noel, and was better known for her commitment to the Fianna Fáil party, and to her husband's career in it. She had a deep love of the theatre, and had acted in the Abbey. Knowing the chronic state of Gemini's finances, she encouraged our efforts and worked for our continued survival. Noel was also an ardent supporter. *Big Maggie* was set for the Cork Opera House, and Pat Murray arranged to have the set built by the stage crew from his own design, and rehearsals began in Dublin.

At this time a sad letter arrived from my sister Doris in America. She had been in shock since the news of Mother's death; our telegram had not been delivered to her until some weeks after the funeral. Doris had been informed about our move from home, and was anxious about us. She instructed James Traynor to ensure that we were facilitated in taking anything we wanted from the old house. Doris found it very difficult to cope with Mother's death. She had made so many arrangements through the years to come home to see her, but it never happened. Being deprived of a last greeting was a bitter blow, and took its toll on her health for many a season.

We learned one day that the house had been sold to a retired bank inspector. He called one afternoon, and strode insensitively through the rooms; he was going to convert the house into flats, and hoped we would be out of it as soon as possible. Gregg and I looked at each other in rage and grief and wondered why he could not have been a little more humane. We learned afterwards that he had bought the house for a song due to the inexperience of Uncle Cecil, the executor. Just before the official date for our departure, Gregg went down with severe influenza and a sky-high temperature, and was forbidden to move as there was a real threat of pneumonia. The new owner was informed, and rushed around in high dudgeon, insisting that we get an ambulance to shift Gregg; his builders were waiting. I asked him to leave; he threatened me with the police. Sensing my rage, he moved to the steps outside the front door, declaiming that the house was his. I slammed the heavy door on his loathsome presence. I then telephoned James Traynor, who promised that he would deal with the customer, and said that we should stay put until Gregg was over the worst.

The day we left was overcast. Most of the heavy furniture went ahead of us. It was quite dark when Etta, Gregg and I, plus Joe's blue cat Sheba in a basket, closed the door behind us in our new home. Although I had arranged for an electricity supply, it had not been provided, and we could hardly see each other. I rang Liam from the house next door, and the lights were soon on. While we waited, the neighbouring family gave us tea, offered help and proved from that first meeting to be the best neighbours one could wish for. Trying to cope with bare boards and uncurtained windows kept us from indulging the misery we all felt. We did not want to be in this cold, strange house. There were not enough bedclothes, so we used coats and woollen jumpers on the beds, and scarves and underskirts to cover the windows. Finally we fell asleep, too miserable to talk.

In the morning we set about putting some order on the confusion of boxes, cases and furniture dumped anywhere in yesterday's darkness. I soon noticed that a suitcase, containing Mother's radio and two bronze statues which had been with us since my childhood, was missing. Etta and I went searching for other treasures that seemed to have vanished; Jacquie's doll collection, made up of gifts from all over the world, was also gone. In our vulnerable state, this loss seemed to us like a fresh bereavement. We had given the job of moving us to a small and trusted firm, but one of the staff had been tempted for small gain. We never got back any of the stolen items, but did not blame the head of the firm, who was genuinely distressed but could offer only money to make good our loss.

We were opening *Big Maggie* at the Cork Opera House, then managed by the genial Bill Twomey. From there we would go to Limerick, at Jack Bourke's City Theatre, and then to Dublin's Olympia Theatre, where Jack Bourke's father, Lorcan, was chairman of the Board. The Bourkes were a colourful lot, a theatrical family who not only distinguished themselves behind the footlights, but were in business supplying lighting, costumes and scripts to theatres all over the country. Lorcan was the original song-and-dance man, the Mr Malaprop of his time, with a big heart and a real love of theatre. His beautiful daughter Grainne married Eamonn Andrews of TV fame when she was a very young look-alike for Elizabeth Taylor. Peadar Bourke, head of the costume department, also wrote original scripts for the stage. The Bourkes were related to the Behans and the Kearneys, one of whom had written 'A Soldier's Song' which became the national anthem of Ireland. Rick Bourke and his wife Ivy were the mainstay of many charities, including the Variety Club of Ireland. At the Olympia, Lorcan's portrait still beams down on artist and audience alike.

Rehearsals began for *Big Maggie* with a great sense of adventure. Marie Kean was nervous about how audiences would take to her ruthless, tyrannical mother-figure, who showed no sentiment and gave no quarter to her children. Maimed by her arid experience of marriage, she was unable to show love for others; but it became clear that this anti-heroine raised echoes in the thousands who later thronged to see the play. Every family, it seemed, had or knew a 'Big Maggie'. Marie Kean was ideal in the role, and we knew that the day would be lost or won by how her character was accepted. It was a great thrill opening in Cork, where John B Keane's plays were very popular, mainly due to James N Healy and his 'Theatre of the South'. The Opera House was packed, and forward bookings looked terrific. John B and Mary Keane, and about thirty of what was known jokingly as the Listowel mafia, were in attendance. Almost from the start, the audience went with Maggie, laughing at her quips, gasping as she savaged her rebellious family. Then there was an uneasy silence as, one by one, her children left her; was this, after all, a tragedy, and would Maggie surrender, alone and unloved, in the end? Those who expected her to weaken were to find the curtain falling on her in unrepentant mood, business as usual, more assured and upbeat than when the play started.

After the tumultuous reception, John B had us all over for drinks, when a member of the Listowel drama group came up to Marie to congratulate her, saying that he had never heard anyone to get so much from a part while playing it in a monotone! Another well-lubricated gent asked us if we had deliberately tried to make the play into a comedy; there were, he said, no laughs in the script. Barry Cassin fielded that one; even he had not realised how funny some of the scenes were. There had, of course, to be light as well as darkness, and this would be a very dark play indeed had the author not spiced it with comedy. Prior to Gemini committing itself to tour this large company, Philip O'Brien, the American actor who had settled in Ireland, asked if he could invest in the production. Richard Hallinan was for it, and I didn't mind, although my instincts told me that we would not lose with this one and we didn't need to hedge our bets.

John B Keane was not understood or valued as a writer in those years as he is today, but his popularity was immense. He himself was charismatic, accessible to all, never changed by his growing fame, but he had to endure begrudgers, especially among those who fancied themselves as intellectuals.

In Limerick, we were booked out for a two-week run, and when we reached Dublin, all previous attendance records at the Olympia were exceeded. It was the same wherever we toured. After four weeks at the Olympia, Marie Kean had to leave the cast to fulfil a film contract, and Joan O'Hara took over for the final weeks. The change did not affect business at all. Joan's interpretation was very different from Marie's, but just as valid. John B was ecstatic, as nothing seemed to stop the *Maggie* madness. The Olympia invited us back, and we had to regroup. Doreen Hepburn, physically our smallest Maggie, took over with force and relish, and the play sailed on.

We lost Arthur O'Sullivan early in the Olympia run. He collapsed one evening in his dressing-room, and was brought to hospital to be dried out. We sent a car around the city to try to locate Cecil Sheehan, who was scheduled to replace Arthur after the Olympia run, having had a tip that he might be at the Eblana Theatre to visit his friend Paul Goldin, a hypnotist. Sure enough, he was there, and was rushed to the Olympia to take over the role at the shortest notice ever. Fortunately, he had been learning the lines, and performed impeccably. He remained with the show for its duration, and was an exceptional company member. *Big Maggie* went on to Belfast, then down south back to Cork, Limerick and Waterford, all sell-outs. When that tour ended, Anna Manahan took over the role, and off we went on another.

There was a downside to the overwhelming success of *Big Maggie* that deprived Richard, Philip and myself of much of our pleasure in it. A small core of players became resentful of the production's success in terms of profit. It didn't enter their heads that it was hugely expensive to tour it with so many actors, to shift sets around, pay publicity and all kinds of other costs. All this had to be financed from the box-office, and a simple calculation would have told them that there could not possibly be large profits. A lot of the sourness was generated by the amount of alcohol consumed each night after the show. At least two of the dissidents looked set to become problem drinkers, and as no one was permitted to touch alcohol before or during performances, they must have been constantly afflicted with hangovers and acid stomachs. Their discontent and grumbling spread through the company.

The build-up of resentment, as audiences continued to pour in to this phenomenal show, took the form of actors refusing to play matinées despite the extra salary offered; impossible terms were looked for and refused. The rest of the company became uneasy, and, but for the staunch support of Mai McFall and Cecil Sheehan, I would have brought the tour to a premature close. Later, when Anna Manahan was playing the lead, the same hard core of troublesome thespians finally melted into the usual Gemini family togetherness, and we were at last able to enjoy the fun of it all. At the end of the tour, we were asked to go back to the Olympia one more time. Richard and Philip understandably thought that *Big Maggie*, after a year of our life and hers, had run its course. I retained the rights, engaged Ronnie Masterson for the lead, again different, and ran the show to packed houses for six more weeks, making our total stay at the Olympia seventeen weeks.

# 28

# *Fresh Fields*

The time came when Richard Hallinan wanted to leave the agency and strike out on his own. We parted amicably, dividing whatever funds were in the kitty. I was advised to look for a new administrator, and did not have far to look. Brendan Connellan, a friend of Brendan Smith's, came into the bar of the Olympia one night for a drink. He was taking early retirement from his executive job in Player Wills, the tobacco company, to follow his real interest, the theatre. He was interested in the vacant Gemini job, and agreed to take on the position of manager on a temporary basis, to see how we would work together. That was one of the most fortunate meetings of my life.

For the next ten years, I had no problems with the business side of my life, added to which I had acquired a good friend and an entertaining companion. Brendan was tough in negotiations, but he was fair, and actors knew that. He was immensely popular, had a great sense of humour and was in every way an ideal partner. His responsibilities included re-staffing the Eblana, and he found dedicated part-time ladies for the box-office and a front-of-house manager. All we in Gemini had to do was to generate the funds to continue operating. We averaged forty-six production weeks each year, and were now a major source of employment, being the premier freelance, or unsubsidised, company in Ireland. Apart from our steady stream of popular and experimental dramas, we depended on our revues to keep us solvent.

Those Eblana revues often featured Des Keogh and Frank Kelly, and Brendan struck up a particular rapport with them. They liked the same things, including a gin-and-tonic at lunch time and Jameson whiskey after six, if they weren't working. Des and Frank had a lot in common, and yet were poles apart in attitudes. Both were versatile revue performers, superlative stand-up comics and excellent straight actors, at times as touchy as tomcats, and at other times the souls of wit and affability. I would travel anywhere with these two actors on board, provided no wise guy was there to ruffle their feathers. Along with Niall Toibin, they rate as first-class entertainers.

I did not know Niall Toibin as well as I would have wished to; we worked very little together. Cyril Cusack and Siobhán McKenna (who as competitive performers had little love for each other), both expressed reservations to me about Toibin. Cyril, well-versed in the art of being centre-stage on and off the boards, always referred to him in mock-sympathetic terms. 'Poor Niall,' Cyril would sigh; 'Such a *good* actor, but he always confuses good with great.' Mac Liammóir once said that Toibin was like a friendly dog who snapped at you when you weren't looking. Siobhán, on one occasion when I mentioned that I was about to engage Toibin for a season, asked serious questions about my health and stamina. But all this happened in the actor's drinking days. There came a time when wisdom and character prompted Niall Toibin to take the dry road; he never drank alcohol again, and never looked back.

Siobhán also had reservations about John B Keane's plays; 'I want to understand those Kerry Amazons he writes about – I want to be sure they exist.' Had she ever played 'Big Maggie', what a revelation that would have been. She did not relate well to Hugh Leonard's plays either, and was not in sympathy with his female characters. But then, neither author provided the kind of star parts Siobhán was then interested in, with her career on an international high. Cyril, Siobhán, Ray McAnally, Mac Liammóir and Hilton Edwards came intermittently in and out of my life and work. Sometimes I would find myself in the middle of the volcanic upheavals that such big personalities called mere disagreements, and even be called upon to referee. Hilton often upbraided the Irish for slovenly diction and fractured English, while Mícheál would accuse Hilton of adding an 'r' to words ending in 'a'. They would fight over the plays they were producing, with snide references about actors favoured by one or the other. Inevitably, one of them would go too far; then Mícheál would dash from the room, leaving Hilton to rumble on. It was impossible not to think that the rumpus was a well-rehearsed performance, somehow essential to both of them. Some of their exchanges bordered on the vicious, and Mícheál would actually cry, but there was always a sense that if there were no onlookers, there would have been no game.

The arguments between Cyril and Siobhán at rehearsals were fiery on her part and cutting on his. They spoke about each other amusingly and dismissively, but no one could mistake the profound respect each had for the other. They were, after all, the two most distinguished Irish actors of their day, and heavenly bodies have been known to collide at times, as they did. Ray McAnally later entered the galaxy with enough power and versatility to gain his place among the stars. This prompted Cyril to ask, in his mock-modest way, if his lead status in Irish theatre could now be challenged. Ray, not unaware of his own abilities, regarded the older luminaries as past history. Actors are delicately balanced people. Des Keogh could not sustain an argument; his gentle nature suffered so much that it affected his work, and he was often sick with tension before going on to perform. Frank Kelly and Niall Toibin shared a devastating wit, which enhanced their stories about other actors, made doubly wicked by their powers of mimicry.

Our Festival play in 1969 was to be Hugh Leonard's adaptation of John McGahern's moving novel *The Barracks*, to be directed by Tomás Mac Anna and designed by Pat Murray. It was like a reunion, having two such dear friends at the helm again, and fortune smiled on me further by enabling Eddie Golden to get leave from the Abbey to play a key role. Aideen O'Kelly and Gerry Alexander were also available, two strong, confident performers, as was that most agreeable of actors, Martin Dempsey. Martin seemed at times to have the gift of bilocation, as he was known to accept two simultaneous engagements, and somehow work around them. He was once discovered playing in the first half of a play in one theatre, and the second half of an opera at a different venue, on the same evening. Gerry Alexander could play in revue and drama with equal facility, and was President of Equity for many years. We got along famously, and I liked his company enough to cause a flurry of gossip. We were both mischievous enough to enjoy this, but it led us dangerously close to making the rumours a reality.

At times when Liam seemed very far away, both in miles and because he was not a free agent, I would lose heart and enjoy the company of other men. But it was always a dead-end effort, and I would tell Liam about these encounters, and why they occurred. This upset him to the point where he considered opting out of my life altogether so that I might be free, but I could never face that. He was too much an anchor in my often turbulent existence and after each argument about the best thing to do, he would admit that leaving me would bring desolation to his own life. We always ended up clinging to each other, no nearer to a solution, but desperate to hang on to what we had.

For *The Barracks*, Pat Murray had designed an ingenious set involving two small revolving stages right stage and left, with one elevated central one. My nervous system went on red alert, perhaps in the knowledge that Mac Anna and Murray were both eager experimenters. Tomás loved flying in walls, doors, trees and anything else that could be flown, with the very good intention of effecting quick scene changes, and had achieved some startling results this way. Naturally, after his discussions with Pat, it emerged that *The Barracks* would both revolve and fly. All I could do was warn the actors that they had better be quick off the mark if they were not to collide with scenery in motion.

At that time, the Olympia often called in part-time stage hands to work on unusually difficult set changes, and in this case extra hands were needed to spin the central revolve, which on one side represented a hospital bed with a dying woman in it. Gerry Alexander, as a surgeon, was also in place, about to play a moving scene in suitably muted lighting. The revolve was to be eased gently into position with all lights dimmed, when a white glow would reveal the actors. It seemed so simple. But on the first night the new stage hands panicked, and sent the revolving rostrum spinning madly around in bright light, showing a shaken actor clinging to the bed while the patient shot up from under the covers to see what was happening. The audience roared with laughter. I saw Hugh Leonard putting his hands over his face, and thanked God that John McGahern had been unable to attend the first night.

The revolve wasn't the only gremlin in the works that night. Tomás had arranged a large piece of scenery, depicting the exterior view of the barracks, to be flown away as the curtain rose, revealing the interior. This worked well, coming in and out of the play as needed, until an actor hung a heavy policeman's coat on a nail on one side of the 'wall', causing the next flight to make a disastrous landing, totally lopsided. Although the actors soldiered on professionally, the whole mood of the play was lost. The audience understood, and there was thunderous applause to show they sympathised with the actors' plight. When I went backstage, everyone was as mad as hell. Gerry Alexander stormed out of the theatre, and there were some tears of sheer frustration. Pat Murray was suicidal, but Tomás tried to comfort the cast and also to identify the culprits, who had made themselves scarce. Despite the technical disasters which marred the first night, the play was well received. Eddie Golden, such an under-rated actor, walked off with the Festival award for his playing in *The Barracks*. He was half-brother to Geoff Golden, both Abbey actors and as different as chalk and cheese. Geoff was handsome, talented and feckless, not at all ambitious. Eddie was more serious and sensitive. Geoff was married to the brilliant actress Máire Ní Dhomhnaill, who threw her career away almost wantonly in her middle years. Geoff and Máire had a restless, maverick approach to life and the theatre, living more like gypsies than settled people.

During the *Big Maggie* days, I had talks with Jack Bourke in Limerick about a possible season of plays to be produced at the City Theatre. Perhaps we were both dazzled by the huge business generated by John B's play; Limerick was not then noted for its devotion to the arts, and it was said that the bones of many a theatre company lay buried in that cultural wasteland. But the idea persisted, and I began to see a second National Theatre co-situated in the City Theatre. I talked to many key figures in Dublin, and had meetings with actors, directors and possible sponsors. My enthusiasm grew as I found a positive response among actors and in the media. The doyen of theatre critics and columnists, John J Finegan, encouraged the idea privately and in his famous *Evening Herald* column. I have never met anyone in the media with such a love of theatre as John, or anyone who helped so many companies and individuals throughout a long lifetime in theatre journalism. While I pondered on funding, Jack Bourke worked to raise sponsorship in Limerick, and phoned to say that Shannon Development, under Brendan O'Regan, would come in as an associate. Brendan Connellan and I were to assemble the company and administer the season, for which I would be Artistic Director.

We decided to call the enterprise the Limerick Theatre Festival, to counterpoint the annual event in Dublin. It was not easy for actors to commit themselves to a long season out of the metropolis, where there was occasional work to be had in the larger theatres, and sometimes in RTE. But the challenge seemed to fire every actor I spoke to. In that first Festival in July, 1970, the company included Geoff Golden, Cecil Sheehan, Liam Sweeney, Robert Carlisle, Dearbhla Molloy, Beryl Fagan, May Cluskey, Maureen Toal, Anna

Manahan, Áine Ní Mhuirí, Patrick Dawson, Robert Carrickford and a host of others who came and went. We staged *Juno and the Paycock*, *On Trial*, *Lovers* and *All the King's Horses*. Arrangements were made for the company to stay at Geary's Hotel, near the theatre, where Jack Bourke was owner/manager, and where we paid £1 per night for bed and breakfast. Jack was tall and dark, with the family good looks. His wife Monica was a small, pretty woman who was well able, despite her apparent fragility, to dismiss her husband's more importunate admirers. He was laconic, not to say abrupt, on first acquaintance, and his hotel was small, with a variety of mixed styles of furniture, old and new, which gave it an aura of old-worldness. Lorcan Bourke had told me in Dublin that all the rooms were comfortable, and that, as head of the company, I was to have the bridal suite, the best in the hotel. The porter opened the door and switched on the lights, and I saw a large bed with brocaded covers, heavy curtains on long windows and a single bed thrown in for good measure. No one ever explained what the single bed was doing in a bridal suite!

It would be impossible to detail all the goings-on in Limerick; the Lord Mayor's civic reception, the support of the press and the amount of publicity Jack Bourke generated all the time we were there. There was a Festival Club with a late-night licence in the George Hotel. Unfortunately, it was mostly Limerick's ladies who supported the theatre and attended all the shows. Their husbands skipped the shows and went to the Festival Club, where there was drinking and dancing. We discovered that there were only two social classes in Limerick, the wealthy and the poor, and that most of our audiences came from those who could least afford the theatre tickets. We admitted later that a ten-week Festival was too long.

In Limerick, Maureen Toal was one of the best Junos I have seen, younger than earlier actresses who were clearly unaware that O'Casey had specified his heroine's age as forty. Robert Carlisle's portrait of Johnny Boyle, Juno's son at the mercy of the gunmen, was one of his finest. Dearbhla Molloy, Bob Carlisle's wife, excelled as Mary Boyle as she did in most things. She had a naturally small voice, with the tiniest hint of a lisp at times, and we had our first and only real disagreement about her lack of projection. The City Theatre was a large, long building not noted for good acoustics; any actor who could be heard clearly there would have no difficulty anywhere. I argued with Dearbhla that she should exercise her voice regularly, and project with a lot more force and vigour; she replied that this would cause her to lose all subtlety and conviction, and that she was not prepared to shout for anyone. But from then on, she took voice lessons as often as possible, and now possesses enough power to tackle the classics.

Arthur O'Sullivan was playing Captain Boyle, and was very suited to the part. May Cluskey was Maisie Madigan, understating the character rather than turning it into a music-hall type, giving us reality rather than laughs. Áine Ní Mhuirí was a memorable Mrs Tancred. Barry Cassin gave the play a fine production, in which the only flaw was the casting of Gerry O'Sullivan as Joxer Daly. He had persuaded Barry to let him try, and turned in a brave effort; but when you're wrong for a part, you're wrong.

Mairéad Ní Ghráda's moving drama about the betrayal of innocence, On Trial, brought great houses, and our hopes of a good season were high. We had decided to do a farce named All the King's Horses, by John O'Donnell, starring Cecil Sheehan and Geoff Golden. One day, while we were rehearsing it, Arthur O'Sullivan crawled in on his hands and knees, ossified with drink. Barry immediately insisted that I replace Arthur, failing which he would take the next train home. Fortunately, it was a small part, and the College Players, Limerick's oldest amateur group, were able to supply a replacement for our disgraced actor. I had no intention of sending Arthur home, but he had to be put back on the rails very firmly. Mai McFall was despatched to his digs to break the news of his replacement, and I waited with Barry for a message of repentance, an abject apology even. When Mai returned, the message she brought was that Barry should go back to snagging turnips, and that f***ing Lady Gregory could go to hell and take the rest of her f***ing amateurs with her.

One of the highlights was Brian Friel's Lovers, that exquisite combination of two one-act plays. We had a superb cast. Anna Manahan had played it at the Gate and on Broadway, Geoff Golden took over the part so brilliantly created by Niall Toibin, and Dearbhla Molloy and Bob Carlisle were the two young sweethearts. Professor Eoin McKiernan, founder and president of the Irish-American Cultural Institute, wanted a first-class Irish company to come to St Paul, Minnesota to open a new arts centre there. He had almost clinched the Abbey, but it had to pull out at the last moment. Someone, and I suspect it was Tomás Mac Anna, had told Eoin of our work in Limerick, and he came over to see *Lovers*. There and then he offered us the privilege of providing the drama content of his significant event. It was a real triumph for Gemini to represent the best of Irish theatre in America. Most of the company had never been there, and they could hardly contain their excitement. The Limerick season had been hard work, with mixed audiences, but we were a light-hearted group, and enjoyed the experience in all its ups and downs. Before the season ended, Jack and Brendan and our Shannon Development supporters met to consider the financial position. All of us had lost money, but not our enthusiasm. We voted unanimously to do it again next year, to try to get more sponsors and to make it a bigger and better (but not longer) event.

We had other invitations to bring *Lovers* to Dublin and Cork after the American trip, this time with Maureen Toal replacing Anna Manahan, who had been offered a role in the West End with the well-known actor, Wilfred Hyde White, and left for London. Niall Toibin replaced Geoff Golden, who was ill, and the production drew high praise from the author. Unfortunately Anna had a most unhappy experience with Hyde White, who was apparently more egotistical than anything she had experienced. Eventually the stress and clash of personalities made her ill, whereupon he replaced her in the part.

Barry Cassin had often expressed a wish to direct an Arthur Miller play, and it happened that we had acquired the rights of *The Price*, and were negotiating with the Olympia Theatre. The casting seemed to fall into place. Westport-born Joe Maher, an actor fresh from an award-winning performance on Broadway, was home on a visit, and contacted Anna Manahan, with whom he had a long-term friendship. He had some time to spare before his next engagement in America, and, when Anna introduced us, I invited him to take the role of the surgeon-brother; we had already decided that Gerry Alexander was perfect for the part of the policeman. Brendan Connellan checked out the Jewish actor, Vic Wise, who had played the part of the antique dealer in the West End; he was free, and keen to come to Ireland. Angela Vale filled the role of the surgeon's wife.

It is a strong, sad play which leaves one with a feeling of frustration for what might, what ought to have been, but Arthur Miller never promises a happy ending. He knows that there are not too many of them. One thing we all became aware of; the actor who plays the dealer Gregory Solomon will, if he is a strong actor, walk away with the play in his pocket. *The Price* did not attract large audiences to the Olympia, despite very good reviews. I think now that the theatre was too big; the play needed more intimacy. Joe Maher went on to continue his rising career in America, and I saw him later in many films, an excellent actor and a good person to work with.

Christmas had fallen into place in Braemor Road. On Christmas Eve, some theatre friends, journalists, writers and others would find their way to our house for a drink and a snack, but mostly for theatre chat, exchanges of gossip and the newest jokes. They came in waves; sometimes there would be perhaps thirty, other times just a few. So long as nothing too serious was discussed, nothing to worry anyone, all were welcome. Regulars included Agnes Bernelle and Maurice Craig, photographer Fergus Bourke, Eddie and Elda Golden, Mai McFall and 'Bunny' Connellan, Alan Stanford and his first wife Patricia McMenamin, Brendan Smith and Beryl, Hugh Leonard and Paule, Des Keogh and Geraldine O'Grady, who described herself to Gregg as a fiddler, leaving him with a vision of her playing her violin in country kitchens. Liam dropped in rarely; he disliked crowds and stayed only a few minutes. Gerry and Bernie Colgan came, but never stayed long, having a large family of their own to cater for. Gerry was then a critic for *Plays and Players*, and had become our friend through years of Leonard plays and receptions. One of the best things I derived from my association with Hugh Leonard was the introduction he gave me to the Colgans. If there is a talent for friendship, they have it in abundance.

One Christmas Eve ended in a few stray revellers and myself going to Midnight Mass at our nearby church, hastily-swallowed cups of tea giving us a false sense of sobriety. We stood at the back, wondering why the lights were waving and flickering. Fortified with wine and optimism, we were grateful that we had come until one of our merry-makers began to walk up the aisle, bowing and showing people to seats already well-filled. We had to retrieve him as stealthily as we could, and make our way home, to return again sober and contrite on Christmas morning.

Then came 1971, the year of the *Playboy*. I am reminded, looking through J J Finegan's invaluable notes from his *Evening Herald* columns, that there was no Dublin Theatre Festival in that year. There was, however, a Limerick Festival, our second, and as it fell within the Synge centenary year, his classic *The Playboy of the*

*Western World* was on our list of productions. *Playboy* was springing up in every corner of Ireland that year, but I determined that ours was going to be the crowning glory.

Barry Cassin was as much in love with the play as I was. We chose Niall Buggy for our Christy Mahon, and Aideen O'Kelly, an auburn-haired actress of sensitivity and strength, as Pegeen Mike. Dermot Crowley, already showing enormous potential, was our Shaun Keogh. Liam O'Callaghan was a powerful Old Mahon, and all we needed was a Michael James who could match the team already in place. We had no doubt that it should be Niall Toibin. Pat Murray designed an entire set from Irish tweed, and the effect was stunning. All boded well.

Within hours of our arrival in Limerick, having completed our Dublin rehearsals, all hell broke loose. Niall went on a drinking spree, and subjected the whole company to vituperative insults. After being treated medically and prescribed sedatives, he got through the dress rehearsal, and the first night was quite a triumph. The press came down from Dublin, and granted my wish by acclaiming ours the finest *Playboy* of the centenary. But the following weeks were like a horror film. There was no peace at rehearsals; Niall seemed incapable of uttering a civil word, and the company was distraught, working in intolerable conditions. Barry bore the brunt of it, but remonstrating with Niall was futile, like prodding a wild bull. We went to receptions and other manifestations of Limerick hospitality, but there was always an incident, or the threat of one, when Niall was within reach of alcohol. Without it, he was merely turbulent; with it he became a belligerent, foul-mouthed adversary, bereft of his formidable intelligence and civilised wit. I vowed that I would never work with him again, and told him so; his reply was unprintable.

Almost a year later, I was at a party and, having caught a glimpse of Niall through the crowd, decided to make a quick getaway. As I moved, I saw him approaching to intercept me with outstretched hand. 'I'm apologising,' he said; 'Shake on it.' Instead, I gave him an impulsive hug, and he told me that he was on the dry, hopefully for good. He had realised that he was hurting his family, his friends and his career, and had gone for treatment. As his health improved, his great talent grew steadily, and he is today one of our best and most versatile entertainers.

There came a time when I needed Ray McAnally again to direct

*The Barretts of Wimpole Street*, the story of Robert Browning and Elizabeth Barrett. I knew that I could get a booking at the Gate. Mícheál and Hilton had at last been honoured with a grant to refurbish and run the theatre, and part of the arrangement was that it would be available to worthy freelance companies. This was arranged by the then Minister for Finance, Charles J Haughey, who told me that Gemini was to have first choice of the 'free' periods.

I asked Ray to direct *The Barretts* but I had a dilemma. My mind and heart knew that he would be the perfect Mr Barrett, but could he both act and direct? As I hesitated, he pressed me to say what was on my mind, and, when I finally told him, took my hands in his and said, 'We'll find a way.' Ray and I sat down to cast. He looked smug when it came to the part of Elizabeth Barrett. 'Have you heard of Kate Flynn?' he asked. I had, but she was fairly new on the scene, and I wondered if she was experienced enough. She came and read for us, and sounded and looked wonderful. Ray told me with total confidence that she would be great, and I believed him. We signed her, together with Dearbhla Molloy, Olivia Shanley, Liz Davis, Beryl Fagan, Liam Sweeney, Patrick Dawson, Frank Melia, Gerard O'Brien and Laurence Foster. It was difficult finding an actor for Robert Browning, but we located one at the Abbey. Pat Laffan was handsome and a fine actor, but he didn't see himself in the role, and consented reluctantly. With the addition of a few others and a King Charles spaniel acquired by Mai McFall, we were ready to go.

Rehearsals were a joy, and Ray was basking in the warmth flowing from a company who worshipped him. Kate blossomed daily, and Ray gave her private time when she had any difficulty with her character. We had some very young actors working with mature players, and they blended wonderfully together. During rehearsals, a remarkably pretty young woman called to see me, saying that she was a friend of Dearbhla Molloy's, and wanted to audition. When I explained that we were already fully cast and in rehearsal, she told me that I had made a mistake casting Dearbhla instead of her, and that if I had seen her perform, I would not have made such a blunder. I asked her name, and she told me she was Jeananne Crowley. I replied that she seemed to me to be a version of the title character in the film *All About Eve*. She was not a bit upset, and told me defiantly that at least I would remember her. And I did, and grew to like her enormously. She is very talented, as an actress and journalist, alarmingly honest and altogether charming.

With one week to go, Ray summoned me to the Gate for the first run-through. I sat beside him as the story unfolded, wondering why I was beginning to yawn, wasn't moved and, by the end, was downright bored. At the end, Ray and I left the theatre together, and went for tea without speaking. After a while, I could not bear his stricken look, and blurted out that it was too long, too slow and too repetitive. 'Right, see you Monday,' said Ray and left quite suddenly. I felt that all would be well, but longed for Monday to come around. When it did, I found that Ray had cut forty minutes from the script, and in the next run-through the play had more texture and was moving with an extra impetus. He added music for the interval and scene-changes, which now seemed to flow from the scenes rather than interrupt them. This was Ray at his finest and most lovable. He was also a fearsome Barrett, coldly tyrannical. It was a memorable triumph for one of our greatest actor-directors.

During the run at the Gate, Ray felt unwell one night, and a doctor was called at the end of the performance. It was then we discovered that Ray's supposed indigestion was in fact angina. He was given medication and ordered to rest, but decided to finish the run, and then re-cast the part for the planned revival. The following day he saw his own doctor, and the good news was that he had a mild angina condition, and it would not hinder his career if he was sensible, and monitored his work-load. We kept all this from the company, as Ray did not want exaggerated rumour spreading around; he wished to do major work, as he always had. Years later it came as a surprise to many in the profession that Ray had suffered from this condition for a long time before his eventual heart-attack, with consequent by-pass surgery. The *Barretts* went on to Limerick, where Barrett was played very well by Godfrey Quigley, if without Ray's degree of icy cruelty.

Coincidentally, the crippling pain that I had experienced at intervals for some years before now began to take over for longer periods. I had been to doctors and had X-rays, and been dismissed as psychosomatic when nothing showed up, a non-diagnosis I resented. My tolerance to pain began to increase, a dangerous attribute, but it got me through quite a few occasions when my presence was considered essential.

We soldiered through six Limerick Festivals before calling a halt due to lack of funds and insufficient audience support. Jack Bourke stood with me outside the City Theatre, which he had refurbished as best he could, and said that they would sell it over his dead body. They sold it, all right. Jack's father and the family brokers could not sustain the building as a theatre when that was plainly uneconomic. Later on I learned with sadness that when the Arts Council helped to fund an Arts Centre at the Belltable, Jack Bourke, it appears, was not asked to be on the board, a strange way to acknowledge the years he had given to the arts in Limerick.

# 29

# *Northern Approaches*

The genial Eoin McKiernan invited Gemini to present a three-play season in the Arts Centre of St Paul, Minnesota, which we had opened earlier. With Barry Cassin, I selected two full-length plays – Shaw's *Arms and the Man* and Hugh Leonard's *The Patrick Pearse Motel* – and a special Synge evening of short plays, *The Shadow of the Glen* and *The Tinker's Wedding*. The idea was to offer a season of contemporary and classic drama. Synge's love of the violin inspired an interlude between the one-act plays, with Des Keogh narrating excerpts from the playwright's life, and his wife Geraldine O'Grady playing some of his favourite melodies, accompanied by her sister Eileen on the piano. The company also included Maureen Toal, Martin Dempsey, Anna Manahan, Dearbhla Molloy, May Cluskey, Robert Carrickford and Teddy Byrne. Pat Murray would design and oversee the settings, which would be built in St Paul.

We rehearsed in the Pioneer Hall off Gardiner Street, where tea was brewed non-stop for our director, Barry, who seemed totally dependent on it, and for the actors whenever they got a chance to drink the stuff. They were coping with rehearsals for three productions in less than four weeks, and facing a dress rehearsal of each as soon as they arrived in America.

Once again I could not accompany the shows to America, although I really wanted to go; the pain from my psychosomatic tummy had now spread to my back. In addition, there was the commitment to a revue which Des Keogh and I had planned to put on in the Eblana when the company came home again. We had the idea of having two versatile ladies in the first half, two equally talented men in the second, with a get-together number as a finale. I had to find material for the ladies, Toal and Manahan, while Des had already collected enough sketches and songs for his part. He had also lined up the pianist Tadhg de Brún, who would be replaced

later in the run by Peter O'Brien. I asked the novelist Terence de
Vere White, who was attracted to me for a year or so, to help me in
my search. He had been interested in my career as a young actress,
but I didn't really get to know him until we began to produce at the
Gate, and we became really friendly during *The Barretts*. I knew he
had a romantic streak, and he made it plain that it was pointing in
my direction. Although my relationship with Liam was firmly rooted,
I was not above accepting dinner dates and having an old-fashioned
flirtation with this charming and civilised man. He was a writer of
note and I had every reason to be seen in his company, and even to
take the odd trip out of town with him. Tongues were wagging as I
dined in the Kildare Street Club, the Gresham, anywhere I was sure
to meet his colleagues.

Terence adapted *Roman Fever* by Edith Wharton into a short
playlet, and made a fine job of it. With advice from Blanaid Irvine,
that splendid actress who should have been a star, we put together a
poetry section, interspersed with two very funny pieces by Cecil
Sheridan. The ladies began to have a show to give Des a run for his
part of it, but he was well able to hold his hour.

The American tour was a great success, especially the Synge
evening. Geraldine O'Grady was a revelation to audiences and
sponsors, and was invited out again almost immediately. *The Patrick
Pearse Motel* was not as well received as we had hoped; its irony
was lost on the Irish Americans. Still, all the reports testified that
Gemini had brought a sense of gaiety to St Paul, and left it a duller
city for their departure. Meanwhile, at the Eblana the hurriedly
rehearsed *Sweet and Sour* had a most uncertain first night, with the
prompter's voice heard often. This was not the fault of the gallant
cast of four, who had simply not had time to learn their numbers. We
were despondent, feeling that we had thrown away a good show.
We were astonished next morning when the reviews were all raves,
and the evening papers were equally ecstatic.

Terence was so pleased with the revue and his part in it that he
came several times, bringing family and friends. He was an insecure
man, always worried as to why his novels were not in the best-
selling lists. I was glad to have his friendship, but when I told Liam
about it, he accused me of giving Terence a false impression.
Afterwards, when I suggested to Terence that we should not go out
publicly or meet so often, I could see that his feelings were hurt –
but not too seriously. He was very helpful to Mícheál and Hilton in

their many difficulties at the Gate, and adapted *The Real Charlotte*, by Somerville and Ross, for them. It was not successful, and Mícheál was cruel in his criticism of the adaptation, leaving Terence devastated. He longed for recognition as a writer, and was easily put down.

*Sweet and Sour* ran for eight months, and still holds the Dublin record for the longest unbroken run of any show. It ended only because of the bomb blasts in the city in December 1972; people were afraid to go into the city centre at night. We decided to close. There had been too much tension in the small, claustrophobic theatre, and our two grande dames were at loggerheads; they had reached the point of shunning each other. Des Keogh and his wife Geraldine hosted a sumptuous party to mark the show's closing, and even there a little acid flowed. Rosaleen Linehan, who had starred in all our previous reviews, remarked sweetly to Anna Manahan how amazing it was that 'you two had the stamina to keep going so long in that show, at your age', provoking the retort that if she herself had equal experience, her shows might have lasted longer.

I was exhausted at the end of the revue, and had begun to accept not being well as a way of life. One read-through of Hugh Leonard's *Da* in his Dalkey home convinced me that here was his 'play for posterity'. He introduced me to an American professor of drama and English in the Catholic University in Washington, Jim Waring, who was also a well-known director of plays during his summer vacations at a place called Olney near Washington DC. He had talked Hugh into writing an autobiographical play about his adoptive parents, and was now set to design and direct it. An American cast, with screen and stage star John McGiver in the title role, was assembled at Olney. John was an actor who, like Cyril Cusack, could dominate any stage just by being on it; the less he did, the more attention was focused on him. According to the author, he caught the spirit and innocence of the real-life father. The guilt and pain we all feel for neglect of our parents, for not releasing our affection for them while they are alive is beautifully caught in this remarkable play. It was a big success in Olney, and an even bigger one in the 1973 Dublin Theatre Festival. John McGiver excelled, and the Gemini cast included Kevin McHugh, Chris O'Neill, Phyl O'Doherty, Dearbhla Molloy, Eddie Golden, Frank Kelly and Pamela Mant. When John McGiver's contract was up, Eddie Golden stepped into the lead, and proved that the play was stronger than any star name. It played at the Olympia to packed houses and fantastic reviews until we had to take it off to make room for another production.

Around this time, I began to plan something close to my heart. Northern Ireland was having its troubles, bombs and killings, and we heard of the lack of visiting companies. Word was that entertainers from the South were deserting the sinking ship, and it was true that we were scared, and there was also a prevalent view that no one should go to entertain a bunch of bigoted terrorists who deserved each other. Ordinary citizens were not considered. Mary O'Malley had founded the Lyric in Belfast, the nearest thing to a northern national theatre. With her husband, psychiatrist Pearse O'Malley, she had cajoled arts councils and other funding bodies to give her the theatre, and to grant-aid its productions to some extent. Her republican sympathies, completely non-violent, were well known, but she persevered, and was now trying to keep her theatre open despite threats and much aggression. I wondered if our touring production of *Da* might serve as a small, cultural bridge between the warring communities

I contacted Mary O'Malley, and she was thrilled with the idea, but wondered if I would be able to get a company to travel north. I had no qualms in the least, and indeed only one actor cried off. His plight turned to our profit when we got the young Barry McGovern to take the role. He was wonderful, and it surprised no one when he went on to be an international actor, and a major interpreter of the plays of Samuel Beckett. Strict plans were laid for our safety. We would be housed in rooms in Queen's University, and would go to and leave the theatre in a group. After the show the theatre would close, and there would be no late bar facilities. We were to stay out of the city centre, where bombs might explode at any time. The company was so nervous that these limitations were accepted as good sense.

Mary O'Malley had a wide mix of political and religious adherents among her actors and crew, all subscribing to one common cause; the survival of the theatre they worked so hard to keep alive. *Da*, starring Eddie Golden and a fine team, packed the Lyric for the two weeks we were in residence. Soon the safety rules were discarded, and company members ventured regularly into the centre to shop. The rules dwindled to just one, to stay out of pubs. We were overjoyed with the experience, and plans began immediately to cement the exchange, which would happen in Limerick in the summer. On our way home, some of the actors had tears in their eyes; not only had they made new friends, but they were leaving them behind in conditions of some danger and isolation. I also had made friends. Mary and Pearse live in Dublin now, and I see them often.

Back from Belfast, I found myself with health problems, and again the X-rays and tests showed up nothing. They gave me injections and tablets for anaemia, but I was in pain for much of the time. At that time, in association with Noel Pearson, Gemini was presenting *Twigs*, by George Furth, starring Niall Toibin, which consisted of four plays with one linking character. Instead of the eleven actors provided for, I used only three. This puzzled Noel, who was afraid people might think him stingy, but it was nothing of the kind. It was simply that the playlets worked with three people changing identities in each. Anna Manahan and Des Keogh completed the trio and Robert Gillespie came over from England to direct.

When the dress rehearsal of *Twigs* was due at the Gate, I could not get out of bed to go to it. The doctor sent me to St Vincent's Hospital, where an emergency operation was planned, X-rays having shown up something possibly serious. It was the August Bank Holiday, and a young surgeon and team had to remove a benign cyst, unwrinkle a twisted colon and pin down a flying intestine. When I surfaced from the anaesthetic, a doctor murmured that I must have been in pain for years. Some day, I thought, I will find the cretin who told me that my symptoms were a figment of my imagination.

Then flowers came, in such profusion that it seemed every garden must be left barren. Cards arrived in every size and shape, and the nurses told me that the telephones were jammed with messages of goodwill. It was a while before I was well enough to appreciate what generous and caring colleagues I had. Every theatre sent its own floral tribute, its own special message, and visitors came from every company. Mai McFall came every day with news of the show, including the odd tremor between Niall and Anna.

In the second week in hospital, when I was finding my legs again, the chief surgeon told me that a deputation from the theatre was coming to see me. The TV room was spruced up, and so was I, even though I had lost weight and looked like a ghost. Sitting in state in a big armchair, I was presented with flowers by Brendan Smith, Gerry Alexander (then President of Equity) and Dermot Doolan, secretary of Irish Actors Equity. They stood around my chair, looking strangely solemn, and finally said they had come to offer me the post of Artistic Director of the Irish Theatre Company, the first state-supported touring company, for which money had been made available by the then government via the Minister for Finance, Richie Ryan. Brendan said that, if I accepted the position, I would be launching the new company; after six months I could rejoin my own company, and a replacement would be appointed for a further period. I thanked them, and pointed out that there could be no such thing as a six-month artistic director. It took years to establish and continue an artistic policy. As I was already artistic director of two companies, I could only consider coming in as Artistic Adviser, to help launch the company, and promised to give them an early reply on these terms.

After a week or two of enforced rest at home, during which I was as weak as a kitten, I managed to go to see *Twigs*, still packing the Gate, and marvelled at the artistry of the three performers who managed to make the audience feel that at least three times their number were on-stage. It was still another fortnight before I could get to Limerick to welcome the Lyric Players in Patrick Galvin's *The Last Burning*, and superb they were too. At first they were suspicious of southerners and how they would react to them, just as we had been when first we went to the north. But they soon warmed to the obvious friendliness around them, and had a week of parties and receptions. They went on to Cork and more hospitality, after which they had to return to Belfast to open a new play. Mary O'Malley wrote to me when they got back home, thanking me and saying that the cast were so hung over from the late night celebrations that she had to give them time off for recovery before they got going again.

The following year I was honoured with a cultural grant from the Irish-American Cultural Institute, one of their awards designed to advance Irish writing, painting and theatre. We were given £5000 to be used for further North/South promotion, and used it to bring down an amalgamated company of Unionist and Nationalist actors from Belfast and Derry, under the guidance of Michael Gillen. In the cast, in the small Eblana Theatre, was a tall young actor named Liam Neeson, shy and easily the best actor in their play. It was called *John Ferguson*, a rather heavy work by the well-known Belfast playwright, St John Ervine. Michael, a head-master from Derry and a dear friend, organised that visit, and many later visits by Gemini and others to Derry. Republican in his beliefs, he was a man of peace who did not think any cause worth the taking of life.

Around that time, I had many talks with Noel Pearson, who entered the theatre as manager of The Dubliners, Niall Toibin and others. He was fascinated by the phenomena of theatre personalities who did not, as he said, make any 'lolly' from their work. He knew that Gemini had won great respect over the years, but could not fathom why I had not been able to turn this into a healthy bank balance. I liked Noel's flair for thinking big, and for getting backers for all his projects; but I did not like the wheeler-dealer side of him, especially in his dealings with Gemini on our second and final association. He saw himself as a Hollywood-type tycoon long before he reached his present status in the world of film. Noel always gave big parties in plush places, smoking huge cigars with sunglasses perched on top of his head, talking of queues of girls lined up for the casting couch. It was a little odd, coming from a small, balding fellow nicknamed 'Blinkie', but his mind ran on such images. He hasn't changed much, despite his film success, his apparently carefully planned takeover as Chairman of the Abbey for a period, and lots and lots of 'lolly'. When presiding over the opening of the incredibly ugly new front at the Abbey, Taoiseach Charles J Haughey made a seriously schmaltzy speech lauding 'my mate Noel', putting his arm around him; how I cringed at these two old jossers who seemed to me to have so much in common.

Hugh Leonard's *Summer* was being cast while I was in hospital, and while I managed to get Des Perry, who proved to be the star of the show, and the magnificent Doreen Hepburn, there were other castings I was never happy with. I don't think the play's promise was ever fully realised, although as usual it was a Festival hit. Shortly after it closed, while a rehearsal group were out to lunch, the pillars supporting the proscenium arch in the Olympia Theatre collapsed and fell outward into the parterre. If anyone had been playing there during the incident, there would have been death and injury, and for a long time I could not sleep without visions of the mayhem that might have been.

Liam Mac Gabhann was still a strong and calming influence in my life, but his health was in poor condition. By bizarre coincidence, he had been in St Vincent's for surgery when I arrived as a patient, having visited him there a week before. He came into my ward in robe and slippers saying, 'I know you're fond of me, but this is ridiculous!'

Tony Ó Dálaigh, then director of the Irish National Opera, was seconded from the civil service to join the new Irish Theatre Company as its first administrator. We had to find a premises, plot a touring circuit and put together a programme of contrasting plays to start the ball rolling. I found Tony an affable partner. In our temporary headquarters in Harcourt Street, he sat at one end of a long table and I sat at the other end. Once I had stopped him from sending me memos, we got along fine. Tony and his wife Margaret were the leading lights in an amateur dramatic society called Strand Players, out of which came some notable names including Lewis Clohessy, who became administrator of the Dublin Theatre Festival for a time; Gerry Sinnott, who became general manager of the Olympia Theatre and Arthur Lappin, who shot from a banking background into the position of Drama Officer of the Arts Council. But if Tony Ó Dálaigh's ambitions had turned early in life to a vocation in the arts, he could have been the saviour of the Gaiety or the Olympia. His natural flair would have made him as able an administrator as Michael Colgan of the Gate, and a much more congenial one to actors. Tony was human and fallible, but made few mistakes and was never a seeker of personal publicity. Perhaps he could have used a touch more steel, entering the ring with a large company of experienced professionals, who were going to have their say in this new venture.

From my point of view, it was disappointing that we had no new Irish play to start off the company, and no time to grow one. I eventually came up with *London Assurance*, a Boucicault which had been revived in London with great success, starring Donald Sinden. We called it *Out of Town*, and starred Godfrey Quigley in a cast which included Niall Buggy, Doreen Hepburn, Gerard McSorley and Veronica Duffy, to be directed by Ray McAnally. The other plays we decided to tour were Molière's *The Miser*, Fergus Linehan's brilliant historical revue *Black Rosie*, and a prize-winning play from Newfoundland called *Leaving Home* by David French. Barry Cassin and Louis Lentin were our two 'resident' directors. We planned to continue rehearsals on tour, and to open in Cork with *Out of Town*. The sets by Alan Pleass were vast and luxurious, and Babs de Monte's costumes were a riot of silks and satins. The then President, Cearbhall Ó Dálaigh, wrote a sensitive foreword for the programme, and made a wonderful speech from the Cork stage on our opening night. The reviews were ecstatic, but the play drew disappointing houses, except in Wexford; still, it was a memorable launching of the new company. *Leaving Home* was notable for the brilliant performance of Joe McPartland, the Belfast actor, and Barry McGovern as the father and son who could not communicate. Des Perry starred in the title role of *The Miser*, a stalwart rendering with Dublin overtones; but Siobhán McKenna always said that Cecil Sheehan, in the role of the chef, stole the show. Lona Moran designed the beautiful set and costumes.

I had really wanted Siobhán to play in the ITC's first season, in a play of her choice, but she was heavily committed that year. I will always remember our walks in the pale Galway sunshine, down by the Spanish Arch. She mentioned to me her desire to play Mrs Alving in Ibsen's *Ghosts*, and her conviction that the play could be adapted to an Irish setting.

After the launching, interest spread rapidly in the company. I had insisted, as part of my brief in accepting the temporary position of Artistic Director, that we must tour the North as well as the South, and we succeeded in booking a theatre in Derry. Some company members were terrified of going there, especially with what they called a provocative show like *Black Rosie*, which took wicked and witty swipes at the Provos, the British army, Daniel O'Connell, Parnell and the mixed blood-lines of the Irish in general. The company board got cold feet, and sent the revue up to Michael Gillen, who was organising our visit, with suggested cuts. He came thundering back by telephone to say that if any cuts were made, the show needn't bother coming. As the board did this behind my back, I slapped my resignation on the table at the next meeting, refusing to reconsider unless the plays went as I wanted them, and those company members who objected were either replaced or made to honour their contracts. The board climbed down, and the company objections fizzled out. *Black Rosie* proved to be an overwhelming success, delighting all creeds, sects and political colourings.

I love Derry to this day. Michael Gillen, a great supporter of the theatre, ferried members of the company on sight-seeing tours, Cecil Sheehan indulged his love of antiques by buying all kinds of bargains, and the actors generally went everywhere without a care. When that first tour had ended, and I resumed my place on the Board, I had mixed feelings about the experiment. For me, Gemini had through the years been ahead of most other companies. Being independent meant that there was seldom real financial benefits for our creative work, but there was joy in our freedom. The ITC ended up with a financial observer on the Board appointed by the Arts Council. Tony Ó Dálaigh had worked with two temporary artistic directors before the Board got the message that such short-term contracts were ridiculous. Joe Dowling was approached by the Board, and contributed shows of such excellence that the reputation of the ITC was considerably enhanced. He then went on to become one of the best artistic directors ever to grace the Abbey Theatre.

The structure of the ITC was notable for its quota of three Equity officers, three management and a Government appointee on the Board. It was eventually killed off quite ruthlessly by the Arts Council, as it had overrun its financial limit and incurred an unacceptable debt. The presence on the Board of the Equity executives spelled doom for the venture. Meeting after meeting saw them approve new pay rates and rises for their members, and it was useless for the rest of us to point out the realities of life. More increases meant more debt, and actors were getting so much subsistence money that many, including some who had been hardly a wet week in the business, never had to touch their salaries. Phelim Donlon, the new administrator, was a nice man with integrity. He believed utterly in a letter from Charles J Haughey promising to see the company right; but Mr Haughey was not a nice man, and did not keep that promise. So the merry-go-round ran down and nobody came to the rescue. The ITC had no chance of generating more cash, as the Arts Council had contributed to the maintenance of Arts Centres dotted all over the country with little, uneconomic theatres which ensured that companies could not survive without aid.

# 30

# *Endings and Beginnings*

Having weathered the late nineteen-fifties, sixties and a good part of the seventies in a subsidy-free world, rising costs began to pose huge problems for independent companies. Gemini went on regardless, one show paying for the next, none making serious profits, but providing a living for a great many freelance actors. But there was something in the air, a lot of talk about a new era in the arts, and the possibility of some independent companies coming under the umbrella of the Arts Council. The Abbey, the Gate, the Dublin Grand Opera Society and the Irish National Ballet were the then beneficiaries of state funds on an annual basis. Now the grapevine was buzzing with news of extended subsidies for other labourers in the field, hit by new financial factors. One of these was Irish Actors Equity, at last emerging as a force able to fight for better terms for actors, and not before its time. Actors were paid appallingly low wages, and the Equity minimum was derisory. The solution seemed to lie in subsidising freelance management, who had no resources other than box-office returns.

But actors need to work, to be part of the living theatre; it is the breath of life to them. So they, and we continued to provide good plays both on tour and in Dublin. We had a serious play from John B Keane called *The Change in Mame Fadden*, which starred Maureen Toal, staged first in Cork and then in Dublin's Olympia. It was very different from the author's other works, dealing with the difficulties of a woman undergoing the change of life. His fans were fascinated but puzzled by this unrelieved drama, culminating in suicide; not even a happy ending.

In 1975 the Arts Council appointed a new director, Colm Ó Briain, who had founded the Project Arts Centre to cater for theatre, film and the visual arts. We waited expectantly for the announcement of his policies. It was widely believed that Gemini, having soldiered down the years and toured widely at home and abroad, would gain some form of subsidy. I began to dream of better productions, improved conditions for our actors and more opportunities for new Irish playwrights, and could not stop myself from making plans, perhaps even to turn the Eblana into an experimental theatre. When the list of Arts Council beneficiaries was published, it read: the Abbey Theatre, the Gate Theatre, the Dublin Grand Opera Society, the Irish Theatre Company, the National Ballet and – the Project Arts Centre.

I could not believe or understand this result. Colm Ó Briain had often expressed admiration for my work, and I felt sure that a further list of subsidies would be announced. Brendan Connellan was very dispirited, being unable to see how Gemini could survive in this new and difficult climate. At home the telephone never stopped ringing, with actors expressing anger and sympathy. I took stock, and decided to write to Colm thinking that there was still hope. Gemini meant many things to so many people, and had served Irish theatre when no one else was even on the horizon; there would surely be some recognition of that. Colm replied briefly, saying only sorry, the cupboard is bare, and I still have his note.

I badgered the Arts Council constantly, but the appointment of Arthur Lappin as Drama Officer did not help my case. I cannot pretend that I was gracious to Arthur and at times it was as if there was a war between us. For a while, between running the Eblana and maintaining the high standards expected of Gemini, there seemed to be little change except in the frequency of our productions. We had to weigh everything very carefully before proceeding, and Brendan Connellan's meticulous accounting kept us afloat. We could not have managed without him as budgets got tighter and costs kept rising. We did some commercial fun shows in association with Des Keogh, and Noel Coward's *Private Lives*, directed for us by Robert Gillespie, was quite one of the finest productions of the play ever seen here. Alan Stanford and Des Keogh, Deirdre Donnelly and Deirdra Morris were all quite superb under Gillespie's observation, often tetchy but always accurate. He was not able to attend the first night because of prior commitments, but pronounced at the run-through that Des and Alan had reached heights in their roles that he had never seen surpassed. Unfortunately, the following day, after the dress rehearsal, he told them that they had lost whatever they had, and were back to square one; he then praised the ladies, and left for his plane. Alan and Des were crushed, and all that I could say to them was that they would shine on the night – and they did. Deirdre Donnelly, an actress of extraordinary charisma, was fantastic in the part of Amanda. I wish her stage appearances were more frequent.

As time went by, Gemini applied to the Arts Council, and got dribs and drabs of grants for this project or that. Occasionally we might get a touring grant, but there were always too many strings attached. Certain venues set up by the Council had to be included, and the choice of plays had to be approved. We no longer had that freedom which before had spurred us on to such heights.

At the Gate, during the run of *Equus*, Mícheál Mac Liammóir was taken ill. For a long time near-blind and unable to read, write or see his beloved hills and trees, he had wished for death. 'Except for Hilton being happy and well', he said in an interview, 'there is nothing.' Mícheál died on 6 March, 1978 at 7 pm, and the whole country mourned. I thought how lonely Hilton would be now. When I heard him quarrelling with Mícheál in recent years, he reminded me of a mother, frightened because her child is sick and railing out of her own fear.

Gregg got his NUJ card at a tender age and, under the guidance of Liam Mac Gabhann, progressed from daily advertising papers to the *Drogheda Independent* as a roving reporter. He was situated in Trim, and came up and down frequently. On one occasion he introduced me to a small, shy girl named Gillian Elliott, and told me that he knew her family, who lived in Navan. She was eighteen, and about to take up her first job, in the civil service in Dublin. Gregg told me that he was keeping an eye on her, as she was bound to be homesick. She stayed with me for a fortnight, and cried every night but it did not dawn on me that being away from Gregg was the cause of her grief. They met at weekends, in Navan or Dublin, and a year later Gregg proposed, going the old-fashioned route by asking for her hand in marriage. After due consultation, the Elliotts and I suggested to them that they should wait until Gillian was at least twenty-one. Gregg was willing, but Gillian had other ideas. She put it to us that she had found the man she loved, and saw no virtue in playing a waiting game; they were both adults and belonged together. They blew us and our arguments out of the water, and never looked back.

After a fairy-tale wedding in Navan (at which Hugh Leonard played the bride's chauffeur in his Rolls Royce), followed by a reception in Slane Castle, the happy couple went on a mystery honeymoon, so that Gregg could share with Gillian some of his favourite spots in Europe. They returned to work in Trim, Gillian in the courthouse there and Gregg back to the *Drogheda Independent*. It was one of the greatest joys of my life to see my son so radiantly happy, with a girl no one could help but love and cherish. Refreshingly natural, she brought a breath of uncomplicated goodwill to all her undertakings. They had two beautiful daughters, Emma and Sarah, and are as much in love today as when they first met.

In 1975, Ray McAnally booked the Eblana for fourteen weeks, to present a play called *Kennedy's Children* by Robert Patrick, which had been well received in London. It was a courageous venture, and Ray put all his money into it, including mortgaging his house. It was a fine production, critically well received, but the audiences did not come. Ray was in desperate straits, and he and his wife Ronnie spent long hours in the theatre going through scripts to see what could be salvaged. The news spread through the theatre community, and scripts arrived from a variety of sources. I had been to Writers' Week in Listowel, and acquired a copy of John B Keane's new book *Letters of a Matchmaker*, it made me laugh all the way back to Dublin on the bus. I went to the Eblana to talk to Ray and Ronnie, and found the advance booking for their play non-existent. I thought of the book, and we sent out for a couple of copies. Barry Cassin had arrived to offer what help he could, and we all read through the *Letters*, convulsed with laughter. I told Ray to phone John B, explain his predicament and ask for the rights. He did so there and then, and John not only gave permission for the adaptation, but set a small percentage royalty which he would take only if the show did well.

Ray and Barry edited the *Letters* between them, Ray and Ronnie played all the characters, Bob Heade designed a simple but effective set for a nominal fee and a success story was launched that is now history. The Eblana was packed for the next eleven weeks. Ray and Ronnie toured the show, cleared their mortgage and made a small fortune. Ray kept trying to repay me for, as he said, saving his home and his sanity. I accepted a lavish supper and a set of Tchaikovsky symphonies. Years later, in 1991, I took Anna Manahan and Frank Kelly on tour in *The Matchmaker*. Ronnie gave it back to me in Ray's adaptation, free of charge, John B again accepted a tiny royalty and the show triumphed again, saving yet another company – Gemini.

My uneasy relationship with the Arts Council continued. I queried everything, and wrote letters to the Council screaming for justice, for a fair allocation of funds for Gemini and for the creation of a client relationship which would not restrict my freedom to choose plays for my company as its Artistic Director. In the meantime, we got on with the business. The prolific John B sent us a new play called *The Good Thing*, which again broke new ground for him. It featured an outgoing, good-natured woman easily mistaken for a loose one, and the turning of the tables on a notoriously unfaithful husband. The play went on a long tour, returning to the Eblana; then Michael Gillen asked us for a new play, and we brought it to Derry. We were not, in the late 1970s, expecting the degree of controversy generated by *The Good Thing*. It seemed that the idea of a wife playing her husband at his own game of infidelity was anathema in country venues, and the moral indignation was bad for business. Even in Derry, which had come to expect realism as well as high standards from Gemini, one could feel a wall of resistance to the issues raised by the play. Maureen Toal gave a wonderfully convincing performance in the lead. This is a play I should like to revive; there is more to be gleaned from it than we managed to extract on its first showing.

In 1978, again in August, the dreaded symptoms that caused my earlier hospitalisation recurred, and I had another major operation, and a longer time out for reflection and recovery. The profession, as before, inundated the hospital with cards gifts, and their presence; and helped me through the trauma and back on my feet. Brendan Connellan was left holding the baby while I fought my way back to health. I confess that I am a rotten patient, and hate being in bed unless I am doing something useful there. In the same year, Liam Mac Gabhann, who had suffered and recovered from a light stroke, was felled by a major one, which left him paralysed and unable to speak. I had talked to him a few days before, when he was full of life, anxious to get on with his memoirs and, some day, to return to his beloved Valencia. It was always his dearest wish to be home again on the island of his birth. He had the same desire to 'speak his love' as Siobhán McKenna had, be it of family, country or any other; and he wrote his last message of love to me in my little red book, the same one that contained his first written words of affection.

Liam could be seen in hospital by very few people outside his immediate family. I went to see him just once, to take his hand and tell him I understood. He was locked away in some strange limbo, unable to move, speak or even blink. It was what he had always dreaded; to be helpless in the charge of others, with no control over mind or body. He had to endure this for six months, and, when he died, I could not regret it.

I had been hanging on to a thread with regard to my religious beliefs, going to Mass occasionally, feeling unwanted and rejected during the sacrament. It was lonely watching people taking the host in their hands or mouths, knowing that I must remain outside that door, or deny the years with Liam by saying I was sorry. I could never do that. I talked it over with a Jesuit priest, who found a way for me to tread with honesty the road back to a kind of salvation. Then, one day, I went into the Pro-Cathedral, and heard a sermon preached by Rev Dermod McCarthy that touched on the importance of human relations and God's awareness of us as lonely orphans adrift in a lost paradise, seeking love, and I gradually settled into a semblance of peace with myself and my Maker. So I went back to work, reconciled to being alone, this time for good.

In 1980, Barry Cassin and I got hold of John B Keane's *Letters of a Love-Hungry Farmer*, and a stage adaptation seemed essential. The central character was a farmer in search of love, desperate for a mate but too shy to land one. His pursuit, aided by matchmakers and others, had a Chaplinesque quality; and Donal Farmer played the character with great delicacy and lightness of touch. Partly miming, moving from crisis to crisis like a character in a Feydeau farce, he gave a brilliant performance, leaving me determined to see him play *Cyrano de Bergerac*. We teamed up with the Cork Opera House to produce another play by John B, *The Chastitute*. An excerpt beamed out from *The Late Late Show* turned uncertain business in Cork into packed houses, as it later did in the Olympia. The magic of Gay Byrne, surely the greatest TV and radio personality in the country, worked wonders with public perception. Unfortunately we could not tour the play; the cost was, by unsubsidised standards, enormous. I can still see Gerry Lundberg as the merriest missionary who ever preached hell-fire; it may have been that performance that drove him into the PR world in which he has been so successful, for he was ribbed unmercifully about it for ages afterwards.

In 1981 I became aware of a strange reticence in friends who were normally garrulous. Actors began to grow evasive when I spoke to them of plans for my next production. Brendan Connellan was acting restively, which was not his style. Ray McAnally kept asking me about my availability on a certain Sunday, 8 November, speaking of a great theatrical hooley which I must not miss. Anna Manahan was acting mysteriously, affecting a vacant smile, and Maureen Toal was at it too, hinting of a big party being planned, and I must be sure to come. When I told her I would think about it, the smile vanished. Michael Gillen rang from Derry to say that he had heard about a big theatre do, and to ask if I would be there. My friends Phyl and Maurice O'Doherty – he was the President of Equity at that time – expressed the thought that it was time the profession got together on a big scale, and showed our solidarity to the Arts Council. Ah, I thought, a protest of some kind, and of course I would support it. When my son Gregg and Gillian telephoned to say they had been invited, and to offer me a lift, I began to wonder what was going on, and to feel a little nervous.

When I arrived at the Eblana, the venue for the party or whatever, there was a reception in progress. I knew almost all the faces in the large assembly, but a few were unfamiliar. As I moved closer to these, I recognised the Mayor of Derry, whom I had met. Seated in a chair was Hilton Edwards, and Brendan Connellan guided me towards him, explaining that the great director had left his hospital bed for the occasion. The occasion turned out to be a gala tribute to *me*. Everyone in the theatre world seemed to be there. I stayed beside Hilton's chair; if this was a tribute, his gesture in coming out of hospital to salute me, as he said, was the biggest accolade of all, and brought tears to my eyes. A bouquet was placed in my arms from Tom Murphy, with a message to say that he was paying tribute from a distance because of work commitments. Derry's Lord Mayor said he was there because of my work in transporting theatre across political boundaries, which few others had done. John B Keane said that he, like many others, owed his very survival to me. Hilton Edwards had written his tribute in the specially-produced programme; I treasured that most of all because, although we were colleagues, we were never friends, and yet he had made this tremendous gesture. Speeches were made about the twenty-one years Gemini had run the Eblana – it was actually longer than that, but it was a nice number to put on the huge cake which was wheeled in.

I felt that I must be dreaming. After the reception, we all crowded into the theatre for a rich entertainment provided by Ray McAnally,

'Professor' Peter O'Brien's jazz trio, Des Keogh and Rosaleen
Linehan, Geraldine O'Grady, Ulick O'Connor, Maria McDermottroe
and the Wolfe Tones, popular ballad singers. The stage management
teams under Mai McFall presented me with a silver tea set, and I also
received a huge card and a cheque. Perhaps the gift which made me
most proud was presented by Maurice O'Doherty, a scroll bestowing
upon me honorary Life Membership of Irish Actors Equity. The
generous, unforgettable phrases written by Hilton, Hugh Leonard,
Fergus Linehan and so many others in the programme, which I will
always treasure, have since spurred me on in less favourable times.
It was a long time before I came down to earth after that night and
experience.

Brendan Connellan retired that year. The last production we
worked on together was Mike Leigh's *Abigail's Party* at the Gate.
Joan O'Hara starred as the impossible, vulgar Abigail, with Liz Davis,
Ann Sinnott and Des Keogh in the cast. It was a successful outing,
but I was deeply saddened to lose an ideal company man and
manager, and a dear friend. I found new administrators, and at first it
seemed as if Gemini would run smoothly enough. But I never again
found a manager so popular with actors, or one who was also such
an excellent companion.

As my first operation had miraculously solved my problem with
air sickness, and I could now fly without qualms, I undertook a
lecture tour for the Irish-American Cultural Institute which took me
to Boston, Philadelphia, Washington, New York and San Antonio. I
learned about American internal flights, with planes shuttling around
like taxis; the only difference was in the fares and the number of
snacks that could be consumed on each trip. I kept a copy of Brian
Friel's *Translations* in my handbag, and used parts of that excellent
play to make points about heritage and language. Eoin McKiernan
first mentioned the possibility of an American tour on that lecture-
trip, and by 1982 it was a reality. The choice of play was Bernard
Farrell's *I Do Not Like Thee, Dr Fell*, and we visited five major cities.
In three of these, we were going into commercial theatres, and I
knew that we would have to be critically beyond reproach. Barry
Cassin had proved his worth as director on our last American visit to
Minnesota, and I was delighted when he accepted the new tour.
Alan Pleass was engaged to design a set which could be brought by
truck from place to place, and we then began to recruit a hand-
picked company. I knew that Garrett Keogh, who had played the

title role in the Abbey's première, could not be bettered. Billie Morton had also been perfect in the part of a phoney group therapy leader. Anna Manahan was an obvious choice for an elderly 'cat' lady, and Nuala Hayes was clearly right for an outspoken suburban wife. I wanted Derry Power to repeat his lovely portrayal of the caretaker, but Bernard Farrell dug his heels in there. The man had to be a Dubliner, he insisted, so we cast Charlie Roberts, who couldn't be accused of being anything else. Des Keogh's humour and sensitivity were ideal assets for the part of the lonely, gay man. Finally we had it all; cast, director, set and a sparkling new Irish play, far removed from stale Irish-American concepts.

We set off for America in holiday mood, knowing that we had a successful play and a production worthy of it. First stop was Rochester, New York State, where we rehearsed for two weeks and played for two nights. The play was uproariously received and the reviews were raves, with the acting highly praised. I met the Mayor, who presented me with the Freedom of the City of Rochester, the tangible form of which was a small blue box with a gorgeous medallion inside. I flew ahead of the company to publicise them in Tulsa, Oklahoma, and appeared on TV news and talk shows. I met Charlton Heston, who was waiting to be interviewed to give a plug to his son's new film. He introduced himself, saying that he loved the theatre, had started there and played every year in summer stock, just to keep his hand in. He was natural and charming, and was really disappointed that he could not stay over to see our play, but not as much as we were. Tulsa loved *Dr Fell*, so did Philadelphia, and even the phlegmatic audiences of St Paul were enthusiastic. The reviews compared us to the best Abbey Theatre players, heartening in the extreme.

We went sightseeing with the enthusiasm of children, held parties in our rooms, bought lightweight clothes and gifts for home. All through that tour there was a consistent joy in the work and in leisure time. We were housed on the campus in Rochester, and in first-class hotels elsewhere. Bernie and Grace Croke, the live-wires of the IACI, were in charge in Philadelphia, and sold out every performance beside looking after our every comfort and taking us on tours. In the middle of the tour we learned that Ray McAnally (who was now Billie Morton's father-in-law) was due to have a heart by-pass operation in Dublin, and sent him a telegram wishing him a successful opening; but behind the facetiousness we prayed.

Although we had folk to get home to, we were a sober group as we took our last look at the blue skies. Billie, Anna, Mai McFall and I became bonded together in even firmer unity of spirit and purpose after that trip. The magic of sunshine and warm appreciation soon diminished as our plane landed in rain, and the familiar greyness engulfed us. Mortgages, bills and the conundrum of the next job came to greet us as the dream was replaced by reality.

Change was in the air. Brendan Smith, founder and soul of the Dublin Theatre Festival was unwell. He had become forgetful, his speech was halting and at times his memory failed completely. He was suffering from Alzheimer's disease, and his wife Beryl and his two sons were to go through an ordeal which would take all their fortitude and strength. The theatre community was shocked and dismayed; we owed so much to this great man, a friend and father figure. With the news of his illness, everyone in or remotely associated with the theatre acknowledged our great debt to him. He died on 30 October 1989, but, as with all victims of that cruel disease, he had left us a long time before that. His family, with typical courage, donated his body for research, to help other sufferers.

# 31

# *The Old Order Changeth*

For many years, Brendan Smith's Festival provided Irish companies and playwrights with a platform which attracted international managements and critics to appraise their work. He begged and borrowed to give the best companies and plays the funding needed for high production standards. Together with the excellent shows he invited from abroad, this made for a mix that brought a healthy quota of foreign visitors and producers to Ireland. Now that he was gone, there was a different attitude and a less familial atmosphere. The new Festival organisers depended mainly on the Abbey, the Gate and other subsidised units. They awarded freelance managements what they called associate status, which meant that both parties funded approved productions.

Lewis Clohessy had been appointed Director of the Dublin Theatre Festival when I first approached Siobhán McKenna with the idea for a new production of *Arsenic and Old Lace* by Joseph Kesselring. She had often talked to me about her wish to do more comedy. 'They never ask me,' she said wistfully. 'They think I can do nothing but 'ologón'.' She had enjoyed playing in Noel Coward's *Fallen Angels* some years before with Ann Rowan and Marie Conmee, in a stylish production by William Chappell which had been a huge financial success. I had been looking for something suitable for herself and Maureen Potter, whose work in pantomime I considered brilliant, and *Arsenic and Old Lace* seemed an ideal vehicle for them both. Siobhán agreed with enthusiasm, and we thought that the Gaiety was the right venue for the show. The drawback was that Gemini had very little money, and this was an expensive show with a large cast and elaborate setting. Despite that, I set about organising matters, and contacted Fred O'Donovan, an old friend and a first-class theatre manager and producer, who had run the Gaiety for many years. He was enthusiastic about the project and said he was certain that the Gaiety would back the show with

these two female stars and that I should go ahead. Maureen had yet
to be coaxed on board, a task Siobhán accomplished over several
glasses of white wine. She telephoned me afterwards with the good
news, and we agreed that William Chappell should be brought from
London to direct. He was happy to come, and asked me to line up
the rest of the cast for him. Later, he accused me of giving him a
motley crew, but agreed that the final result showed how gifted Irish
actors can be.

The motley crew included Jonathan Ryan, Liz Lloyd, Maurie Taylor,
Breandán Ó Dúill, Kevin Flood, Gerry Alexander, Des Nealon, Garrett
Keogh and everyone's favourite, gentle Liam Sweeney, who was
playing a cameo role. With Fred O'Donovan's help, we began
rehearsals with more than the usual degree of fellowship and goodwill. For a week or two, a happier group of thespians could not be
found. Billy had emphysema, and his walking was restricted, so he
ate lunch and took tea in the rehearsal room, entertaining us with a
marvellous repertoire of high camp theatre stories.

One evening, after work, Liam Sweeney went in high good
humour to meet a few old friends in a pub near his flat. He was
found dead next morning in the nearby canal, his house-keys
clutched in his hand. The police called to ask how he had been the
previous day, and whether he had history of illness. I remembered
that he had mentioned attacks of dizziness, for which his doctor had
given him medication. There was no doubt in anyone's mind that he
had suffered a blackout and fallen into the water, which was not
very deep. Billy thought that I should break the news to the cast,
who were shocked and saddened. We contacted his relatives in New
Zealand, who wished us to proceed with the burial, and Father Brian
D'Arcy conducted the ceremonies. Siobhán and Maureen offered to
deliver the readings. Billy called us for rehearsal when the funeral
was over; a wise move. He also told me not to re-cast Liam's part for
the moment; it would be too hard on all of us to see another actor
fill his shoes while we were still shocked. Liam Sweeney was a fine
actor. Often, when he played cameo roles, he stole both reviews and
applause from the lead actors. When his coffin was wheeled down
the aisle after the final prayers, applause broke out and became
thunderous and prolonged; a tribute to a shy artist and a great
humanitarian.

We found a suitable actor to replace Liam after a while. Pat Nolan,
well known to Gemini from the 1960s, stepped easily and quietly

into the gap. As it must, the play took over our thoughts and
energies, and soon we were approaching the first night. Siobhán and
Maureen were working magically together, leading a cast that was
uniformly superb. The opening performance vindicated my faith in
the venture for the reviews were all raves. Siobhán sent me two
beautiful letters, the first, with flowers, on the opening night, to
thank me for bringing this play and pairing about. Dear loyal,
generous Siobhán. Even then I was beginning to notice a look of
frailty I had not seen before. She was, she told me, committed to
John Huston's film of *The Dead* and to Tom Murphy's *Bailegangaire*,
then she was going to have a very long rest.

At that time, Siobhán and I were shareholders of the Abbey
Theatre though we were both wary of the political nature of changes
in both policies and personnel. On the shareholding body also sat a
shadowy, remote figure who bore a ghostly resemblance to the lover
in my youthful dream world. The wheel had come full circle, and
Professor Hugh Hunt of the chair of drama in Manchester University
and Phyllis Ryan were both shareholders of the Abbey.

Siobhán, ill and visibly losing weight, went to Galway to star in
*Bailegangaire*, and gave a performance with the Druid company that
was a tour de force. Critics were left without adjectives to sing her
praises. Even that journalist who had wounded her most in previous
years struggled vainly for a worthy summation of her achievement. I
am sure that the same Fintan O'Toole, who wrote scathing criticisms
of her work could never have intended to hurt this deeply sensitive
soul as much as he did. His views on drama seemed to me to lack an
instinct for or comprehension of his subject. As a political
commentator, a writer in depth on social issues, he is very able, but
the theatre appears to be a maze in which he loses his way. Siobhán
dreaded enemies she did not deserve, and indeed she had none,
other than those few who envied what she was. At the end, she
fought a terminal illness to give Tom Murphy's fine play its ultimate
realisation.

Siobhán died on 16 November, 1986. I was at my son's house in
Kildare when the news came through on the radio. I stood quite still
for a long time. Two days later I cried because I loved her, and knew
I would miss her to the end of my days. Johnny Hippisley, her close
friend and manager, racked with grief, told me that Siobhán had
been awarded the Harvey's Trophy for best performance that year;
and that, knowing she might not be well enough to attend the

ceremony, she had asked that I accept it for her. Gregg came to comfort and support me, with Johnny Hippisley, Pauline Forbes, Siobhán's son, Donnacha O'Dea and his wife, and Rev. Dermod McCarthy, a priest who was her friend, and was fast becoming mine. Siobhán was mourned and eulogised in the Irish, English and American press. Television and radio tributes and letters poured in from all over the world. The torrent of grief and love coming from multitudes of ordinary people who wept for her passing would have delighted her.

Siobhán's worst fears about loss of ideals and standards in the Abbey were to be realised. I have seen some dark years in the Abbey since Tomás Mac Anna was dislodged from the Board. The permanent acting company, containing some of the strongest talents in the business, were ignored, treated with contempt and cruelty. They were made to feel superfluous and unwanted, and advised to retire. Watching shows at the Abbey which were a disgrace to professional theatre, some shareholders grew very angry. The author Ulick O'Connor, Mary O'Malley, Mícheál Ó hAodha, Seán White and myself, together with members of the Players' Council, began a movement of resistance. Ulick O'Connor, in particular, gave unstintingly of his time and expertise to further our cause. Our primary aim was to restore the members of the permanent company to their proper position.

Audibility, the first requirement for any actor, had almost vanished from the Abbey stage. The new company members, young and old, mumbled their lines or gabbled at a speed that made nonsense of coherence. Classic plays lay in ruins, badly acted and badly lit, with no firm director's hand discernible. Audiences naturally began to dwindle. Necessary changes were made, but not until, after several private meetings, the shareholders confronted the board. It appeared to some senior shareholders that key positions might be taken over by individuals who could use them for personal gain and that the Abbey's name could be sold to the highest bidder outside Ireland. Legal advice was taken, and that threat was averted; but the money-changers had, for a while, successfully invaded the temple.

With the arrival of the artistic and articulate Patrick Mason, a great deal of ground has been recovered, albeit painfully slowly. Tradition will have its place amid inevitable change, and standards are on the way to making us again proud of our heritage. Mason has already established an enviable record in discovering new playwrights, and in bringing international drama to us. His award-winning production of Brian Friel's *Dancing at Lughnasa* has been hailed in every country where theatre exists. Michael Colgan, who restored the Gate to brilliant life, has now to face competition from a resurrected national theatre. We can look ahead to a new era of excellence. Already, all over the world, Ireland's star shines brightly in theatre and film circles; our actors can hold their own anywhere and our designers and directors win universal acclaim.

Colm Ó Briain, despite having almost brought Gemini down, held out a lifeline to me which kept me afloat. When he discovered that, despite all Gemini's successes, I was earning a salary well below the accepted poverty line, he came to the rescue, and enabled me to keep going. We have shaken hands, and closed the door on past acrimony. Today's Arts Council includes some worthy names, along with the customary quota of management and grace-and-favour appointments. The same outrageous rules apply. Managements may benefit from extra funding by their presence on the Council, no reasons are given to rejected applicants, and the Council is still responsible to nobody. We have at last a Minister for Arts and Culture, Michael D Higgins, and I am waiting to see if justice may become more than just an empty word. I have the minister's personal assurance that he holds me and my work for the Irish theatre in high esteem and that my company must continue.

Gemini goes on, and there are still victories to be had. We produced at the Dublin Festival in 1989, in association with the Abbey, an adaptation by Thomas Kilroy of Ibsen's *Ghosts*, dedicated to Siobhán McKenna. It starred Doreen Hepburn, who struck sparks from her material, and the smooth, sardonic David Kelly. The adaptation had been created with skill and fidelity to its haunting original, and the production, directed by the imaginative and colourful Michael Scott, was hailed by the critics. It was selected for inclusion in the Stoneybrook International Festival, Long Island, USA, and we flew there the following year. We played to packed houses but received indifferent reviews from writers who seemed to dislike Ibsen's work, and saw no merit in tampering with it.

My sister Doris, now widowed, who suffers from arthritis and cannot travel, writes frequently to give me news of her life in Redwood City, California, and of her son Blair, whom I have not yet met. My own visits to America have stopped short of making the journey to Redwood City; I always seem to be going in the opposite direction, burdened with some responsibility which limits my time away from home. Jacqueline shares a house in Dorset, and is studying for law exams. Gregg lives in Kildare, now a respected transport research journalist and an ordained priest in the Anglican church. My two grandchildren are the loves of my life. My work in the theatre keeps me alive and able to appreciate the wonders in the world about me. I have good and true friends, fewer now since so many have passed away.

The only new friendship to take root in my life in recent years occurred in the Dublin Festival of 1993, during a production of Boucicault's *The Streets of Dublin*, creatively adapted by Fergus Linehan. It was financially backed by Athlone solicitor Edward Farrell. We assembled a fine cast, but crucially lacked the most important player in melodrama; a villain. Finally Edward persuaded Ron Moody, famous for his Fagin in *Oliver*, to come to Ireland. Ron was superb, and loomed over the proceedings. He warned us that he had a reputation for being temperamental, and had walked out of two shows, but I knew that our Irish actors would envelop him in the warm atmosphere he needed, and he was tremendously happy with us.

I don't know why this show, starring Ron Moody, designed by Robert Ballagh, with a cast including Anna Manahan, Des Nealon, Tom Murphy, Tina Kellegher and Mark Lambert, was not more successful. I think it was mainly that there were too many cooks. The only people who stood to lose financially were Edward Farrell and, in a much smaller way, myself. Yet, outside of the acting company, everyone seemed to want to assume the mantle of producer, to meddle with schedules, musical numbers, posters, royalties and who owned which part of the show. Rave reviews, however, were earned by Ron Moody and the dedicated cast. In one of his first forays into professional production, Edward Farrell encountered egos which almost sabotaged our original plan, and lost money in the process. He also produced two other loss-making shows during that period, and endured his hard luck with enviable cheerfulness. And though my own finances plummeted to a new low as a result of this production, in Ron Moody I gained the friendship of a deeply religious, honest man and it was a privilege to have worked with and known him.

On the smaller scale which had become obligatory, Gemini toured with Anna Manahan and Frank Kelly in John B Keane's *Matchmaker* and again in Tomás Mac Anna's new production of P J O'Connor's *The Tailor and Ansty*, adapted from the book by Eric Cross. These tours covered north and south, and were immensely popular. But all good things must end, and Frank is now starring in the award-winning TV series *Father Ted*, while Anna has moved to her native Waterford, well within reach of work and friendship. We have soldiered through many years, she and I; perhaps the best 'part' of her lifetime may still be around the corner.

I still have the joy of working occasionally with Tomás Mac Anna, who believes in magic and may be a true sorcerer. There will always be magic; witness Donal McCann's recent wizardry at the Gate, in Sebastian Barry's *The Steward of Christendom*. The play, like all Barry's work, is poetic, moving and illuminates the truth. Donal McCann, powerful and magnetic, towered not over but within the framework of this exploration of past lives. I have now seen acting greatness unrivalled since McCormick, McAnally, Cusack, and McKenna. At the Peacock Theatre recently I met two ferociously talented young ladies, Marina Carr, author of the searing new play *Portia Coughlan*, and gifted actress and playwright Gina Moxley, whose play *Danti-Dan* has earned her plaudits at home and abroad. In the foyer, I spied rising young actress, Derbhle Crotty, whose singular magnetism was palpably evident as Portia Coughlan. Their success ensures a healthy future for Irish drama. Also set to conquer new worlds is Rough Magic, the young company which has become a leading dramatic force in the country and whose early years of hardship are now somewhat alleviated by an Arts Council subsidy. The famous Druid Theatre from Galway has recently celebrated its twenty-first birthday, and shows every sign of continuing excellence.

I meet Hugh Leonard and his wife Paule mostly at first nights now. They are a large part of Gemini's history, as is Norman Rodway, who pursues his successful career in London. I met him in Dublin early in 1995, and we talked ourselves hoarse for hours. Nothing had changed. John B Keane and Mary continue to inspire me with their loyalty and affection in bad times and good. As always, my friends are the most important part of my world outside my family. Gemini, abandoned while I complete this memoir, beckons me invitingly to carry on, as does the Play Circle and other projects. Shades from the past point me to the future, their inspiration urging me forward.

# Index

Mac, Mc and Mhac are all treated as Mac.
St is treated as if spelled out.
Numbers in italics are for illustrations or their captions.